Twayne's English Authors Series

Sylvia E. Bowman, *Editor*

INDIANA UNIVERSITY

Mary Renault

(TEAS) 98

Mary Renault

By PETER WOLFE

University of Missouri—St. Louis

Twayne Publishers, Inc.   ::   New York

TO MR. FRISBEEN'S BEST CUSTOMER,
MILTON B. WOLFE

Preface

My critical methodology in *Mary Renault* involves rather more plot summary and character description than would be needed in a book on a better-known writer. The descriptive methodology can be justified, I think, on the basis of subject matter. Although I have tried to be critical and analytical in my readings, I felt that my first duty—both to Miss Renault and the reader—was to convey the flavor, the sensation, the whatness of Mary Renault's novels. This procedure also explains my liberal quoting of passages.

For the sake of uniformity, I have followed the novelist's practice of using the Greek spelling of proper names from Classical antiquity. Thus the reader must not be shocked to encounter *Sokrates*, the *Kentaurs*, and *Mykenai* instead of the more familiar *Socrates*, the *Centaurs*, and *Mycenae*.

An introductory study like mine has three major obligations: to fit its subject in a cultural tradition, to show where the subject belongs in this tradition, and to judge the artistic merit of the subject's work. Wherever possible, I have allowed Miss Renault to reveal herself directly to the reader. This practice gives the reader both an intimate view of Miss Renault's world and a chance to make some independent judgments about that world.

The strong critical stand I have taken on the artistic merit of each of the ten novels may strike the reader as untactful, premature, and foolhardy. It is true that I have not been guarded or tentative in my judgments. But my outspoken remarks on Mary Renault's artistry take root in her inability, to date, to attract serious critical attention. There is no question that she deserves a higher standing among literary scholars than she now has. So, although my esthetic judgments may prove unsound, they reveal Mary Renault as a developing artist who deserves to be taken seriously.

I want to thank Miss Renault for her patient and generous comments on my readings of her work; Lee Lemon, Mordecai Marcus, and James Hazen for their kind help with matters of organization and style; Elias Kapetanopoulos, Howard Norland, and Stanley Vandersall for pointing out important historical and mythical themes; Audria Shumard for typing the manuscript; and the Univeristy of Nebraska Research Council and the University of Missouri-St. Louis Research Council for grants to cover expenses connected with the manuscript's preparation.

The combined help of the following people amounts to a major contribution: Mrs. Joel N. Calhoun, Garland Cobb, Marco Fessel, William J. Gallegos, John Higbe, Tom La Grange, Oscar Louik, Walter Benway Stuart, and Joseph P. Vincenti, Jr.

I must also gratefully acknowledge the unflagging help of Marie, Philip, John, and Rhea, who encouraged me lovingly at every step of the book's preparation.

PETER WOLFE

St. Louis, Missouri

Acknowledgments

The author and the publisher join in expressing their thanks for permission to quote copyright passages from the following: *Promise of Love,* Copyright 1939 by Mary Renault, *Kind Are Her Answers,* Copyright 1940 by Mary Renault, *The Middle Mist,* Copyright 1944 by Mary Renault, *Return to Night,* Copyright 1947 by Mary Renault, *North Face,* Copyright 1948 by Mary Renault; all reprinted by permission of William Morrow and Company, Inc.; *The Charioteer,* Copyright 1953 by Mary Renault; *The Last of the Wine,* Copyright 1956 by Mary Renault; *The King Must Die,* Copyright 1958 by Mary Renault; *The Bull from the Sea,* Copyright 1962 by Mary Renault, *The Mask of Apollo,* Copyright 1966 by Mary Renault; all reprinted by permission of Pantheon Books, a Division of Random House, Inc.

Acknowledgments

Contents

Chronology

1905 Mary Challans born September 4 in London; first of two girls.

1921– Attended Clifton High School, Bristol.
1925

1925– Attended St. Hugh's College, Oxford.
1928

1933– Attended Radcliffe Infirmary, Oxford.
1936

1937 Completed nursing training.

1938– Worked as a hospital nurse and returned to Radcliffe In-
1945 firmary, the brain surgery ward.

1939 Publication of *Purposes of Love;* entitled *Promise of Love* in the United States.

1940 Publication of *Kind Are Her Answers.*

1944 Publication of *The Friendly Young Ladies.*

1945 *The Friendly Young Ladies* published in the United States as *The Middle Mist.*

1946 Publication of *Return to Night,* which wins the annual Metro Goldwyn Mayer prize of $150,000.

1947 American publication of *Return to Night.*

1948 Went to live in South Africa; publication of *North Face.*

1953 Publication of *The Charioteer.*

1956 Publication of *The Last of the Wine.*

1958 Publication of *The King Must Die.*

1959 Elected a Fellow of the Royal Society of Literature; American publication of *The Charioteer.*

1961 Elected President, P. E. N. Club of South Africa.

1962 Publication of *The Bull from the Sea.*

1964 Publication of *The Lion in the Gateway,* a children's history of famous Greek battles.

1966 Publication of *The Mask of Apollo.*

1969 Publication of *Fire from Heaven.*

CHAPTER 1

The Cultural Milieu

MARY RENAULT has virtually no standing in the world of literary criticism today. Although all but one of her novels are in print, she is not a popular author in the same sense that Thomas Costain, Leon Uris, or Taylor Caldwell are sneeringly labeled "popular authors." Although Miss Renault is technically bold and even original, she has never invited the term of "writer's writer"; nor has she captured a fashionable coterie. On the other hand, literary critics—readers who write about serious literature in a serious way—seem uniformly convinced that she does not merit any kind of critical discussion. To prove this point, I offer the fact that no recent study of modern British fiction ever refers to her either as an influence, as a phase in a larger literary trend, or as an original creative force. Frederick Karl's *The Contemporary English Novel*, James Hall's *The Tragic Comedians*, William van O'Connor's *The New University Wits*, G. S. Fraser's *The Modern Writer and His World*, John Edward Hardy's *Man in the Modern Novel*, Walter Allen's *The Modern Novel*, and Anthony Burgess' *The Novel Now*, by neglecting her completely, establish that modern criticism gives her no substance, either artistically or philosophically. But the critical establishment has ignored a writer of quality. For Mary Renault is, first of all, a sophisticated artist. As an artist, she neither has nor needs a systematic philosophy. As we shall see, she is chiefly concerned in her later novels with deepening and reconstructing myth for the purpose of describing contemporary problems.

Before discussing her use of anthropology and existentialism, I must first recreate the basic social principles which nourish and shape her art. All writing, it scarcely needs saying, requires selectivity; the dual aim of this chapter is to clarify both her method of artistic selection and her understanding of the general context from which she selects.

I   *Two Decades*

Although Mary Renault published only one novel before 1940, it is hard to find a better term for her than that of a 1930's novelist —a label that will sit more easily when we have distinguished the cultural milieu of the 1930's from that of the 1950's.[1] (In that the great economic unrest and the human suffering bred by the Depression boiled into the war mentality of 1939–45, we need not discuss the social character of the 1940's.) An irony of our times is that the generation which reached adulthood in the 1950's is much more conservative and is much narrower than the corresponding generation of twenty years before. In general, the futilities of Korea and Suez, the uneasy repose generated by the Eisenhower and Macmillan administrations, and the rising popularity of Billy Graham fostered an age of grey-flannel conformity which young intellectuals and coffee-house preachers first began challenging in the mid-1960's.

Although the 1950's stimulated dissent, the content and tone of protest lacked point and pep, respectively. Instead of opposing the cold-war policies of the Power Establishment with creative alternatives, the young dissidents marshalled only blind rage and a shrill fatalism. The prospect of nuclear war not only created excesses; it excused them. A tendency to disbelieve, encouraged both by Sartrean Existentialism and by the reluctance of the logical positivists to discuss ethical questions, clouded the moral atmosphere. The pointless wanderings and Oriental passivity of the Kerouac-Ginsberg clan in America and the close, spontaneous living favored by the Angry Young Men in England failed to rout the opportunism of the administrators.

The standard fictional hero of the 1950's subsists either beneath society or on its fringes: Joe Lampton, at the end of John Braine's *Room at the Top*, grumbles that moral responsibility has disappeared in modern society; Arthur Seaton, in the social jungle of Alan Sillitoe's *Saturday Night and Sunday Morning*, shrinks from any values less tangible than those of a teddy-boy suit, a good meal, or a woman in bed; Osborne's Jimmy Porter is exhausted by his search for personal identity and social coherence in post-war England. On the other hand, the outcasts in Mary Renault's *The Charioteer* (1953) all perceive the value of social solidarity, even if they, as homosexuals, can never really partake of it. By volunteering for military service—an act utterly inconceivable to heterosexuals like Amis's Lucky Jim or Donleavy's Sebastian Dangerfield—these men freely submerge their personal needs in order to join in a common cause.

The rallying of young intellectuals to the banner of Spanish Republicanism in 1936–37 and the enlistments of 1938–40 had no counterpart in the 1950's, either at Korea or Suez. As different as Mary Renault's works are in political attitude and artistic technique, no one born after 1915 could write anything after 1950 like *The Charioteer*, Noël Coward's *Cavalcade*, or W. H. Auden's "Spain 1937" without being considered quaint. To assume that one was a force in a creatively evolving society was jejeune and anachronistic; the best one could wish for was to maintain an uneasy truce with society and to remain anonymous for as long as possible.

The major difference between the two decades, then, centered around the question of the individual's role in society. Practically everyone in England in the 1930's believed that the social order was simply dead, not a shapeless web of power extending inscrutably to all phases of life. Edwardian ideals like abstract duty or the bracing powers of a cold bath and a brisk walk were categorically rejected by Conservative and Communist alike. Julian Fleming's mother in Mary Renault's *Return to Night* (1947) and Mr. Straike in *The Charioteer* are evil not because of any basic flaw in their characters, but because they cling so stubbornly to obsolete standards of conduct. They are the rare exceptions to the general social mentality, however.

Although leading intellectuals shared the belief that the prevailing social code was dead, they also insisted that they could restore society to life; therefore, the 1930's was an age of social and political faith. Cecil Day Lewis suggests in his autobiography, *The Buried Day*, that to many of the people who grew up in the 1945–60 period, the 1930's seemed to be the last time anyone believed in anything. Unemployment and the threat of war failed to quell English optimism. At one political extreme, Lord Beaverbrook and Lord Rothermere, two notable press lords, sought salvation in British nationalism. The popular slogan of "Buy British" grew out of Beaverbrook's program for the removal of all trade restrictions between the various parts of the Empire. Rothermere, founder of the United Empire Party, later leagued with Beaverbrook to support Oswald Mosley's British Union of Fascists.[2]

The failure of reactionary movements quickened hope in other circles. Although the world was complex, it was knowable, and knowledge could grant the control necessary for a workable social ethic. The supremacy of science, and especially of the scientific method, created a collective belief that modern life could be firmly grounded in reason. Sir James Jeans had explained the universe; J. M. Keynes had formulated an economic theory acceptable to almost everybody except zealots of either political extreme; A. J. Ayer's *Language, Truth and Logic* and other writings of the logical positivist movement brought a fresh spirit of detached inquiry to Western philosophy. Nor were these works unread. They and books like Lancelot Hogben's *Mathematics for the Million* and *Science for the Citizen* fostered a sense of public faith that was to ramify in many directions. Changing the world looked like an easy job. The application of detached inquiry to international affairs, like trade, finance, and disarmament, promised to be merely the next logical step in an encompassing social program. This attitude acquired force at home due to a widespread tendency of writers to relate art to politics, morality to esthetics, and science to society. People found signs everywhere of a social system which could flourish without adopting expediency and materialism as its ruling principles.

It is commonly accepted that the most distinguished social literature of the 1930's was written by the Auden circle. Although he later changed his mind, Auden believed that the artist could help create the social change so drastically needed in the middle of the decade. In accord with this belief, he reversed his earlier practice of addressing a coterie. The elliptical allusions, the in-group jargon, and the private group myths he toyed with in *Poems* (1930) and in *The Orators* (1932) reached too few readers to have value as social expression. Accordingly, as the decade advanced, he began to exploit the folk ballad and the popular song. Instead of the sour, blunt imagery of the pit-works, he turned to the heroic couplet of Pope and to the more relaxed cadenzas of dramatic verse.

Chiefly responsible for dissuading Day Lewis and Auden from their pseudo-aristocratic verse techniques was Communism. Day

Lewis writes in retrospect, "What attracted me most, perhaps, in the Communist philosophy was the concept that we discover reality by acting upon it, not thinking about it. . . ." [3] The patrician family backgrounds of Day Lewis and Auden had severed them completely from the working class. Their sense of public commitment was refreshed and strengthened by the promise that poetry could perform an important public service. By embracing Communism with missionary fervor, the two poets could finally reduce the chasm between the artist and the man of action while at the same time resolving the needs of personal and public necessity.

All of Mary Renault's English novels (in contrast to the works set in Greece) take place in Great Britain during the 1937–46 period. Written, as it were, after the fact, they lack the urgency and timeliness found in much of the 1930's writing. Although the perspective of time—her English novels were published between 1939 and 1953—allowed for an objectivity and critical distance unavailable to Day Lewis, Auden, and Christopher Isherwood, the authors of *The Magnetic Mountain* and *The Ascent of F6*, Mary Renault grounds most of her social data in assumptions current during the 1930's. One obvious borrowing occurs in her first novel, *Promise of Love* (1939). In keeping with Stephen Spender's distrust of power, mechanical efficiency, and impersonality in "Pylons" and in "The Express," Miss Renault makes imaginative use of the massive factories built during the 1930's along roads outside of London. A chemical warfare experimental station observed by two of her characters is said to operate through the night. The sinister nightly preparations of poisonous gasses, suggested by the hulking factory, square well with the character associated with it—Dr. Donald Scot-Hallard, a ruthless and tenacious physician who dispatches his surgical chores and his sexual conquests with the same lank efficiency.

Parallels between fictional events and the milieu of the 1930's are also present in the Classical novels. In these works, the author, like Isherwood, Rex Warner, and Orwell before her, turns to the arena of public affairs and political choice. The Athenian polis (*The Last of the Wine* [1956]) and the office of kingship in the two Theseus novels (*The King Must Die* [1958], *The Bull from The Sea* [1962]) suggest the same strenuous blend of private and social values found in the works of the Auden group twenty-five years before. The events leading to the collapse of the polis invite

loose comparisons with the totalitarian threat of the 1930's. Although the novelist attempts no consistent historical parallels, her
portrayal of Spartan force and discipline suggests affinities with
Nazi Germany. This cult of racial destiny undermined all diplomacy and statesmanship involving Germany in the 1930's, just as
it destroyed the Athenian ideals of grace, proportion, and all-
around excellence. Like the Nazis, the Thirty Oligarchs—the
Spartan puppet government that controlled Athens at the end of
the Peloponessian War—replied to civilized dialogue with violence and to balanced wholeness with the secret police. The end
product of their butchery was the law forbidding the teaching of
philosophy and, more pointedly, the execution of Sokrates. Sokrates's trial, along with the collective trials conducted by the
Thirty, bring vividly to mind the infamous Moscow purges and
the Reichstag Fire trials in Germany.

These dramatized statements on the cancerous nature of power,
although not historically consistent, are too pointed to allow us to
overlook Mary Renault's method of historical selection. A writer
cannot willfully extend his artistic range beyond his personal experiences or values. The mood and the movements of the 1930's
provide a cultural framework to which Mary Renault imaginatively responds. But she is not a political propagandist. Her social
views must be seen as absorbed, not applied—as artistic events,
not political manifestoes. So long as we see her writings as assimilated works of literature, we will not ask misleading questions
about partisan doctrine.

II   *Firming Up the Ranks*

The 1930's are so prickly with meanings that any attempt to
compress the decade into a formula would be fatuous. Various
currents interacted with one another in ways that resist classification or labeling; furthermore, since men's lives are not controlled
by the calendar, any model designed to explain an isolated historical period contains within itself the seeds of inaccuracy and distortion. One reliable constant that may be applied to the 1930's,
however, is the principle of cooperative action. Indeed, to discuss
the period without using terms like the "Auden group," the "Left
Book Club," the "Jarrow marchers," and the "Russian-German
Non-Aggression Pact" would drain much of the flavor of the
decade. Although large numbers of people disliked alignment of

any sort, the general insecurity of the times created a need for collective, rather than individual, action. Vivian Lingard wonders in Miss Renault's *Promise of Love* "whether one has the right to attach any value to oneself whatever apart from one's function in the community" (49). The frightening success of totalitarianism in Spain, Italy, and Germany discredited the public serviceability of personal relations. Private values, the young poets such as Auden, MacNeice, and Spender, warned, must be shaped by public conscience. As has been suggested, literature promised to become a political weapon rather than a form of self-indulgence. While Day Lewis tried to synthesize Marx and Lawrence in *A Hope for Poetry*, Auden was promoting "disciplined love" and the intellect at the expense of spontaneity and the instincts.

British public policy, both domestic and foreign, expressed the same endorsement of collective security. Social services were widely extended in the areas of slum clearance and public education. The World Economic Conference in London (1933), the League, and Chamberlain's visits to Germany characterized an era of international conferences. After the failure of diplomacy and arbitration to deter fascism, the cry for cooperative enterprise grew more shrill. Thus we see Louis MacNeice, who was not a Communist, writing in his *Autumn Journal* (1939):

> For from now on
> Each occasion must be used, however trivial,
> To rally the ranks . . . .
> The nicest people in England have been the least
> Apt to solidarity or alignment
> But all of them must now align against the beast
> That prowls at every door and barks in every headline.

As has been stated, the structure of the closing sections of *The Last of the Wine* echoes the disintegration of European society that was taking place while MacNeice was writing his *Autumn Journal*. Although Mary Renault refers to the 1930's intuitively rather than systematically, the spirit of the decade provides a usable esthetic and social past which frequently recurs in her novels. We may compare, for example, the following passages from totally unrelated books. The first, from *Lions and Shadows* (1938), explains Isherwood's public school friendship with Edward Upward; the second characterizes the relationship of Theseus and his male retainers at Eleusis in *The King Must Die*. When we project these two quotes against the group tendency of the 1930's, the esthetic and cultural gap between them diminishes. No less than the workingman's recreation club, the intellectual coterie gained many followers in the early years of the decade:

Our conversation would have been hardly intelligible to anyone who happened to overhear it; it was a rigmarole of private slang, deliberate misquotation, bad puns, bits of parody, and preparatory-school smut.[4]

. . . .
As we got used to each other's speech, we had a language of our own, Greek-Minyan laced with our own jokes and catchwords. No one else could understand it. (80)

    While Auden and his circle were swelling their audience from the clique to the class, similar alignments took place in the theater. The emergence of the cinema had been undermining legitimate theater all over England. Movies offered actors better salaries, a wider public exposure, and fewer theatrical demands—like reducing the number of lines and cues to be memorized. Corresponding to the departure of actors from the stage were the numerous borrowings from film techniques in novels like Aldous Huxley's *Brave New World*, Graham Greene's *Orient Express,* and Isherwood's *The Last of Mr. Norris*. Like the stage production, the novel could not rely on traditional presentational modes to compete with the vividness and the novelty of the camera. Less able to adapt itself to the new photographic realism and to the glamor of Hollywood, the theater sank in popularity from 1918 to 1935.

    At about that time, however, the trend toward public solidarity rescued British stage drama. New theatrical concepts developed in England and in the United States directed themselves to the principle of collective unity. Eliot's *Murder in the Cathedral* grew out of a movement to restore drama to the church, where it had originated. In the case of Eliot's play, dramatist, producer, and ecclesiastical hierarchy joined forces with the aim of promoting spiritual values and a unified church tradition. There was also the ever-present question of the class war. New companies like the

Group Theater and the Unity Theater formed rapidly to promulgate leftist doctrines. Julian Fleming, in *Return to Night,* himself a member of the Lynchwick Dramatic Society, speaks of several left-wing amateur groups his friends have joined.

In *Kind Are Her Answers* (1940), Mary Renault's treatment of amateur theaticals is even more ambitious. We are taken into the wings and the audition room of Brimpton Abbey, where we see the costumes, properties, and makeup kits of the company. The novel abounds with backstage color; we hear, as well, the players discussing the social-esthetic tenets of Agitprop drama: audience involvement and the need to diminish esthetic distance between actors and audience. The chapters devoted to the Brimpton players are in many ways the most realistic in the book. For our immediate purposes, however, they serve to suggest that, although Mary Renault has a firm historical grasp of theater, the modern theater she understands best is the one associated with Clifford Odets, Auden, and Isherwood.

Another popular trend reflected in *Kind Are Her Answers,* which the novel criticizes more sharply, refers to contemporary developments in humanistic religions. In the 1920's Frank Buchman, a youthful American minister, founded an organization called the Oxford Group. Very prominent among the gentry in the early 1930's, the Group dedicated itself to self-improvement through religion. Buchman operated the Group along promotional lines, eliciting statements from well-known athletes and politicians that God had changed their lives. Mary Renault expresses her animus for Buchmanism by naming the leader of the Group's fictional counterpart Dagger. The novel recreates the weekend outings, the confessional intimacy, and the jargon of its prototype. (The young members of the Group revere terms like "Share," "Guidance," and "Absolute Honesty.") An astute psychologist, Mary Renault is not impressed by this Frankness. Janet Anderson sails for Africa on a Group outing because she cannot face the challenge of marriage; Timmie Curtis uses the Group as an escape from the rigors of the university. Further comment on the blighting effects of groupism is found in *Promise of Love,* in the scenes in which Mic and Vivian Lingard encounter noisy parties of hikers. (Hiking, an import from Germany and America, became widely popular in England in the early 1930's.) The belt worn by one of the hikers conveys the idea of stunted sexuality: "In a mo-

ment or two there appeared, along the narrow path that fringed
the lake, a company of Girl Guides. . . . At the back was the
leader, a bright adolescent in the late thirties, with a solid waist in
a shiny leather belt, a well-soaped pink face and eager pale-blue
eyes. Vivian saw her throw back her head and give a jolly, inspir-
ing laugh, looking as if she had just received guidance to do so"
(190). The belt symbol reappears in *Promise of Love* and again in
The Charioteer in conjunction with group relations, but on these
occasions the context is nursing rather than hiking. Since nursing
was Mary Renault's own profession for several years, her description of the tension between group values and private commitment
carries the authority of personal experience. Like many other novelists of the 1930's, she uses psychology, and particularly psycho-
sexuality, to make this tension resonate.

Nearly all of her major characters are dogged by guilt, loneliness, or failure—often by the failure to love. Kit Anderson (*Kind
Are Her Answers*) and Hilary Mansell (*Return to Night*) are two
doctors who use their work to circumvent deep personal problems. Leonora Lane (*The Middle Mist* [1945]) and Julian Fleming (*Return to Night*) both have aptitudes for acting: each is a
fine impersonator and a quick-change artist who enjoys entertain-
ing audiences. But, like Eddie in Elizabeth Bowen's *The Death of
the Heart,* both characters are obsessively defensive; and acting
serves as a mask or a disguise of their true personalities. Leonora
and Julian, however, are even more self-distrustful than Eddie:
not only do they try to hide their personalities from themselves
and from others; they also deliberately redirect their fine energies
away from acceptance of mature responsibility. Julian's acting
ambitions do not extend beyond playing character roles in an obscure provincial company. Leonora runs away from home at the
age of seventeen; ten years later, she is living with another woman
in a Thames-side houseboat and supporting herself by writing
pulp melodramas of the American west. Leonora's fear of men
and the fact that the houseboat is not seaworthy provide two well-
orchestrated motifs which convey the depth of her failure. By
avoiding challenging relationships, she can never emerge as a
first-class writer *or* as a person.

Like Lawrence, Mary Renault urges, therefore, the explora-
tion of the spontaneous, unlaundered self. Like Lawrence, she
seems also to advance an encompassing social ethic in her later

fiction, the contours of which sharpen when we place them within the intellectual framework of the 1930's. Two motifs she borrows from the Auden circle without amplifying upon significantly include underground imagery and the figure of the mountain climber. Subterranean imagery in Day Lewis, Auden, and Warner suggest the dark naked self that usually operates as an untapped source of health. Although Julian Fleming's descent into a Cotswald cave in *Return to Night* figures largely in his moral and social regeneration, the novel indicates nowhere that Mary Renault has universalized her theme. Her use of the mountain climber, although artistically valid, gives the same impression of serving aptly as received doctrine without providing exciting variations. Auden's archetypal mountaineer, especially in *The Ascent of F6*, has rejected his corrupt society. Although he understands that he too is ailing, he usually fails to exploit constructively the new vision which his mountain perspective offers: "The man on the mountain has the hawk's view, the airman's perspective, but is nearly always a failure; for escape from the world of sickness does not always ensure health. Indeed, the mountains are usually associated with self-deception and suggest that the corrupt world will not be rehabilitated by merely escaping from it. . . ."[5]

Leonora Lane climbs mountains with Tom Fawcett and Joe Flint. But in neither case is she renewed with the strength to act creatively in the valley of human involvement. Resigned to an existence on the quaking margins of life, she either flirts with men or flees them when she sees her false security imperiled. Neil Langton recoils from his child's death and his unhappy marriage in *North Face* (1948) by perfecting the austere, exacting discipline of mountain climbing. His most difficult job, although he fails to recognize it, is to overcome his fear of the suffering and guilt that accompany life. Again, the displacement of values is not effected by an independent act of will. Although Neil is self-responsible and self-legislating he cannot exist alone; he needs the love of Ellen Shorland—the name is significant—to regain access to the human community.

Mary Renault reacts with more force and originality to the question of power, particularly social power. Although this theme generated its own fictional tradition in works like Graham Greene's *England Made Me*, Christopher Isherwood's *Goodbye to Berlin*, Rex Warner's *The Aerodrome*, and Anthony Powell's

What's Become of Waring, it was such an urgent presence in the
1930's that Mary Renault's response to it is more osmotic than intellectual. The trend of the hero raised and later shattered was
begun by Joseph Conrad's novels and by Lytton Strachey's icon-
oclastic biographies. Freud's belief that the outstanding man
drives himself to excel in order to compensate for an emotional
void was applied widely to notable public figures of the decade.
The suicides in 1932 of George Eastman and Ivar Kreuger, the
Swedish match-king, invited various psychological interpretations,
most of which discredited uniqueness in the interests of the class
struggle. T. E. Lawrence (d. 1935) and Shakespeare's Coriolanus
also attracted great interest because of the strong aroma of psy-
chosexual disorder they imparted.

Standing at the center of this trend was the figure of Hitler and
the public's complex reaction to him. Like the character of Alkibiades in *The Last of the Wine*, Hitler was viewed as a prodigal son
or errant lover, a charismatic leader openly reprimanded but later appeased and forgiven his excesses. Both Hitler's Chaplinesque
appearance and his naïve theory of creative evolution evoked a
curious sort of comic relief in British hearts. Despite warnings in
Italy and in Spain, the average Englishman found a deterrant to
Bolshevism rather than alarm in Hitler's declaration that his race
of blond giants would some day rule the earth: his program
sounded so ridiculous and extreme that it seemed self-doomed.
For many reasons, people identified with him and even saw themselves as part of his Hegelian world-drama. While they could
siphon their frustrations and anxieties into his self-image, they
were also comforted by the utter folly of his schemes. That he was
both an artist and a writer suggested a crack in his character
which would sooner or later manifest itself in a self-defeating act.
Later, when Western civilization understood that it could not wait
for this blunder to occur, the theory of power as an expression of a
warped mentality gained fresh currency at all levels.

Mary Renault's ideas about power differ subtly from those of
her counterparts. Isherwood in his Berlin fiction sees power as a
reflection of a deranged sexuality; Anthony Powell develops it in
the *Music of Time* sequence as an ugly middle-class movement
that has sprung to hideous life owing to the decadence of British
high society; Greene, in his books of the 1930's, describes power as
a heartless, often faceless, impersonality. In Mary Renault, power

is a trap and a curse. More often than not, her strong characters evoke pathos because power is a quality they neither understand nor want. The ethical, morally sensitive individual often has the responsibility of power forced upon him by the mediocrity, or even the downright moral weakness, of his associates. Power usually afflicts the exceptional person. Dion has been called the wisest and best leader in Classical history after Perikles, but his death in *The Mask of Apollo* (1966), after his short but contaminating reign as ruler of Syracuse, is described as a blessing. Vivian Lingard and Hilary Mansell master their men, but their mastery carries with it self-denial and unexpected moral demands.

Like Vivian and Hilary, Neil Langton and Ralph Lanyon of *The Charioteer* (the names suggest Auden's "tall" men) have an obsessive desire to give. What they cannot do is share; they fear chiefly the responsibility of accepting another person's love. Together with these two men, Vivian Lingard's brother Jan ("He has everything . . . and seems to need nothing." [7]) suffers because he cannot channel his noble qualities into a sustained emotional commitment. Neil Langton's divorce makes him a drug addict and an escapist. Ralph Lanyon is expelled from school after his manly refusal to contradict an immorality charge. Later, when he performs the Prospero-like act of saving Laurie Odell's life, he is rewarded first by an insult and then by rejection. Like Elsie Lane of *The Middle Mist*, he cannot find anyone to accept him even after he has learned the regenerative force of love. Driven from leadership and power by his courage to suffer unjustly, his only recompense is continued loneliness. Jan Lingard is another pathetic Prospero: although he brings Vivian and Mic Freeborn together, he fears intimacy himself. His Grecian smile and the witty remarks he habitually makes to conceal his defensiveness anticipate Neil Langton, a teacher of Classics who also uses wit to cloak an emotional void.

The subject of parent-oriented sexuality has less force in English fiction today than it did in the era from D. H. Lawrence's *Sons and Lovers* to the end of World War II. Mary Renault, however, uses this Freudian-Lawrencian doctrine in most of her work. The only person Jan Lingard ever felt close to was his mother. Julian Fleming gravitates to Hilary Mansell, eleven years his senior, to compensate for his mother's rejection of him. Alexias, whose mother in *The Last of the Wine* died giving him birth, finds older women decidedly more attractive than girls younger than himself; when he does marry, he characteristically chooses the widow of his former idol. Laurie Odell's father was a hard-drinking journalist whom Laurie never saw after the age of five, a fact that may have imparted the romantic glamor to men which forms the basis of his homosexuality. The novelist's most arresting treatment of parent-directed sexuality, however, resides in *The King Must Die* and in *The Bull from the Sea*. These companion novels blend power, sexuality, and politics in a bright embroidery, deepened through point of view. Although Theseus is the ruler of Athens, Eleusis, Megara, Crete, and Thebes, he is not conscious of himself as a success. Political expediency keeps him from marrying Hippolyta, the only woman he ever loves; and, since she later dies defending Athens from an Amazon attack, Theseus also sacrifices her life as well as her honor to the state. As a lover, a king, a husband, a father, and a son, he ultimately defines himself as a failure.

The father search, the fatherland, and the archetypal killing of the father interpenetrate Theseus's personality. His rise to power consists of a chain of murders of either kings, fathers, or father-surrogates. He restores political hope to decadent Crete by killing a king who reminds him of his own father; later he kills Oedipus, Antigone's father-brother, an act which eventually leads to the absorption of Thebes into the Greek federation. These killings and others like them—the slaying of the Year King at Eleusis and the betrayal of his father, Aigeus, king of Athens—contribute so vitally to a unified Greek state under his leadership that we cannot readily distinguish between his private and his public acts. The father, or the father-surrogate, is Theseus's *moira*, a word we may loosely define now as the sum of a man's secular and spiritual potentialities. Theseus's excesses may surprise or even shock us at times; but we must understand that to the ancients morality was not governed by religious scruples. Theseus is not acting irreverently or hypocritically when he prays to Poseidon for strength before sacking a city; in fact, his piety is a major ingredient of his kingship. When he accepts Poseidon unquestioningly as his tutelary deity and sacrifices to him regularly, Poseidon becomes his source of life. Defined variously as the earthquake god (the "earth-shaker"), the God of bulls, horses, and of the sea, and as Theseus's own natural father, he presides over all his "son's" actions. It is no surprise, therefore, that Poseidon's role in Theseus's undoing is as strong as the one he plays in his rise to power. By pridefully banishing Hippolytos from his kingdoms, Theseus unleashes the sea fury which both kills his son and destroys part of Troizen. After Hippolytos's death, Theseus, drained of purpose, lives out his life an unhappy exile.

The figure of Theseus allows Mary Renault to break new ground as a social commentator. Retaining the idea of power, she uses him to explore the problem of reconciling social and personal motivations. I must say, emphatically, however, that her choice of a protagonist reflects no romantic fascism. She renders his personality with all the ironical awareness evident in her portrayals of earlier hero-types, like Jan Lingard and Ralph Lanyon. Theseus succeeds so remarkably because he is not afraid of probing what Auden punningly calls "the burrows of the Nightmare": to adapt onself to one's limitations is to overcome them in part. Morbidly sensitive about his shortness as a youth, Theseus perfects skills in wrestling and bull-leaping. These skills prove, finally, not only useful in themselves but important for the self-discipline and self-knowledge they demand.

His conquest of himself, on the other hand, is imperfect. Throughout both novels he persistently compares his mistresses to his mother, and his insecurity betrays him into taking grave risks for negligible rewards. Even as a mature man, he asserts himself blindly and stubbornly. (We think of Isherwood's remarks in *Lions and Shadows* about "The Test," a dangerous act which men undertake to prove their masculinity, mostly to themselves.) Instead of weighing critically Phaedra's accusation against Hippolytos, he seizes the opportunity to discredit his son and thus to remove the major threat to his aging manhood.

Because both novels are written as an extended memoir, we only view events from the perspective of Theseus, who often misjudges or refuses to face the moral consequences of his choices. Although we shall later present a detailed analysis of his character, what I am now interested in establishing is Mary Renault's use of cultural principles from the 1930's to develop her portrait of him. By dramatizing the psychic identity of a great leader, by telescoping his father-fixation with affairs of state, and by describing his urge to power as the expression of a personality flaw, Mary Renault has perhaps established this point herself.

III *Beyond Pamphleteering*

To overlook the subject of homosexuality in Mary Renault's works would be evasive. Fortunately, the subject can be easily compressed into a survey of the sexual context of the 1930's. The age's endorsement of freedom of any kind dovetailed with the overall repudiation of received moral imperatives. As Muggeridge and then Graves and Hodge indicate in *The Sun Never Sets* and in *The Long Week-End*, sexual freedom was viewed in the 1930's as a solemn duty. Young people discovered sexual permissiveness to be sanctioned by prevailing psychological techniques. Attacking the archaic medical procedures of the 1930's, Mary Renault censures the hospital in which Vivian Lingard works by mentioning the absence of psychology textbooks in its library. In both *Promise of Love* and *Return to Night,* the author works Freudian causality into her characterizations: Julian Fleming dreams of killing his father, and Vivian is reported to have "held down a man recovering from an anaesthetic who kept begging her to get into bed with him and telling her she reminded him of his mother" (82). Vignettes like these do not occur often in more recent British fiction; although writers like Durrell and Iris Murdoch portray sex outspokenly, the sexuality they describe is not schematized; individuals do sleep together in the *Alexandria Quartet* and in *The Flight from the Enchanter,* but they do so with more freedom and gusto. Sexual interaction in today's novels, both in England and America, is merely a "given" or an assumed ingredient of a private relationship.

Attitudes toward homosexuality also differ strikingly today from what they were thirty years ago. Although it has become virtually impossible to attack Jews and Negroes publicly anywhere but in the deep South, people are rarely more liberal than they have to be. Our age of escalation, computers, and national Research and Defense budgets has endorsed Negro rights so uneqivocally in certain legislative areas that other minorities have become scapegoats for people's aggression. The upshot of this trend is that homosexuals are getting a great deal of scorn, as can be seen in most reviews of Baldwin's *Another Country* and Isherwood's *A Single Man.*

The solemn permissiveness of the 1930's yielded a far different attitude. In line with the decade's misguided conviction that it could control things by understanding them rationally, homosexuality inspired considerable sociological inquiry. The traditional segregation of the sexes in expensive public schools explained why homosexuality was more popular among the gentry than among laborers; for the first time, it became fashionable to seek membership in homosexual enclaves at schools, universities, and nursing dormitories. In *The Charioteer,* which was denied publication in America until six years after it had appeared in England in 1953, Charles Fosticue's circle of friends at Oxford is known by homosexuals from all over the British Isles. Laurie Odell, in the same novel, attends a party comprised of homosexuals, most of whom are on active military service. That these men arrange their own social gatherings reverses radically an earlier tendency to denigrate homosexuality as a shameful disorder which must either be submerged or indulged in furtively.

The status of the homosexual, therefore, was continuous with the general relaxation of morals, the collective instinct, and the reductive scientific tendencies which characterized the period. Although Mic Freeborn kisses Vivian Lingard because she reminds him of her brother, Jan, she is not outraged. Accordingly, she aborts herself without any remorse and later asks Jan for money to go on a vacation with Mic: " 'We've been living together, technically, since June, but this is the first chance we've had to do it actually, so it would be fun if we could' " (173–74). The letter, needless to say, is read in the same permissive spirit in which it is written. Jan sends the money without any moral reproaches, and the two lovers enjoy a rapturous vacation together.

As the novel continues, however, this rapture wanes. Indeed, all of Mary Renault's lovers must moderate their romantic idealism. In spite of the period's attempt to make fun a category of reason, the continued suffering, the decline in childbirth, and the suicide increase evidenced in the 1930's prove that the permissive social code was desperate. Critically conscious of this moral bleakness, Mary Renault nevertheless resists the label "social critic." The historical details of her earlier books are much less carefully documented than the intangibles of social dynamics. And although she recommends firmly at times that society can only be improved by critical self-analysis and by the improvement of close human relationships, we cannot place her historically as a disciple of either Lawrence of Forster. Unlike these writers, she has no carefully

developed theoretical program; furthermore, she published nothing until 1939. As timely social criticism, her novels appear too
late and are written from sidelines too intellectually safe for their
commentary to signify.

When we understand that Miss Renault's use of cultural materials from the 1930's is not documentary, we may begin to appreciate her artistic merits. Her awareness of the decade, intuitive and
organic, allows her to fabricate a well-specified context for her
plots. Her imaginative thrust is inward, not outward. Although
novelistic conventions demand a solid temporal and physical setting for dramatic interplay, her abiding fictional interest is consciousness in the Jamesian sense. For this reason, we must describe her as a social moralist rather than as a social critic. She
uses the 1930's as a palpable social medium through which she
communicates her social observations. Although, as I have suggested, a fundamental lack of creative intensity and, possibly, of
judgment prevents her work from rising to the artistry of writers
like Lawrence and Auden, within her natural limitations she can
be very fine indeed. The moral focus of her novels and the importance she grants to the sensitive reaction to event places her work
within the best humanistic traditions of English fiction—the strain
familiarly associated with authors like George Meredith, Henry
James, Virginia Woolf, and Elizabeth Bowen.

CHAPTER 2

Of Love and Hospitals

A BRIEF summary of the characteristics of popular fiction indicates that, from the outset, Mary Renault opted for a literary artistry rather than for popular success. Although her early works are disappointingly uneven in quality, they do avoid many of the concessions to public taste which popular novelists often make only too willingly. The galloping narrative tempo, the slipshod style, the sentimentalized happy ending, the avoidance of evil or human suffering, the predominance of surface action as opposed to psychic depth—these novelistic clichés, which are traps to the careless writer and solid capital to one with an eye on the cash register, have little place in the fictional world of Mary Renault.

Accordingly, her view of human love—an area of human activity tremendously appealing to *all* novelists, popular or otherwise —is uniformly serious. Instead of resorting to the banalities of love-at-first-sight, closely detailed sexuality, and fake romanticism, she insists that people always face deep problems when they intensively involve themselves with others. Additional evidence of her artistic integrity can be found in her use of setting and character types. Her preference for hospitals and doctors' offices, and for characters either pursuing or possessing a Medical Doctor or Registered Nurse degree squares in no way with the fictional stratagems of many of her counterparts. An astute, witty article, "Nurse Novels," by Bill Casey, distinguishes sharply between the stock-nurse heroine and the conventional heroine of popular literature. The nurse heroine, Casey says, is utterly absorbed by her profession. Chaste, sober, and icily unemotional, she has repudiated all values divorced from the operating theater or the hospital ward. The following excerpts from Casey's article summarize deftly the ethics and the ludicrous limitations of the prevailing nurse archetype:

She does not write letters to her parents or receive letters from them, she never phones them, and she never consults their known opinions or biases in making a decision. She is incredibly unrooted and unencumbered, a self-made, self-sufficient blank. Nothing in the past has any reality except her nurse's training . . . . She is a good nurse, she is frequently praised as such, and she takes herself seriously.

. . . .

She is too self-sufficient to be very excited about new experiences, she is morally irreproachable and thus cannot feel guilt or remorse, she is not the victim of gossip, she seems to have little interest in food or clothes . . . . As for affairs of the heart, they hardly seem real enough to cause any discomfort . . . . Nothing seems to matter very much.[1]

The most casual reading of Mary Renault's *Promise of Love, The Middle Mist,* and *North Face* reveals that her hospital workers have little in common with contemporary modes of character presentation, both in the so-called nurse novel and in television. Within the anatomies of Vivian Lingard, Helen Vaughan, and Miss Fisher beats the heart of a woman, not that of a well-trained nurse. These characters are primarily human beings. They are as easily confused as Mary Renault's other characters; they fall in love, and their decisions reflect as much muddled emotion as reason.

Her recurrent use of nurses is, therefore, no more than a reflection of her personal experience. Like her use of the conventions and the social conditions of the 1930's, the nurse and the hospital milieu represent a climate she knows well and, hence, can readily draw from to supply the raw materials of her art. Having worked as a nurse during World War II, she is able to provide her books with a given social situation or fictional *donnée* on the basis of firsthand experience. That she does so without resorting to the reductive fallacies of her counterparts signals a keen wit that blends unity and diversity in an original way.

I   Promise of Love (*1939*)

Although writers like Graham Greene and John Wain have had poor luck with the titles their American publishers have given their books, both the English (*Purposes of Love*) and the American (*Promise of Love*) titles of Mary Renault's first novel express aptly the work's major thesis. The governing idea of this remarkably good first book is that life is an active moving process: and, more pointedly, that the romantic prospect of human love always fails to prepare one for the exacting demands which love, as a process, requires. This bold, complex theme voices what many critics, notably Walter Allen in *The Modern Novel,* believe to be the two richest veins in the British novelistic tradition: first, the difference between appearance and reality; second, the idea that we only learn about ourselves and about others through social interaction.

One of the reasons *Promise of Love* is so impressive is its intelligent multi-dimensional presentation of English life in the 1930's: while Mary Renault adroitly builds her novel around the relationship of Vivian Lingard and Mic Freeborn, she also exercises great care both in sub-plotting and in creating a social milieu which permeates the lives of her characters at all levels. It is important to note, first of all, that—although *Promise of Love* contains the novelist's only excursion into social criticism, the criticism of social institutions—her bias is never proletarian. As hospital employees, Vivian and Mic are underpaid, but they never state their resentment in Marxist terms. The only argument they have with the prevailing economic order is that their meager salaries limit their freedom and range of choice.

The hospital is loathsome mainly because, instead of providing a noble cause for their humane impulses, it is merely a jumble of sordid details smeared over with a veneer of smug professionalism. Most of all, its academic curriculum deliberately avoids the facts of reality: "Their nursing lectures told them nothing. They traced the growth of babies from the first cell, but dismissed their cause with the brevity of a diagnosis. She thought of the elementary psychology, outside their course, which in her brief leisure she had imperfectly assimilated. There were so many things, never adequately explained, which could go wrong" (124).

This same Victorian podginess extends to both the hospital's architecture and its grinding work routine. The grim, iron stairs, the stiffly starched uniforms and the rigidly stratified social hierarchy form an airless web of misery which destroys any personal dignity that the nurses may have hoped to find in their work. Although this criticism may no longer be applicable, Mary Renault describes convincingly the nursing profession in the 1930's as a kind of death. The various wards in the massive, colorless hospital are named after famous battlegrounds, Verdun, Trafalgar, and

Ramillies. But these scenes of glorious battle are burial places, as well, mostly for the young and idealistic.

This irony, which escapes the characters in the novel, is not lost on Mary Renault. At times her satire may grow heavy-handed: "She [Vivian] got a serious reprimand from Sister for breaking off her dusting to address an envelope for a girl with a broken arm" (30). As a rule, however, her attacks are well managed. Sudden changes in staffing and in scheduling make any private life outside the hospital virtually impossible for Vivian. Accordingly, any attempt to cultivate interests or friendships away from the rigors of hospital duty is considered by the hierarchy to be indifference, disloyalty, and moral cowardice.

While the facts of chilly professionalism and of working close to death make nurses emotionally susceptible, numerous restrictions deprive them of emotional outlets. The result is wanton sexual indulgence in the forms of lesbianism and nymphomania. Although Mary Renault keeps the excesses of Colonna Kimball and Fat Collins discreetly in the background, Vivian's inability to resist the sexual advances of both Colonna and Mic unifies the book's social criticism and private drama. This union is made dramatically convincing by skillful descriptions, like the following, which conveys the death-dealing self-denial nurses and nurse-trainees must submit to as a matter of course in their everyday duties:

Her apron-strings held back her shoulders, her high round collar kept up her chin, like a scold's bridle; her cap, rigidly pleated, circumscribed the movements of her head. A white stiffened belt, whose constriction she could feel whenever she tried to breathe-deeply, gripped her waist . . . . Its [i.e., the uniform's] purpose was partly that of a religious habit, a remainder of obedience and renunciation; partly, as such habits generally are, a psychic sterilizer, preventing the inconvenient consciousness of personality. (102)

Social criticism and private drama mingle again in Mary Renault's use of the hospital as a common meeting-ground for Vivian and Mic and, more significantly, as the sterile framework within which they must conduct their relationship. Their work schedules are so wearing that they often find themselves too exhausted to deal with the tensions their relationship generates. Whereas they might ordinarily smooth over minor conflicts with a small gesture of tact or affection, at the end of a day's work they no longer have the physical and mental reserves to offer each other anything but a frayed cantankerousness.

Ironically, the two lovers share a relationship which needs enormous reserves in tact, patience, and endurance. After they are casually brought together by Vivian's brother Jan, Mic explains that he is "free born" in the legal sense as well as in name. Consequently, he is morbidly afraid of siring a bastard himself. This fear manifests itself in two overt ways: a leaning toward homosexuality and evasiveness in all of his social and professional dealings. Although he is an extremely able pathologist, Mic needs to overcome his self-doubt before asserting himself in the competitive world. He must, in short, accept himself before accepting responsibility of any sort. This dual theme is executed with humane sensitivity.

The first outing of Mic and Vivian is a trip to a country inn, called the "Hawk and Ring." Although both characters are in their mid-twenties, they are extremely naïve in sexual matters. Standing on a hill near the inn, they experience a mystical continuity enclosing both themselves and their surroundings. This Whitmanesque merging of personalities constitutes their understanding at this point of love. And as their relation grows more complex and demanding, they continually struggle to recapture this first moment of sublime intimacy: "They embraced as though they were trying to break through one another's bodies" (179). But all future attempts to fuse a single personality out of their unique selves fail.

Mary Renault, incidentally, is careful enough to work her social theme into this first idyllic encounter and also to sow the seeds of their future conflicts. Still reeling from the effects of a long draft of cider, Vivian reacts to Mic in a way that, although extreme, is dramatically valid: "She had slipped somehow from his knees, and he was lying beside her. Her shirt was open to the waist. When had that happened? She couldn't remember. What did it matter, they had been such fools so long. 'Poor Mic,' she murmured, stroking his hair; 'and you were being so good'" (95).

Her grinding, thankless routine at the hospital renders this exaggerated response feasible. Further, her frustrated yearning for self-expression also prompts her to declare her love for him first and to suggest sleeping together the next time they meet. Vivian, then, has finally found an outlet for her submerged aggression. Thanks to a shrewd handling of her expanding point of view, we come to understand along with her the dangers she has unleashed: although the two lovers enjoy sex together, they are not prepared for its emotional consequences. Again, the promise of love proves widely different from the decidedly unromantic demands or purposes they must ultimately face.

Their relationship brings one shock after the other; at each stage, Vivian learns more about herself and about Mic than she can handle. Mary Renault describes love uniformly as a charged encounter that is, at once, unmanageable, abrasive, and vigorously new. From the start, Vivian's expectations are outstripped; when she first begins seeing Mic, he is merely an intellectual companion or, at most, a tactical exercise. Although they later reconstruct their relationship, they continue to have their ease and self-confidence battered by unexpected developments. Their consummation of sex, for instance, is certainly a major hurdle, especially when we link Mic's hidden fears with the fact that he and Vivian are both virgins. Yet they soon discover challenges beyond any physical act. Mary Renault presents with stark honesty the difficulty of sustaining love on a dignified daily basis. Love often takes a long time of nurture, but it may be fractured in a moment. Without understanding what has happened to them, Vivian and Mic discover more than once that a childish act has damaged irreparably the intimacy they have lovingly fostered.

Their relationship can be best described by referring to the bleak statement Auden makes in one of his poems: "After the kiss comes the impulse to throttle." When Vivian and Mic have accepted the importance of emotional involvement, pain and suffering follow remorselessly. By making Vivian accountable for most of the friction, Mary Renault brings home the ferocity inherent in love. Vivian, as the novel's central intelligence, has defined herself from the start as a person of more than ordinary insight and compassion. Yet her romance with Mic automatically brings out her worst traits. It is not by chance that she twice challenges him to race and that twice more she offers to fence with him. Although she knows that power is a corrupting force, she drifts unconsciously into situations which cause her either to test or to hurt Mic. When she accidentally becomes pregnant, for instance, she sees that, to protect him from his worst fears and to safeguard his career, she must abort; but she later tells him of the abortion. Accordingly, in an earlier chapter, she dresses herself in his clothes and parades before him for the dual purpose of reminding him of his homosexuality and of reinforcing his subservience. Vivian is much more competitive and sadistic than she understands. Her greatest challenge is to help Mic overcome his fears without resenting his moral independence. The following passages bring out the obscure contrary rhythms her protectiveness begets in her troubled mind:

Why had she told him about the drug she had taken? Not only a second's thought, but instinct even, should have warned her that it must hurt him. Something hidden in her secret self had seized on this unguarded moment for its purposes. His suffering . . . had revived her sense of power. (192)

. . . .
Mic was growing up. It was a process so rapid that it could be watched . . . . At school he had been alone a good deal because he could not discuss his people or ask other boys to stay; and at Cambridge . . . want of money had produced much the same effect. Now, by imperceptible degrees, even the manner was disappearing. He talked about his work with a confidence that verged often on authority; the resident staff, the physicians first and now the surgeons, had begun to notice him and treated him as one of themselves, a thing not usual in his position. (209–10)

Before Vivian learns the danger of competing with Mic, she makes one final lunge for power at his expense. During an afternoon party given by a friend of her deceased mother, she meets Donald Scot-Hallard, a senior staff physician at the hospital. Selfish, arrogant, and tenacious, he already invited comparisons with Hitler in her mind (106). His scorn for warm human values finds expression in his reiterated suggestion that Vivian has more reality for him as an idea than as a person. But, even though she realizes that he has no personal interest in her, she is content to be his plaything. Scot-Hallard, himself a failure at the deepest emotional level, is her logical sexual partner. Intolerant of pacifism and hotly eager for war as an outlet for his energies, Scot-Hallard seduces her as a finale to her self-betrayal. Mary Renault modulates beautifully the female psychology involved in her choice:

She had dismissed his invitation without a second thought, because the time he had asked for belonged to Mic: but it occurred to her now that as her holiday did not cover a weekend she would be alone all through Mic's working hours. Scot-Hallard, she recollected, had added a postscript suggesting lunch, or tea . . . . It seemed to her that, after all, a brief encounter with him might make a good *apéritif* for the more important meal of life to follow . . . . It seemed sinful to come to it listless if anything could give her a fillip. Unfair, too, to Mic.

. . . .

A new dress was overdue; she had not bought one for the daytime for a year . . . . She owed Mic something fresh; he had much more taste and observation than he laid claim to and she had nothing new to speak of since she had known him. Besides, a new dress was imperative if she was not to wear the same one for Scot-Hallard a second time. (222–23)

Vivian, then, feels guilty about meeting Scot-Hallard but does it anyway. The consequences of her act, which are deepened by the fact that Mic works under his supervision at the hospital, follow relentlessly: Scot-Hallard will not release her from his power until he has had his way with her. Moreover, while her self-deceit betrays her into infidelity, she is made to see her playful act of self-assertion through Mic's eyes: "So as not to see his face any more, she looked in the glass at her own. . . . She saw what he had seen; her mouth and eyes sagging with fatigue which her heavy make-up had masked into dissipation . . . the new hat tilted too far: at one corner of her mouth the lipstick blurred in a small, unmistakable smear" (236).

Vivian misjudges Mic's response to the news of her escapade. In keeping with the feeling of worthlessness foisted upon him by his birth, he believes he has received his due; her faithlessness proves to him that he deserves no better from any woman. As a way of restoring his self-confidence, she sends for her brother, Jan, Mic's good friend, and soon thereafter the two men suffer an auto wreck that eventually takes Jan's life. After the funeral, Mic submerges himself completely in his work. At the end of the novel, he is redeemed by his work, not to mention Jan's sacrifice. He has put on weight, he has stopped coughing, and he is about to take an important job in a new cancer clinic, which will enable him to eclipse his former chief and love-rival, Scot-Hallard. Most significantly, he has acquired the self-acceptance requisite for marriage and even for paternity. He has, in brief, retraced the paths of traditional fictional heroes like Tom Jones and Dickens's Pip of overcoming his illusions, and he is therefore able to root himself securely in the life of his society.

Vivian, however, admits to herself that she can never truly share his success. Even though she will marry him, her sadistic craving for power has stained all their future dealings. She has learned too late the lesson of "disciplined love"; although she and Mic have hurdled many emotional crises, their refurbished relationship excludes her from his trust and confidence: "In the secret battle which had underlain their love, of which she, only, had been aware with the mind, she was now and finally the loser. . . . Like water, she had found her own level; this was as it was, only because she had fought in the conscious craving for self-certainty and power, he in the simple instinctive reaching of his spirit for the good" (192-93). Ironically, then, she cannot partake of the manhood she helped bring about.

Mary Renault operates faithfully within the loneliness and estrangement she has posited as inescapable to the human condition. Mic has endured the cycle of sin, guilt, and redemption; Vivian, too, has come to absorb the Lawrencian credo of female passivity. The last sentence of the novel conveys Mic's growing independence from her and, furthermore, his acceptance of this mode of life: "His mind wandered back to the new laboratories: lying on his elbow, watching the smoke recede and mingle with the shadows, he began planning the work he meant to cover in the first year" (361).

The smoke rings he casually blows throughout the book develop, then, into a symbol of marriage. Yet, in spite of the flimsiness and the evanescence of their union, Vivian and Mic are in a sense morally renewed. By accepting their mutual estrangement, they have outgrown the romantic illusion of transforming themselves, through the power of love, into a single entity. This knowledge is definitely constructive; for, when Mic accepts his apartness from her, he can help her overcome her guilt, her loss, and her despair. The reader's final impression of their relationship is curiously soothing: although they have undergone tremendous misery and waste, they have attained the maturity to understand each other's needs and to communicate as responsible adults. As flawed as their relationship is, it has nonetheless survived the acid of Mic's frustrations and Vivian's sadism.

Like Virginia Woolf and Iris Murdoch, Mary Renault understands that everything in our contingent world is imperfect. But, also like these writers, she cannot be called a defeatist in her attitude toward human purpose. Mic's bitterly gained self-acceptance and Vivian's watchful repentance will keep their marriage from becoming one-sided and imbalanced. Accordingly, neither person will be able to absorb the other. When we align these facts with the love, however imperfect, which has guided them through their numerous crises, we may reasonably assume that the two have supplied the undergirding for a satisfying life together.

As has been suggested, Mary Renault took great care in her first novel to convey the reality of life apart from her two main characters. In addition to serving as Vivian's confidante and as a character in her own right, Colonna Kimball also reflects Vivian's plight. The hospital where both women are nurse-trainees offers as little creative outlet to Colonna as it does to her friend. Tall, gracious, and cultured, Colonna had previously worked as an actress before coming to the hospital. Her mention of Marlowe's *Edward II* early in the novel, therefore, is not accidental; for, in addition to being an actress, and a nurse, Colonna is also a homosexual. Her lesbianism is artfully developed, however, as an adjunct of her response to life in general. As her play-acting and her favorite pastime of reading cowboy stories suggest, she shrinks from the important challenges of life. Lesbian relationships prove attractive to her because of their accessibility, their casualness, and their usually short life-span.

Yet, she finds even these relationships less manageable than she had thought. As soon as Valentine, the nurse with whom she is having an affair, begins going out with one of the house surgeons, she suddenly finds herself jealous. Her innocent romance has grown unwatched into something she is extremely reluctant to sacrifice. At twenty-seven or so, she foresees an empty life; in the future, she will not be able to attract many more Valentines or Vivians; and she cannot continue taking orders in the hospital from her intellectual and social inferiors. To escape the trap, she leaves her job. The sight of Jan Lingard dying has filled her with genuine concern for another person for the first time in many years. She is now ready to face the responsibilities of life directly and maturely. Jan's death and his flip attitude toward his survival teach her the waste of her past. The world is rich, complex, and exciting; to continue neglecting it is an act of both surrender and suicide.

Colonna profits from Jan's tragic example because she is so similar to him. When we first meet him, Jan seems to be the complete man, imperially graced in looks, education, and mental endowments. He has just returned from Germany, Scotland, and Cornwall, where he has caused one person after the next to fall in love with him. Presumably capable of enjoying himself anywhere with anybody, he indirectly reveals himself to be an emotional void. While Vivian is said to take after their scholarly father, Jan favors their mother, the former actress, Mary Hallows. (He does, in fact, address her in his delirium after the car crash.) Yet Vivian overcomes the hollowness of self-sufficiency in a way that her brother does not. Her remark, " 'I suppose I like to think I'm satisfying my personal needs in a way that isn't entirely useless to the community' " (26), falls outside his range of experience and values. By choosing a nursing career, she demonstrates her willingness to seek identity within the arena of human frailty and suffering. Her stormy association with Mic also reveals to her that selfhood is attainable only through direct involvement with others. Although love may quicken our worst impulses, the only alternative is an empty loneliness. Jan never does make the existential leap of commitment, either to a cause or to another person. Despite his extraordinary endowments, he lacks the moral imagination of his sister. Her relationship with Mic, then, regardless of the pain it causes both of them, allows her to outdo the more gifted Jan in human understanding.

Like Forster's Fielding in *A Passage to India*, Jan dramatizes eloquently the humanistic shortcomings of reason, detachment, and self-reliance. One of his first acts in the novel is to console a crying baby; later, his death brings comfort to Vivian and Mic by reuniting them. On the other hand, his intrepid detachment prevents him from bringing any comfort to himself. In the scene in which he introduces his sister to Mic, he is fascinated by the swirling patterns in a can of green paint: " 'It makes all the classic forms. . . . But it's too thin for anything romantic' "(39).

This casual statement anticipates Jan's shortcomings as a man. Form or design dominates his vision of things at the expense of

content or substance. Human relations are events he interprets
esthetically rather than emotionally: "They would make lovely
patterns, intricate intersecting traceries of sinuous lines, like the
tracks of skaters, or of skiers in a snow-slope" (293). Mary Renault's choice of language and of snow symbolism explains her fa-
miliarity with Kantian esthetics. According to Kant, the understanding limits itself to forms and patterns at the exclusion of
morals or ethics, the province of the reason. Jan's sudden revelation, or epiphany, which occurs just before his fatal car crash,
brings home his personal failure in these very terms. Like
Maugham's Philip Carey in *Of Human Bondage,* Jan realizes that
life is a design or embroidery we must weave ourselves; yet, unlike his predecessor, he forfeits his chance to create a rich design
of human involvement:

Before him, the headlamps turned the moths and midges that crossed
their beam to motes of fire. Suddenly, one of their mazes, scattering,
made what seemed to Jan the loveliest and most significant pattern he
had ever seen. It startled with certainty, it linked and illuminated ir-
reconcilables. He knew all at once what he ought to say to Mic; he
knew that it would succeed. He knew, too, the answer to an older
question of his own, an answer he had always been seeking.

. . . .
 He seemed to have awaited, for many years before it reached him,
the great blow, like the swinging blow of an axe, that drove into his
back. (294–95)

Jan dies as he had lived. One of the most important lessons in
anybody's social education is to accept the help of other people.
As a self-made, self-absorbed man, Jan finds this task very difficult. While in the hospital being treated for a fractured spine, he
says that sickness is a state of being during which one does not
belong to oneself. He has, meanwhile, been told that the only
thing keeping him alive is a blood transfusion. The knowledge
that he needs other people is more than he can bear. When Colonna briefly leaves his room to help another patient (this departure, incidentally, is her third, suggesting Peter's three-time denial
of Christ), he kills himself.

We cannot leave *Promise of Love* without remarking upon its
outstanding unity. The book opens with an image suggesting
suffering in the lives of the young and the innocent: "At a white-

tiled table a young girl was sitting, sucking a bullseye and sewing a shroud" (3). After the camera pans over the dingy ward, picking up various details, it settles on Vivian: "Vivian Lingard stooped in a pool of blurred light from the windows, sorting laundry and entering the numbers on a long printed list" (4-5). The drabness, the misery, and the loneliness which strike so sharply hold force until the novel's final sentence. The effect of the novel is one of harsh unity. This promising apprenticeship, ironically, can only cause regret; for, as we shall see, Mary Renault delayed seven years and three novels before writing another work of comparable merit.

II Kind Are Her Answers (*1940*)

Kind Are Her Answers is written with the same clarity and control as its predecessor. There is nothing clumsy or amateurish about the book; the action is well paced without being slick, the dialogue is crisp, and motivation is almost always sure and convincing. The novel fails, not because of any flaw in execution, but because of its triteness. It is craftsmanly because it fails to try anything new or exciting. Whereas the characters in *Promise of Love* were portrayed with sociological and psychological depth, the persons in Mary Renault's thinly designed second novel never transcend their immediate actions. Like humor characters in Roman comedy, they are reducible to a single ruling passion which causes their downfall; but they are not sufficiently fleshed out to discover anything new about themselves *or* their society. The things which imparted scope and power to *Promise of Love* —the struggle for identity, the reverse father-search, the ironical treatment of human emotions—do not reappear in *Kind Are Her Answers*.

Most of the faults of this second work are, indeed, traceable to its narrow concept and design. While Mary Renault's first novel was the carefully deliberated product of many years, her second seems to have leaped onto the printed page without self-criticism. We can discover no clear line of artistic growth between her first two novels because the basic narrative materials are so skimpy in her second work. If dramatic event and character enriched each other to such a degree in *Promise of Love* that the book defies classification as a novel of action or as one of character,[2] *Kind Are Her Answers* is clearly a novel of character—a novel of character, moreover, in which the persons represented are pasted so hurriedly against their moral and social background that they neither please nor surprise.

The story element contains interesting possibilities. Janet and Christopher Anderson, a diligent young physician, have been married about two years. The marriage has failed, largely because of Janet's selfishness and immaturity. In the opening paragraph, Mary Renault conveys economically the facts that the Andersons sleep in separate rooms and that Christopher, or Kit, as he is called most of the time, has fallen out of love. Their first encounter in the book, which begins two pages later, describes both the reason for the blighted marriage and the personal shortcomings of each partner. For Janet quickly reveals herself as such a cormorant that only a person as unformed as Kit would have ever married her in the first place.

Although Janet has little of the energy, the cunning, and the tenacity of Ford Madox Ford's Sylvia Tietjens (*Parade's End*) or Elizabeth Bowen's Anna Quayne (*The Death of the Heart*), Janet stands squarely in the fictional tradition of the self-willed destructive society woman. Bored, impeccably modeled, and unable to sleep, she is both a hater and an eater of men. Presumably caring little for Kit, she only married him for the purpose of having attractive children. About a year before the novel opens, however, she bore a dead baby and, soon after, had a hysterectomy. She and Kit, meanwhile, have not made love since her pregnancy. Now that her mothering instinct has curdled into a hatred for sex, she blames him for her unhappiness. Their marriage is held together, then, only by his pity and her chronic need to punish him. Most of her objections to him are directed to men in general, an indication that her response to him has never been deeply personal. At the same time, she demands the profoundest and the tenderest loyalty on his part; she resents deeply any lessening of the guilt she has transferred to him or any sign that he is tiring of serving as her psychological whipping-boy:

She wished that she had not told Kit that she was sleeping better. Kit was forgetting . . . how sensitive she was, how acutely she felt small coldnesses and failures in response that most women would never even notice . . . . Perhaps if she were to be ill again—as she easily might be, with the cold weather ahead and all this worry—he might realize. She noticed, now, that her head was beginning to ache.

Yes, it really was aching. She felt cold, too. She must not let herself be ill again, for Kit's sake. She would ask him for the tablet after all. He would hardly be asleep yet. Or, if he were, he was so used to being called up that he would soon drop off again; how lucky men were to have no nerves! (13)

Her need for self-justification bars her from understanding her problems, let alone overcoming them. If she does admit that she cannot ask Kit to remain servile, she phrases this concession to him in such a stupid way that it can only breed further resentment: " 'It won't take a minute to finish what I wanted to say to you. It was only to tell you how wrong I feel it was of me to have let the—the physical part of our marriage go, just because it didn't mean anything to *me*. I should simply have told you honestly that it didn't, and fulfilled my part of it for your sake. And that's what I've resolved to do, Kit' " (130-31).

Her decision to join the Group—a quasi-religious organization fusing asceticism, social snobbery, and collective self-improvement—tallies with her self-delusion. After attending three meetings, she becomes a Grouper and begins mouthing heartily the stock creeds of her counterparts. But, while she attunes herself quickly to the mechanical routine of the Group, her values remain unchanged. Instead of learning to become sensitive to other people's needs, she flirts with Timmie Curtis, an impressionable cub of nineteen. But even Timmie, as smitten as he is with her frosty charm and glitter, fails to worship her with the unqualified adoration she demands. She attacks him when he meekly criticizes her for not devoting enough unselfish energy to her marriage. The knowledge that Kit has a life free of her and that she has also lost Timmie's esteem drives her to Africa on a Group excursion. This retreat from responsibility becomes an escape from society and self, for she soon decides to stay in Africa as a governess in a nursery school run by a woman friend:

Janet had found someone to take his place. The new relationship was likely to be free from the inconveniences of the last, for it was a woman. Janet had begun to write about her friend Rachel some weeks before; her influence in the Group, her sympathy, her understanding, the nursery school she kept for children under five. Later it had appeared that Janet was helping with the smallest childen two afternoons a week. In this last letter she said that if she stayed Rachel wanted her to help permanently, and they were thinking of sharing a flat together. (308)

Janet's downfall is well charted: she regresses from her husband to a fawning teen-age admirer and ends her descent by taking care of other people's children. Her self-destructive urge to dominate people has carried her to a remote outpost of civilization where she can exercise her will unchallenged—over very small children.

Although this satire on the nature of power and revenge (the name of Janet's African friend suggests the German word for revenge) is skillfully executed, it creates artistic imbalances elsewhere. Janet is too arbitrarily shipped to Africa to avoid her interfering with the romance of Kit and Christie Heath, which forms the substance of the novel. And, although Janet and Kit are no longer in love, Mary Renault does not convince us that they ever were. Unlike Lawrence in *Sons and Lovers,* she never discusses in this novel the subtle, yet powerful, intangibles growing out of marriage. Kit is as vapid as Janet; neither is capable of feeling pain, as opposed to insult or pique; and neither seems aware, in contrast to Vivian and Mic in *Promise of Love,* that certain human ties unconsciously transcend our overt acts.

Mary Renault has obviously tried to avoid in *Kind Are Her Answers* the standard love triangle of husband, wife, and mistress or lover. But by allowing Kit to detach himself so effortlessly from Janet, she robs her novel of humanistic import. Kit does nothing to dignify his marriage, either through love, understanding, or sheer endurance. When he wearies of shouldering the guilt for Janet's biological incapacity to have children, he simply loses interest. Apart from his folly of marrying her and his meek acceptance of her judgment, he merits our contempt for the lack of creative involvement he brings to his marriage. Where James's Isabel Archer in *The Portrait of a Lady* perceived the moral sanctity of marriage and John Osborne's Porters in *Look Back in Anger* finally reconstruct their marriage within its workable limits, Kit Anderson is morally inert. He either conforms to a degrading situation, or he rebels from it. If his wife does not care for him, this lack of affection is understandable—for neither do we have any for him.

After Kit's frictionless emotional break from Janet, he resolves to avoid women. Almost immediately, however, he meets Christie Heath, grandniece and nurse to the ailing Miss Amy Heath, an elderly heart patient he has been treating. Christie and Kit become lovers the third time they meet at Laurel Dene, the elder Miss Heath's Victorian Gothic estate. His shallowness is conveyed by his automatically recoiling from a super-civilized wife to a mistress completely ruled by sensuality and romance. The Christina-Christopher word play suggests that she represents the aspect of his personality that Janet has suppressed. And Kit does, indeed, oscillate from one extreme to another with little control or self-awareness. When Christie summons him late one night to treat her declining great-aunt, he finds himself putting on a clean collar and taking his midwifery bag with him—his next expected case being a delivery. And on several occasions, he grips her arm or shoulder so forcibly that he hurts her. The man of science cannot cloak his instincts within the musty folds of detachment and objectivity.

As the midwifery bag suggests, Kit is reborn on the stormy night of his third visit to Laurel Dene. But the symbolism of the third visit, the tempest, and the Christina-Christopher doubling motif bring no redemption. As has been suggested, Kit merely shifts from one uncomfortable extreme to another: the unfettered romantic will is just as corrosive as an excess of reason and sophistication. It is consistent with the novel's social philosophy that most of Christie and Kit's meetings occur at night, in the secluded haunt of his childhood, or at the Brimpton Abbey Theater, of which she is a member. Their union is too syrupy and romantically charged to survive in the daylight, civilized world of bank accounts, mortgage payments, and weekend family visitors. Kit, still reeling from the excitement of his rediscovered sensuality, grants her complete charge of their relationship—an obligation she gleefully accepts. And, as her play-acting intimates, she allows them both to be swept dangerously along by her romantic illusions. Presumably enraptured with the idea of having an affair with a handsome young married doctor (Mary Renault's leading male characters are often stunningly handsome), she subjects Kit and herself to an ordeal neither can handle.

Christie seizes every possible opportunity to parade her emotions; in line with her theatrical temperament, she burdens all of her intimate relationships with more intrigue, romance, and emotion than they can bear. Perfectly willing to go to bed with Kit before learning his name, she rebuffs him when they meet the next afternoon. It is not at all surprising that she lets him appease her with a minimum of effort. Consequently, she devises a cipher by means of which they can exchange letters; she arranges the tatty summerhouse on the lawn of Laurel Dene as a trysting place; and she feeds him éclairs, Turkish delight, coffee creams, and coconut biscuits in her zeal to sweeten an intrigue already sultry and overly sticky. Even Kit, as unable as he is to view the relationship in its proper moral or social perspective, sometimes wearies of the romantic excess:

> Kit had been astonished, at first, to find out how quickly Christie had lost any kind of tragic feeling about their necessary deceit. Once she began, she had taken to stratagems as small boys take to playing Red Indians . . . . Her favorite plots were concerned with the exchange of notes; he had assured her that there would be no harm in her occasionally using the post, but she preferred to conceal them in his gloves when he left them in the hall, to throw them, wrapped around stones, into his car as he came up the drive, or to put them in his bag, where they were liable to fall out embarrassingly at the next case he visited. (89)

During one of their summerhouse vigils, she invites him to climb beneath the eiderdown; unanticipated by her, the air is quickly consumed, and they must roll back the eiderdown in order to breathe. Her mode of life, and especially her contempt for practicality, is just as suicidal. At one stage, she is nearly cheated of her life's savings by a sharp theatrical agent who promises her a career on the London stage. Accordingly, she cannot transact an everyday experience like shopping or dining in a public restaurant without friction; when Kit buys her an expensive beaver coat, she makes an undignified scene—which, of course, she later smoothes over with a burst of affection. Most of their ructions, in fact, take place in the afternoon in such locales as city streets, restaurants, or shops. Whereas Janet was a creature of fashionable salons and afternoon teas, Christie's natural milieu is the illusory world of the stage, of rain-scored Gothic mansions, and of lonely romantic glens. Her sensuality and hyper-emotionalism are an oasis after the stylized dryness of Janet, but Kit seems to have learned nothing from his earlier failure. Although he is often disgruntled by Christie, he displays no more courage or initiative with her than he had with his wife.

Anyone with as sweeping an emotional range as Christie delights in the woes of other people. Her emotional susceptibility proves, as well, but a small distance from sexual gluttony; lacking rational control, she is easily corrupted by the sorrows, feigned or otherwise, of anyone who cares to seduce her. Supposedly in love with Kit, she falls prey to the cheap theatricals of a fellow actor; although she knows she is transgressing, she cannot resist the opportunity to indulge her pity:

"Really it was because I felt so sorry for him. You see he's always wanted to go on the stage, and he's good too, but his people are dead and he's got a sister in a sanitorium with T.B. and has to work at insurance, or something, to pay for her. His father died of it and of course secretly he thinks he will too in the end, though he doesn't actually say so." (183)

. . . .

"No, don't you see, it's like being in love in a play. He does it all rather well, you know—I don't mean he ever actually poses, he's quite a sincere sort of creature, but he has what you might call a sense of situation. And when he reaches a specially artistic moment, I think what my part ought to be as you might remember your part in a play, and before I've time to think, I've picked it up. I'm often like that." (185)

Later, she becomes engaged to another member of the acting troupe. Her moral degradation strikes its nadir in this undramatized episode, for her fiancé, Jimmie Burford, is an undistinguished schoolmaster who only wants to marry her to escape living as a tutor in a student dormitory. The engagement is broken the day before the wedding by an unforeseen happening.

During her stay at Laurel Dene, Christie may have offended her great-aunt's servant, Pedlow, a prying, self-righteous spinster who, as Miss Amy's private retainer for many years, could well resent the intrusion of a young helper. At any rate, Pedlow learns of Christie's affair with Kit and explains it in a carefully timed letter to Jimmie. Her motives are never made clear, nor is dramatic motivation important in this curious episode. Harmless and even ludicrous, she represents no outward threat to anyone's tranquillity: "Pedlow opened the door. She was a subterraneous-looking creature with a cachetic skin, and moved with faint crepitations which Kit could never certainly assign to her black alpaca dress, her corsets, or her bones. She still wore the little round cap, like a frilled doily, of two generations back, and . . . two lumps of hair in front and one behind—necessary to support it" (16). Pedlow's letter, then, like the tormented acts of Graham Greene's demonic heroes, explains the power of the unspectacular, the unascertainable, and the seedy in our lives. Decisions need not only concern the person who makes them: the lives of Christie, Jimmie, Kit, and their families are deeply rocked by Pedlow's unexplained act. Christie's sense of pity defines itself ironically as utter selfishness rather than a selfless concern for others. And it is this very selfishness which renders her defenseless; unable to perceive individuals as anything but resonators or sounding-boards to her emotional posturings, she is easily destroyed by the reality she refuses to see. Pedlow's flat colorlessness aptly represents this undramatic but twitchingly real world.

Despite Christie's lapses, she keeps returning to Kit with pledges of everlasting fealty:

"Don't be unhappy, darling," she whispered. "I'm going to take such care of you. Everything will be all right. You'll never be allowed to be unhappy for a minute, even when I'm not there." (149)

. . . .

"Kit, darling, I'll never go away from you any more. Until I see you again, I won't think for a single moment of anyone but you . . . . I promise I will. You do believe me?" (187)

. . . .

"Darling Kit. I'm here to look after you now." Warmly, securely, her voice enclosed him, like the walls of a firelit room. "Everything's going to be all right now. You're never going to be unhappy any more." (314)

These assurances are so heart-rending that Christie believes them herself. As the book's title suggests, she does have the answers; but she fails to support them by honor, restraint, or moderation. Her answers, then, are kind—in that they temporarily assuage Kit's discomfort—and they also correspond to the kind of person she is. In a sense, Christie is, however, untouched by her own emotional vagrancies, including, perhaps, her affair with Kit. She is likened by him at one point to a houri, a member of a Moslem harem whose virginity is perpetually renewed. Kit adds, however, that Moslem women are said to have no soul. Christie, then, one may argue, is Kit's unlaundered anti-self, divorced from her acts by the knowledge that she is merely play-acting. Yet, from an existential standpoint, she is fully accountable for her conduct; hence, she is both soulless and a harlot.

Janet's voyage to Africa and Jimmie's decision to cancel the wedding knit the fortunes of Christie and Kit more closely than ever before. As has been mentioned, however, the religious symbolism accompanying their union carries with it no spiritual transformation. Christie's stirring portrayal of the virgin mother at the Christmas crib in a stage production and Kit's assignation with her during the Abbey's Easter School underscore the novel's basic theme: raw emotionalism and sensuality offer no adequate solution to the problem of conducting close human ties. Although the book has the weakness of failing to posit an intermediate realm between Christie's conduct of life and Janet's, it does develop its ironical religious symbolism clearly and logically. Kit has assumed, at the end, the sexless role of Christie's confessor as well as that of her lover. His medical practice will prevent his obtaining a divorce to marry her, and Christie has given no sign that she will behave any differently than before. As a result, her answers will be kind, tender, and reassuring, but filled with promises she cannot keep.

Kit, meanwhile, has become a grotesque, a sort of Pedlow, trapped by the indignity of his position. His alternatives are, indeed, unpromising. He may, in the future, be redeemed by the Marxism of his friend McKinnon; but this solution is never indicated. Another dubious path to redemption is adumbrated by his senior partner Fraser and the Victorian doctrine of work; but Kit, although workmanlike and energetic, has no exalted sense of vocation or any outstanding gift for medical research. A more feasible possibility is that he will have his license revoked and perforce resume life apart from Christie. His recitation from the last act of *Othello* during an audition suggests more logically, perhaps, that this decision may not be available to him. Christie's continued infidelities, which neither of them seems able to control,

may well infuriate him to the point of murder. The only trouble
with this interpretation is that Mary Renault never conceived him
with enough fire to make murder plausible.

These are the possibilities. Unfortunately, they do not interest
us. Although most of us endorse E. K. Brown's judgment in
Rhythm in the Novel that only bad novels conclude with a simpli-
fied morality, we are neither pleased nor instructed by a fictional
ending in which the characters reflect no new maturity of insight.
Kind Are Her Answers contains several artistically handled motifs. But it advances no theme, moral or otherwise, beyond Sunday School homily. Practically all of the book's weaknesses refer
back to Kit. In her second novel, Mary Renault simply lacked the
artistic seasoning to use a male character as her central intelligence. Her next book, *The Middle Mist,* is much more prudently
executed; Joe Flint and Peter Bracknell only appear when essential to the novel's tempo, and rarely do we view or interpret the
action from their perspectives. Although James, Ford, or even
Isherwood can place an indecisive, self-deluded male character at
the center of a novel, they also provide a lively social background
against which his acts resonate surprisingly. Mary Renault was
not ready for this kind of artistic feat in 1939-40. Kit Anderson is
all too predictable for the novelistic weight he carries. His flimsy
morality and his stupid choices prevent us from caring about him
or about anyone boring enough to associate with him.

III   The Middle Mist (*1945*)

The Middle Mist, published in Great Britain as *The Friendly
Young Ladies,* opens at the Cornwall home of the Lane family.
Although Maude and Arthur Lane have managed to live together
for nearly thirty years, their marriage has been a failure from the
start. We are told that they married because of their youthful romantic illusions; regarding each other first as an extension and
then as a condemnation of themselves, they have been unable,
over the years, to coexist, let alone live romantically. Their views
differ markedly on all the major issues of life—marriage, politics,
education, child-rearing, and religion. We never see them skir-
mishing over a specific question, but their heated arguments develop from a basic incompatibility. The tart fruit of their endless
bickering includes two daughters—Leonora, who, nine years be-
for the novel opens, decisively and definitively left her parents;

and Elsie, ten years her sister's junior, who is still living at home.

The early chapters of the book are dominated by Elsie. Most of her family life consists of her being wantonly used as a shuttlecock by her parents. Their habitual insistence that each is conspiring with her to bring about the ruin of the other has reduced the child to a furtive, cowering animal; and her earliest memory seems to be hiding under a table to avoid getting caught in her parents' verbal crossfire. We are not surprised to learn of her that "her calculations were instinctive, like those of a mouse; she had been making them ever since she could crawl" (1). Wherever she turns, Elsie has no room in which to grow; although she enjoys reading books and writing a diary, she cannot muster the concentration or the self-acceptance to succeed in school. Her poor academic record and social backwardness only deepen her guilt, driving her deeper into a fantasy world of unattainable romantic visions.

In a frighteningly real sense, her family situation is encouraging her to repeat her parents' mistake of choosing an entirely unsuitable mate. Although she has not yet considered the question, marriage is her only refuge from her family. Later in the novel, Elsie herself summarizes what life with her parents is like:

"I wanted to be good to both of them, and for everyone to be happy . . . . You don't know what it's like to think up something that will please one of them, and know if you do it the other will behave as if you'd done it to hurt them. And in the end you just never do anything, you're afraid even to *be* anything, you just go on one day after another, making yourself smaller, and flatter, and duller; you daren't say yes or no because it's sure to be taking sides, you feel mean and wicked if you go out of a room and mean and wicked if you stay. You've forgotten what it's like to try extra hard to be good and find you're more in the wrong than ever . . . ." (77–78)

Her first act in the book is to go for a walk by herself in the rain. Although the brief outing does spare her from another family quarrel, she catches a bad cold and is forced to spend a few days in bed. Although she does not understand her predicament, the only immediate alternative she has, aside from becoming a chronic invalid, is either to invite additional emotional suffering or to leave Cornwall. The only place she can safely read her mail without interruption is the outdoor lavatory; analogously, she can only buy inner repose at the unfair price of endangering her health. As the novel develops, Leonora's abrupt departure from home bulks larger, both for Elsie and the reader.

Elsie not only lacks the grit to repeat her sister's act; the blunt finality of Leonora's departure strikes her as heroic. Leonora, or Leo, as she prefers to call herself, beckons to her suppressed, impressionable sister. From the very beginning, Mary Renault carefully develops a vivid contrast between the Lane girls, which is first to prove the hope and then the loss of Elsie's dreams for happiness: "As she moved, she remembered that her sister Leonora, in the dimly-remembered days when she lived at home, used to cross the room . . . with three flying strides, slam the door, and be half-way down to the beach before there was time to say anything. Elsie had been, and still was, as incapable of following her example as she would have been of soaring through the air" (1).

When Elsie is not punishing herself for parental ingratitude, she envisions her wayward sister as living a wild, adventurous life in London. These thoughts become translated into action because of Peter Bracknell, a young doctor who treats Elsie while the family physician is on vacation. As the first man outside her family she has spoken to between the ages of sixteen and forty, he impresses her tremendously. His youthful charm, his unorthodox opinions, and his jaunty independence exalt him in her eyes to the status of a T. E. Lawrence who has stepped out of Arthurian legend. Himself the son of a divorced couple, he easily convinces her that, by leaving home, she can free her parents from *their* unhappy union. This new vision of herself—as a free agent whose magnanimity will be rewarded by adventure and by Peter's esteem—spurs her search for her sister in Mawley, a small Thames-side village about an hour's train-ride from London.

Elsie's initiation into life is conducted with a good deal of formal ritual, which is undercut and deflated by elements of the picaresque. (Mary Renault remarks that Elsie enjoys ritual, and it is indeed dramatically valid that a person as sheltered and emotionally stunted as Elsie should inflate her pleasures to the level of ceremony or ritual.) She first meets Peter as she comes out of a deep sleep during her illness. This neo-Prince Charming restores her health and then prepares her spiritually for her journey across England by hearing her confessions about her home life and about Leo's heroic escape nine years before. Her discovery of Leo's address, hidden among her mother's private effects in a locked chest, corresponds to the initiation rites undergone by figures like Theseus, Alexander, and King Arthur before their mighty feats. Elsie, however, does not soar to any heights, mythical or otherwise, in her travels. The man she fears as an abductor on the train turns out to be a friendly, polite gentleman with a daughter her own age. Mary Renault incorporates archetypal elements into Elsie's education to convey satirically her heroine's mentality. To celebrate the true beginning of Elsie's education—which will consist largely of disencumbering herself of the romantic illusions into which her parents have forced her to retreat—she exchanges reading material with her fellow rider and eats one of his sandwiches.

All of Elsie's assumptions and expectations are unmet. Mawley, first of all, has a small, dim train station, which fails to square with the romantic image she has imposed upon it. Her meeting with Leo takes place in a seedy wharf-side pub, and each sister fails to recognize the other. Elsie's brief elation upon hearing that Leo lives in a houseboat is punctured by the discovery that the houseboat is no proud, sea-going craft; it is a landlocked imitation tamed by running water, electricity, and comfortable furnishings. But, before Elsie is allowed to judge Leo, Mary Renault shifts her narrative focus. Elsie begins to be seen from Leo's perspective.

As an intruder upon the casual housekeeping routine of Leo and Helen Vaughan, Elsie rapidly becomes a burden and a tactical problem. Her status as a missing person rules out the possibility of her returning to school; on the other hand, she is too young to take a job. At seventeen, she is an anomaly—neither a child nor a young lady—and she is entirely without prospects. To rid themselves of their unwanted responsibility, Helen and Leo try to reunite her with Peter Bracknell, now working as a resident in a London hospital. Having heard her romanticized accounts of life aboard the *Lily-Belle*, Peter is only too glad to see her again—but only as a maneuver to display his charms to Helen and Leo. Elsie soon learns that he does not care for her for herself.

Elsie's plight, at this point, resembles that of young Portia Quayne in Elizabeth Bowen's *The Death of the Heart*. Elsie and Portia are used by their authors to convey the pathetic situation of a young person unable to find anyone to love her. Like Miss Bowen, Mary Renault dramatizes the death of the life of feeling in modern British society. Although Elsie shames several of the other characters by her eagerness to love another person, such as Peter, she is restored to the domestic hell of her parents. Upon learning that they have moved to London, she mistakenly feels that their love for her prompted the move from Cornwall. Soon after, the knowledge that she matters to at least someone drives her to surrender herself to a policeman.

One of the dead hearts in the novel belongs to Peter Bracknell. Because of his juvenile self-esteem, Peter fails to develop as a conscious mind. His role is that of a catalyst, for his advice gives Elsie the strength to leave home. Accordingly, he also causes other patients and nurses to fall in love with him, but without understanding the change he has wrought in their inner lives. Impressed with his wisdom, his manner, and the great power of his position as a doctor, he enjoys gaining the confidence of his associates—especially nurses and female patients. His detachment and clinical objectivity make him both a younger Donald Scot-Hallard (*Promise of Love*) and a Meredithian egoist. Life to Peter is a thought process, based primarily upon abnormal psychology; when people resist modeling themselves on his precepts, he takes offense.

The novel's richest satire occurs in Chapter XIX, when Peter brings Norah Haynes, a nurse he has been trying to educate and impress, aboard the *Lily-Belle* to see how she will react with Helen, Leo, and Elsie. A psychological drama is enacted, but at more levels than he had anticipated. To shield Elsie from the pain of seeing her male ideal scatter his wit and charm among four females, Helen and Leo appropriate Norah. Peter is thus maneuvered into a position where he must waste his talents on Elsie, the person on the houseboat who least interests him. The classic biter-bit device works beautifully: not only does his entourage of female admirers refuse to function predictably; the man who enjoys controlling people is himself manipulated by the goodwill and human compassion he has ignored.

The motive force behind Elsie's choice to leave home is her wish to gain Peter's esteem and approval. By encouraging her to join Leo, he infuses her with new life. Yet when he makes clear his obvious lack of interest in her, he demolishes that life—driving her back to her parents and to a fate worse than the one she had suffered before. Concurrent with this ambivalent presentation of Peter as both creator and destroyer is his top-storey room in the

London hospital where he is a resident surgeon. The panoramic view afforded by his lofty perch suggests the classic ambiguity of either God or Satan surveying his earthly realms. Peter represents an artistic advance from Donald Scot-Hallard in Mary Renault's condemnation of scientific technique and its lofty place in modern western civilization. *The Middle Mist* closes with Peter congratulating himself for the influence he has gained with Helen, Leo, and Elsie. The warm humanity he has overlooked would have enabled him to see the Lane sisters as persons rather than ciphers in a mechanistic formula. It is, after all, the differences between people that make them, at once, human, unique, and irreducibly precious. By closing her novel with Peter's complacent musings, Mary Renault states indirectly that science, or logical analysis, must always come after the fact. Only when things are finished and safely in the past can science do its work. About life as an organic, disorderly process, it can explain nothing.

Peter's structural antithesis is Joe Flint. Whereas Peter is a scientist, Joe writes novels. Instead of organizing and labeling people's lives, Joe accepts them as they are, a fact that accounts for the allegedly high quality of his books. As Elsie learns, when she casually begins reading one of Joe's novels, he doggedly shrinks from smuggling any doctrine or fantasy between himself and reality:

> She read a paragraph, a page, three pages, with growing sensations of discomfort and surprise. No politics, no economics, no pro and con; instead a clear and meticulous description of a dead baby . . . . Elsie had never seen a baby, or, for that matter, anyone else dead. After reading a hundred words, she felt that she had, and that her previous ideas on the subject had been inaccurate . . . . Without a word of generalization, only a picture built up with a detail here and a detail there, one was left not simply with a dead baby, but with death itself. (118)

This directness colors Joe's friendships as well as his books. Although Mary Renault uses too much introductory paraphernalia to establish his thematic importance, he does stand solidly as a sincere, forceful presence when he begins to act on his own. A former Oxonian born in Arizona, he is now writing a new book and supporting himself as a brewer. His island shack near the *Lily-Belle* makes him a neighbor to Leo and Helen, whom he often visits, allegedly, to discuss books, music, and seamanship. If Peter is Mary Renault's conception of the modern scientist, Joe is her prototypical artist. He is too genuinely curious about other people to take on the airs of a writer. And, while his voluntary exile on the island is only temporary, his need for direct experience prevents him from supplying his shack with modern plumbing or electricity. Likewise, he is the only character who acts unselfishly on Elsie's behalf. During a party subtly arranged to provide a suitor for Elsie, thus hopefully shortening her stay aboard the *Lily-Belle*, only Joe tries to relieve the discomfort she feels when the group begins singing smutty songs.

Joe's goodness, however, brings him no happiness. Counterpointing the failure of Elsie's inchoate relationship with Peter is the more complex and deeply felt romance of Leo and Joe. These two encounters differ sharply: if Elsie simply never quickened any sexual response in Peter, Leo and Joe have been fencing erotically with each other for several years. The obstacle which destroys their relationship is no outgrowth of the scientific temper; it refers directly to Leo's flawed rebellion. In order to appreciate the deft orchestration of *The Middle Mist*, we must, therefore, explore her past and her muddled reactions to it.

Leo had run away from home with a man; yet her romantic escapade with Tom Fawcett proved both sexless and tedious, a fact that blighted her attitude toward all the men she has met since that time. Elsie's fantasy that Leo is leading the feckless, carefree life of an artist's mistress also proves accurate to a point; the woman she is sleeping with is a technical illustrator for medical journals and books. And, if Leo has the more creative occupation of a novelist, she grinds out juvenile melodramas of the American West under the pen-name of Tex O'Hara. When the author of *Silver Guns, The Mexican Spur,* and *Quick on the Draw* is censured by her literary agent for eliminating love from her books, we gain further insight into her personality. Leo simply does not understand human love well enough to write about it, even at the level of escape fiction.

Elsie's first glance tells her that Leo has not changed at all since leaving home nine years before. That she is not so tall as Elsie herself suggests also that Leo's rebellion from her family and conventional morality in general has a false ring. The character of Helen Vaughan, the young woman she is living with, provides still

another structural contrast to Leo's stunted emotional development. Helen is poised, relaxed, and self-composed. Her natural-
ness and balanced personality gain expression through the green
dresses she favors and the earthy green and buff appointments of
her room on the *Lily-Belle*. Leo, conversely, submerges her feminine instincts. A quick-change artist and a woman of many guises,
she is reluctant to reveal her femininity to anyone, including herself. When Elsie sees her stylishly dressed, just before the houseboat party, she is understandably confused: "A slim young
woman in a plain, but excellently-cut scarlet frock, her back
turned, was lighting a cigarette, and taking what seemed to Elsie
a rather ill-bred interest in the arrangement of the drinks. Overcome by nervousness at the thought of being left alone to make
conversation, she was about to vanish again, when the stranger
turned round. It was Leo" (122-23).

The epithets applied to Leo, like "the slim shabby boy" (142)
and "the lad in the blue shirt and corduroys" (144), grow in force
as the novel progresses. At one point, Leo falls sick after falling
into the Thames River during a punting contest with Joe. In order
to preserve their rough male comradeship—the only kind of relation she can sustain with a man—Leo endangers her health. Competing with men in masculine activities, especially during her period, signals an obsessive compulsion to mask her sexuality. Her
preference for the nickname Leo, shortened from Leonora, indicates both a truncated life and a willful distortion of her womanhood—one that is conveyed by the Ibsenesque overtones sounded
by the omitted part of her name. By the time Mary Renault remarks of Leo, "There came over her, like a kind of sickness, the
consciousness of being a woman" (240), the novel's fine-grained
structure has demonstrated that Leo's wrong-headedness is as destructive as Peter's.

Self-fear and self-deceit, then, describe the novel's most liberated character to be the one most suppressed in both her personal
life and her vocation. Never having known love in her childhood,
she has not gained the self-command to extend love to another
person. Although Mary Renault retains the vivid contrast between
Leo and Elsie, by degrees the terms of the contrast shift radically.
Both girls have rebelled from their parents. But whereas the
plucky Elsie is eager to love somebody, Leo has never stopped
running from involvement. Even Elsie's chance appearance in

Mawley is a major upset to her shaky composure. She has always excused her leaving home on the grounds that her departure, however unnerving to her parents, did not leave them childless; Elsie's appearance in Mawley blasts this self-justification.

The unfeeling treatment Leo extends to her younger sister is psychologically consistent with her treatment of men. Leo's sexual responses are more lively than she is willing to admit. Although she persistently tries to blunt her erotic impulses, she instinctively retains enough kittenishness, as her name suggests, to enjoy arousing men. Yet, after rousing their interest, she claws them for responding to the woman in her. This network of guilt and suffering is indeed complex. As the reactions of Tom Fawcett, Peter Bracknell, and an off-stage character named Roger Brent show, she awakens a good deal of bewilderment and self-doubt in others. The repercussions of her psychological block upon herself are even more withering. Ironically, she can only hurt the people she likes; and this compulsion, which she understands to a point, is both beyond her control and a constant source of guilt.

A paradigm case is her visit to Peter's room. While he has convinced himself that his goal of making love to her is but a short distance away, *she* is conducting a complex double-game with her emotions. Peter is affable, witty, and physically attractive. In addition to these more obvious advantages, her knowledge that he is a charlatan, gleaned from direct observation and from Elsie's ingenuous remarks about him, makes him an ideal outlet for her need for affection. She feels perfectly safe with him. But although he is no less an impersonal experiment to her than she is to him, she pays a much heavier price for the experience. "She seemed, oddly, to have become more feminine as she grew more malicious" (179), Leo learns of herself somewhere during their session of drinking and kissing. (Matters progress no further than this.) The added burden of knowing that she has betrayed Elsie's love for Peter—which she feels guilty about to begin with—increases the shame she feels for having sacrificed one more victim to her neurosis.

The thematic peak of the book is Leo's affair with Joe Flint. But the loss of her virginity is not accompanied by any significant moral change. To Leo, their relationship until now has been completely satisfying—intimate, but unfettered by sex. For a number of years she and Joe have written, sailed, and climbed mountains together. By encouraging comradeship without emotional involvement, she neglects the fact that she and Joe have already ratified their temperamental and emotional compatibility. She does admit to Helen that her mountain-climbing expedition with Joe has been the happiest day of her life. But she refuses to ask why this episode has taken on such personal importance. The bifold experience of sharing danger with one's beloved and of relying upon him for survival provokes a galvanic thrill.

Yet she will not complete the circuit. After two rather clumsily staged events make them starkly aware of each other's sexuality, Joe insists that their old relationship is dead. By inviting her to join him at his family's Arizona ranch, he offers to renounce the island of self-isolation. Leonora, on the other hand, recoils from the challenge of Joe's manhood. When sex destroys the screen of hearty male fellowship between them, she hastily erects another—her responsibility to Elsie. Leo has not escaped the contagion of suffering. Rather than facing the raw, unaccommodated fact of Joe, she punishes him for loving her; worse, she deprives both of them of a real chance for mature happiness.

At the end of the novel all is confusion and loose ends. In addition to the general sexual frustration, nobody understands anybody else. Elsie, who has outstripped her sister, ironically believes that Leo's self-command has enabled her to confront life candidly and forcefully; Helen regards Elsie as too dreamily adolescent to suffer deeply; Peter, ignorant of the pain he has caused, is still labeling and organizing the lives of his associates. He and Leo are incapable of love; Elsie and Joe seek love but cannot find it. Although all the ingredients for at least two satisfactory relationships are present, they exist in improper combinations. Everyone is left to wander in the "middle mist" of loneliness, ungratified passions, and moral cowardice.

As persuasive and inevitably right as this bitter conclusion is, it rests on a shaky novelistic substructure. Like her parents, Elsie drops out of the action before we have learned all we want to know about her. Leo increases in importance as a character, but we are not prepared for the sudden shift in focus. The novel, as has been suggested, divides into two disjointed halves. Leo's half, furthermore, is not executed with the same charity and warmth extended to Elsie in the opening sections. And, although the author dramatizes brilliantly the contrast resonating between the

Lane sisters, we may well indict her for using abnormal psychology to develop character in a novel that attacks psychology and
scientific technique in general. When we reach *Return to Night,*
we shall also see that between 1944 and 1946 Mary Renault
gained great skill in portraying male characters. Although both
Joe Flint and Peter Bracknell are certainly more convincing than
Kit Anderson of *Kind Are Her Answers,* they are used sparingly
and in situations which evoke an easily worked-out response. If
none of the characters seem capable of surprising themselves or
their author, this criticism applies most directly to Peter and Joe.
Different as they are, they stand chiefly as exercises in static male
psychology.

    The Middle Mist is a much stronger work than *Kind Are Her
Answers.* Yet, like its predecessor, it fails because of its dim male
characters and its faulty structure. A more forcible grasp of Joe
and Peter would have perhaps diminished the effect that the
novel gives of having been written according to cold formula. As
it stands, its tight, carefully balanced structure wars against nov-
elty, surprise, or freshness of vision. As the author's interest in her
work wanes, she blatantly manipulates her characters, especially
Joe and Peter, to conform to a pattern too rigid to allow for the
spontaneity or humane generosity it needs. *The Middle Mist* is a
tired novel.

CHAPTER 3

The Coils of War

PERHAPS the most perplexing, disturbing, and exciting job facing the literary critic involves the classification of a writer's work into clearly defined groups. This task perplexes, first of all, because it demands the application of certain value judgments or descriptive statements and the omission of others. Even if we admit that very few writers develop in a predictably linear way, our job is still maddeningly vexing. The closest we can come to an accurate and just classification is to forget critical absolutes and study the writer on his own terms. Instead of asking whether fiction should be paradox, myth, moral judgment, or an explication of the class war, we must begin with the specific artifact as the expression of a specific mind at a specified time.

But this methodology, as sensible as it appears, brings little reward because there is no general critical agreement on the best way to study a writer as a developing organism. Even after we collect and assemble the various materials a writer uses and indicate the ones he neglects, we still face obstacles. There is simply no *best* critical technique. Although most readers agree that prose fiction is rich territory for the discovery of knowledge and of beauty, we dig in different places. Our needs, our training, and our attitudes differ so widely that we cannot escape falling prey to a methodology conditioned by some kind of special pleading in disguise.

Such are the general objections to any overall statement about a writer's growth. To anticipate some particular objections to my ranging of *Return to Night, North Face,* and *The Charioteer* as a body of work which differs from the three novels studied above and the four later novels, I offer my grouping as tentative. *The Charioteer* has enough affinity with *The Last of the Wine* to stand anomalously as a "post-English" or "pre-Classical" novel. *North Face,* as well, defies classification. As an unsatisfactory work which presents critical problems not found elsewhere in Mary Renault, it too qualifies as an anomaly. On the other hand, the critic's job is to reduce distinctions whenever possible, not to multiply them.

Although *The Charioteer* may be a transitional work, it resembles its two forerunners in many important ways; and it supplies us an observation point from which to study several major preoccupations of the middle period. To dismiss it as a transitional novel would be like omitting the keystone of an arch. And, if *North Face* is an artistic failure, it is a different sort of failure than *Kind Are Her Answers* or *The Middle Mist*. Like James's *The Awkward Age* and *The Sacred Fount*, *North Face* is a stylistic eccentricity, or virtuoso piece, which taught Mary Renault how far she could carry fictional experiments without snapping or losing her novelistic thread. As we shall see, she can even be seen modifying her original intentions within the novel itself. An abortive tour de force, *North Face* figures nonetheless as an important landmark in her artistic development. Not only can we see her learning fictional technique within the body of the work; we also observe her using many of the same narrative modes of *Return to Night* and *The Charioteer* after she keys her book to a more conventional literary register.

Although Mary Renault's middle novels exploit the same provincial English setting of the first three works, one obvious difference between the earlier and the later novels is style. A poised, vivid stylist in all her work, she first displays in *Return to Night* an ability to convey character through sharp and precise physical details. Thus she introduces Elaine Fleming, a major character, by describing briefly but aptly the studied casualness of Mrs. Fleming's appearance: "The correct tweeds, halfway between sporting and urban; the discreetly-toning cashmere jumper with the permissible small pearls; powder but no lipstick; fading fair hair becomingly, but not fashionably dressed, under the inevitable Henry Heath; the tense concealment of emotion before the maid" (37).

This sartorial simplicity, we soon learn, is an outcropping of Mrs. Fleming's chilly personality. Similarly, the rustle of the operating gowns, the sharp ring of the surgical instruments, and the pungent-smelling antiseptics in the hospital scenes of both *Return to Night* and *The Charioteer* demonstrate a new ability to convey mood by means of terse, accurate description. The three works of Mary Renault's middle period contain much solid good writing. Especially noteworthy are the mountain-climbing passages of *North Face*, which look ahead to the mastery of *The Last of the Wine* and *The King Must Die*, where her sure grasp of descriptive detail recreates the color and spirit of Classical antiquity. The rendering of the Athenian temper and the dramatized reconstruction of the Minoan Court both have their artistic roots in Neil Langton's footholds along the crags and escarpments of Devonshire. Where Mary Renault had summarized Leo Lane's mountain-climbing incidents with Tom Fawcett and Joe Flint, summary gives way to scenic immediacy in *North Face*—the result being that Neil and Ellen Shorland enact their exploits before our eyes.

This same stylistic attention to sensory objects extends to Mary Renault's presentation of character in the middle novels. As her writing acquires vividness, her awareness of people reflects a similar growth. Although the leading male characters in this second group of novels are as unformed as their earlier counterparts, Mary Renault justifies them as real persons. We have seen her retreating into both satire and female point of view after her flawed portrayal of Kit Anderson in *Kind Are Her Answers*. *Return to Night* marks a more positive development in fictional strategy. From this point in her career, one feels her portraying more intelligently the inner reality of her male characters.

Instead of serving as fixed references or stimuli for female psychology, Mary Renault's men now take on a genuine life of their own. Beginning with the works of her early maturity, she grounds her method of artistic selectiveness on the principle of "enactment," to borrow a term from F. R. Leavis. The novels after *The Middle Mist* reduce esthetic distance between described, rather than explained, event and the reader's own experience. This telescoping of esthetic distance enables us to observe firsthand the described events as real experiences happening to real people. The happy result is an enormous gain in dramatic immediacy: the immediate becomes immediately rendered. Mary Renault's artistic growth in her middle period, then, may be accurately called "organic." By fusing her new sensitivity to physical details with her humanistic observations, she creates a body of fiction at once more taut and more penetrating than anything she had written before.

Our last justification for studying *Return to Night*, *North Face*, and *The Charioteer* as a roughly unified whole pertains to the common mood and social milieu of the three works: each is a war novel. Except for that brilliant apprentice-piece, *Promise of Love*, Mary Renault had not yet presented the wartime mood as carefully as she does in her middle novels. Neil Langton's marriage is wrecked because of the presence of American military bases in England during the World War II. Practically all the action of *The Charioteer* centers around a British military hospital in 1940. And, in *Return to Night*, not only does Julian Fleming's impending call-up figure largely in his choices; his mother married and bore him during the war of 1914-18, when she succumbed to the same collective tension and frayed nerves about to rampage through England once more at the novel's conclusion.

Again excluding *Promise of Love*, these wartime conditions differ markedly from the social landscape of Mary Renault's earlier and later novels. War is never a presence in *Kind Are Her Answers* (Janet Anderson sails to Africa without any mention of Mussolini's conquest of Ethiopia). And, though Leo Lane's fear of men and Peter Bracknell's lack of concern for people as legitimate ends in themselves create the kind of moral vacuum which makes Fascist excesses possible, *The Middle Mist* never rises to the level of political comment. Accordingly, the blending of myth, history, and anthropology in Miss Renault's classical novels attains a grandeur that eclipses the range of domestic fiction. The major difference between Mary Renault's first brace of novels and her second resides in concreteness, immediacy, and clarity of focus. Perhaps it is not premature to suggest that, in her Classical phase, she subordinates the sharp specification of her middle period to broader cultural themes. But the question of her continued artistic growth must await its proper place.

I   Return to Night (*1946*)

Set in 1938-39, *Return to Night* records the erratic love affair of Dr. Hilary Mansell and Julian Fleming, a rusticated Oxonian eleven years her junior. Although Julian's psychological predicament forms the narrative center of the book, Hilary is much more than a passive central intelligence or sounding-board. We meet her in the shrewdly constructed first chapter when she is just leaving the local hospital, where she had been summoned on an emergency call: "A small keen wind was stirring; she felt cold, and thought with dejection of the two hours, an interval too short for sleep but far too long for breakfast, which stretched ahead" (5). Another lost wayfarer in the middle mist of loneliness and shallow personal relationships, Hilary is a thirty-four-year-old doctor whose scientific impulses have no outlet in her dull Gloucestershire parish.

Competitive, sensitive, and eager for creative challenges, she is vocationally liberated but professionally and personally frustrated. Her hospital routine of incompetent nurses, snide administrators, and archaic equipment not only fails to re-channel her stunted inner life; it also robs her of the self-knowledge she has eluded since her unhappy love affair of ten years before. Mary Renault soon makes it evident that the title of the book applies to Hilary as much as it does to the more spectacular Julian. Their awkward age difference, the approaching war, and Julian's lack of prospects make them an oddly mated, if not mis-mated, couple. In that Hilary's choice of him is conditioned by boredom and loneliness, the path she traces in the book goes from uncertainty and overcast emotions to darkness. (The novel begins at five in the morning and ends in the blackness of a winter midnight.) Whether her return to night is a regression or a creative descent into the dark core of prime experience forms one of the book's major themes. We shall return to it as soon as we see how it operates in line with some of the other narrative elements of the novel.

After leaving the hospital in Chapter I, Hilary drives to a remote field of larches and flowers, where she soon falls asleep. She then finds herself suddenly awakened by the stunningly handsome Julian, who is riding his horse. Although her first reaction to him is academic, her defensive denial of his dashing sexual appeal reveals that she has been touched: "She felt a little detached from reality. The light, the setting, the hour, seemed a theatrical extravagance, exaggerating, needlessly, what was already excessive, the most spectacularly beautiful human creature she had ever seen. Because her habit of mind had made her hostile to excess, she thought irritably, It's ridiculous. It's like an illustration to something" (14).

This excellent first chapter has strong Conradian overtones. Although Mary Renault traces Hilary's actions consecutively, something Conrad would not normally do with a character in an opening chapter, she develops her chapter around a sharp image rendered through point of view—Hilary's sharp visual impression of Julian. He materializes as a medieval knight, riding his plunging steed and awakening at dawn his sleeping mistress. His unfitness for the role of the heroic Prince Charming is disclosed in the second chapter, where Hilary rediscovers him as an emergency patient in the hospital. In this episode, Mary Renault stresses his immaturity and helplessness rather than the heroic profile of Chapter I. Lying unconscious with a broken collar-bone, the proud knight is now ministered to by females—the Matron, Nurse Jones, and Hilary herself. His most striking feature now is his passive boyishness. Hilary thinks him twenty or younger, while actually he is twenty-three. Totally dependent and incapable of action, he can only survive if he is acted upon—by women, no less —and he even sinks below the boyhood level to that of an infant when he vomits and gropes wildly for Hilary's hand.

His regression from flaming manhood to infancy is presented against the backdrop of a delivery Hilary performed before coming to the hospital, and we should note the similarities between the scenes. The first two quotations are extracted from the earlier episode:

Moving . . . in undirected protest, a hand, perfect and slender like an adult's, closed round one of Hilary's fingers . . . . (17)
Hilary carried the shoe-box over, and tilted it. "We mustn't uncover any more of her. They feel the cold." (18)

.   .   .   .

He drew in a long, gasping breath; she saw the iris of the eyes contract, trying to focus, then relax into blindness again. His fingers, at first loose and unresponsive, closed round hers . . . . (28)
Hilary . . . noted with speechless exasperation the open window, and the long motionless form of the patient lying in its draught, exposed down to the loins. (21)

Julian's swift descent to the hand-seeking infant does not eradicate the heroic imagery dominating Chapter I. Indeed, the two opening chapters of *Return to Night* are of a piece, not only with themselves but with the rest of the novel. While Hilary is treating Julian in Chapter II, she expresses more than just a clinical interest. Although she was correct in warning herself of the danger of overestimating surface glamor, she *has* been charmed by Julian's looks. By lingering at his bedside longer than necessary and by unconsciously arranging her hospital rounds so as to visit Julian last, she defines herself as a human being—as a creature capable of acting in clear opposition to her rational impulses. Good-humored glimpses like this one into Hilary's character furnish the light irony needed to balance her solemn image of herself as a detached, workmanlike scientist.

Several months lapse before they meet again. This time they come together, accidentally once more, at the hospital's annual Christmas party, where Julian surprises her by impersonating a monkey to the delight of two small children:

> Squatting on the last few steps of the staircase, in a doubled-up simian crouch, was a man whose face it was first difficult to see, since it was partly obscured by his knees. He was scratching his armpit, reproducing a monkey's sporadic but earnest concentration. When he moved, she glimpsed a prognathous-looking jaw and a hideously grimacing mouth beneath a mournful stare. Christine, hopping on one leg with delight, was handing him an imaginary morsel. He snatched at it, and went through motions of peeling a banana so lifelike that she could almost see the skin when he threw it away. (65)

When Hilary and Julian leave the party briefly to walk in the hospital's adjoining garden, she is again surprised—this time by his practice of shredding the leaves from the garden shrubbery: "Julian broke another sprig from the yew, turned it round to catch the light, and stripped it, ruthlessly and systematically, like the first" (83). This willful destruction of natural beauty and Julian's monkey-imitation, we soon learn, are curiously consistent. A born actor, he later explains that he greatly prefers character roles to straight parts: " 'Actually, I never feel myself on the stage unless I look different, I really don't know why' " (125). His favorite role, which he performed in an Oxford production, is that of Caliban in *The Tempest*. And when a last-minute emergency forces him to portray a grizzled buccaneer in a pirate melodrama, his impromptu rendition of the scarred, twisted villain is chillingly authentic. Morbidly ashamed of his beautiful appearance, Julian can only act after he has made himself physically repulsive.

This drive to self-abasement exerts the same power off the stage. Mary Renault joins the various threads of his psychological predicament in Chapter XII, which seems on the surface a jumble of unrelated events rather than the brilliantly organized artistic unit it really is. In a bald factual account of the action of this fifty-eight-page compositional whole, Julian visits Hilary at her home, his mother having left town on a trip to her sister; he takes Hilary to the larch-wood of Chapter I, where he fights with a drunken passerby; Hilary accompanies Julian to his home, where she cleans and dresses his wounds; they then return to her cottage and become lovers.

As has been suggested, this varied action and scene-shifting are more closely unified than they superficially appear to be. Julian's hatred of his physical beauty compelled him to mar his face before offering himself to Hilary as a lover. Moreover, this mental acrobatic tallies with the imagery of Chapter I. As the self-abasing knight of medieval romance, Julian must earn his lady's love by performing a valorous act. By picking a fight with Ted, the visiting Cockney wedding-guest, he also risks his life; his decision to fight while still recuperating from his brain surgery conveys both his self-contempt and his latent death wish. No lesser danger than jeopardizing his life can convince him of his worthiness to be Hilary's lover; and, if he dies in the fight, he reaps the gain of acquitting himself honorably.

As Mary Renault did in the episode describing the car accident in *Promise of Love*, she again introduces minor characters into *Return to Night* to portray physical violence. But the scene in the later book is more cleanly written. Jan Lingard's fatal accident, though well reported, was necessary to open a path for the stalled relationship of his sister Vivian and Mic Freeborn. The fight in the larch-wood is admittedly no less essential to the plot of *Return to Night*. But, aside from bristling with psychological suggestion, it also foreshadows Hilary's future with Julian. While he is being buffeted by the cumbersome factory-hand—solid life in its most coarse and most surprising manifestation—she must stand helplessly at the sidelines, doing nothing.

The ensuing visit to Julian's home is concurrent with the rapidly unfolding psychological and moral drama. As we shall see, Julian's most formidable challenge is to see Hilary as a person in her own right and not merely as a phase or a projection of his troubled mentality. Earlier, he had noted the sheer dread of bringing her to his mother's home: "It was practically impossible to think of her as an entity of the polite world who had a right to expect that one should return her hospitality suitably, and even, of all impossible incongruities, invite her home. (But please God, not today.) It was a violation of her mystery; one should go to her, always" (160).

By allowing her to enter his mother's home, significantly by the back door, Julian demonstrates a marked advance over his earlier psychological inertia. Although he could not have entertained her as a close personal friend in his mother's withering presence, the absence of his mother prepares him, along with the fight, to have the first sexual experience of his life. This twelfth chapter is remarkable for more than its wealth of sensitively perceived data. The various degrees of awareness—Hilary's, Julian's, and the reader's—are angled from overlapping fields of vision. Although the events are framed within the recording mind of Hilary, she does not yet know Julian well enough to grasp their meaning. Julian's own knotted mind acts as a distorting lens over his actions, inviting both Hilary and the reader to search for inferences in regions where none exist. This slanted web of viewpoints, finally, creates a perspective the reader can later use to observe the progress of the love affair.

Julian's basic conflict recalls several literary creations of the 1930's: Michael Ransom of *The Ascent of F6*, Isherwood's Arthur Norris in *The Last of Mr. Norris*, and Greene's Kate Farrant of *England Made Me*. Perhaps the most obvious of these antecedents is Ransom of *F6*, which Julian avidly reads. The obscure maternal attachments of Ransom and of Shakespeare's Coriolanus, a figure widely discussed in the 1930's, furnish the psychological undergirding of Julian's problem. Elaine Fleming, Julian's mother, has broken his spirit by decrying his theatrical ambitions, by upbraiding him in public, and by continually reminding him that his good looks are a handicap instead of an advantage.

The most maddening aspect of her disparagement is that he can never pin it to a specific issue or action; there is simply no talking point or ground for improvement. Mrs. Fleming's admonitions to her son involve nothing less than a total rejection of his person: "That was the worst of all, that she never allowed any crisis, any definition. Punishment would have seemed like forgiveness, rather than this withdrawal which was a reaction of the whole self. The loneliness it left was absolute; there was no appeal because, till the unknown moment of her return, nothing was there to receive appeal" (168).

Julian's hoped-for deliverance from his mother's tyranny is complicated by the facts that she is a patron of Hilary's hospital; and, that during Julian's confinement for his head-wound, she openly derided Hilary's professional competence. It is also suggested that, as his elder, Hilary represents a threat to Mrs. Fleming's maternal position. These various complications swell to a new dimension in Chapter XIX, where Mrs. Fleming reluctantly divulges her reasons for her jaundiced opinion of her son.

If Mary Renault ever gains academic critical attention, it is hard to imagine any other passage in her fiction spurring more controversy than Elaine Fleming's mental inventory in *Return to Night*. First, this retrospective passage is far too long; dropped upon the reader in the form of undigested summary, it arrests the action for seventeen pages. Perhaps worst of all, this important background material is too arbitrarily unloaded by an act of authorial will. Rather than serving as delayed information, like Ibsen's master builder's chronic fear of heights or the alcoholism of Brian Moore's Judith Hearne, this undramatized summary strikes the reader as deliberately withheld data. It is only included in Chapter XIX because it could not have been included earlier without spoiling the plot. In extenuation, however, Mrs. Fleming's long recitation is entirely in character. She never apologizes or suggests that she might have acted differently toward Julian. Furthermore, when she finishes talking, he understands clearly the line of action he must take to free himself from her blighting influence.

In spite of Mrs. Fleming's efforts to the contrary, her recitation reveals that, like most of us, her character has been formed by facts and concrete events rather than by abstract principles. While serving as a volunteer nurse in France during World War I, she was wooed and won by Andre O'Connell, a swaggering Roman Catholic stage actor from Canada. Although Captain O'Connell could not boast of important social ties or material wealth, his dash and the general climate of war broke down her sober resolves concerning honor, duty, and family. When she accidentally learned that her new husband was *already* married, she abruptly left him and then reported him to his commanding officer. What Elaine O'Connell overlooked completely was the depth and the sincerity of her actor-husband's love. By violating both canonical and civil law to marry her, he risked eternal damnation as well as a long prison term. Instead of viewing his conduct as a supreme declaration of love, she punished him with a divorce, a court-martial, and a dishonorable discharge from the Army; and Mary Renault keys this part of the recitation in an extremely ironical register. Mrs. Fleming never indicates that her wounded vanity prompted her indignant march to O'Connell's commanding officer; instead, she regarded herself as a disinterested public benefactor, assuming the mantles of judge, jury, and executioner out of goodwill and humanitarian zeal: " 'One has a duty to society. There might have been other women. I informed his commanding officer myself' " (394). " 'I assured him that all I wanted was ordinary justice, and to protect other people' " (395).

Although she never faces the truth, her brief marriage to O'Connell deadened both her emotions and her esthetic sense. Lacking the elasticity and the moral fiber to risk romance again, she married Major Richard Fleming, a solid, reliable Englishman with a Victorian sense of duty and with an established landowning family. This choice of a husband shows that her attitude toward life has gone full circle. Having renounced beauty and excitement, she has retreated into a safer, less challenging relationship. Yet, even here, the picture may not be complete; for, at this point in her discourse, we sense the absence of important data. Either Mrs. Fleming has intentionally omitted or has chosen to forget certain particulars of her second marriage.

Richard Fleming, for instance, reacted to Elaine's earlier marriage as a British gentlemen should: " 'Shortly before we were married, he told me again that he thought we should be happier if we decided never, in any circumstances, to refer to the past. I agreed, and we never spoke of it afterwards' " (392). This bromide from the Victorian apothecary's cupboard may not have worked, however. To claim acceptance of a deep personal affront (Fleming courted Elaine before her first marriage) is not the same as living with it on a daily basis. Although Fleming may have been willing to sacrifice his principles to uphold the shattered dignity of British womanhood, the inescapable knowledge that

Elaine married him out of prudency rather than passion may have rocked him psychologically beyond the purlieus of conventional British morality.

The supposition that his death in battle was intentional takes on weight when we observe that Julian may be O'Connell's son. An aspiring actor gifted with exceptional beauty, he certainly resembles O'Connell more than he does his legal father.[1] Mrs. Fleming, naturally, never offers this as a possibility. Like her conduct, her long recitation mirrors accurately the social order that died with her second husband in World War I: dutiful and stalwart, yet stiffly evasive and blind to anything not reducible to a concrete act of will. Although we must admit that her lengthy account is bad novelistic technique, it holds up well both as social history and as closely documented character portrayal.

If Chapter XIX explains why Elaine Fleming has driven beauty and romance from her thwarted life, it also clarifies her wholesale rejection of Julian—a living reminder of her painful failure with O'Connell. Never having enjoyed the warm security of mother-love, he gravitates naturally to women older than himself. His not-so-random daydreams project his female ideal as a thinly veiled mother-image: the throbbing bosom of the earth, enclosed by a sunsplashed fan of undulating trees: "Heaven was warm and enclosed, secure from intrusion; the branches and leaves of the tree of life encircled it, the sun through the leaves making it warm and sleepy; the river flowed through it, sun-warmed, and one could live and breathe in the river like a fish in a summer stream. As long as he could remember, he had thought of heaven like this" (157–58).

His sexual experience before meeting Hilary consisted of an inchoate attraction to an actress twice his age whom he had never met personally and whose leading-man he had aspired to be. Hilary, however, brings his frustrations and obscure yearnings to a sharp focus. As an older woman and his doctor, the healing Hilary represents to him a new promise—a mother-image that has not rejected him. As such, she is a positive goal to be relentlessly pursued. Julian's actual pursuit is enacted at this level: when he sends her a bouquet of flowers for Christmas, the greeting card is attached by a silver cord, *The Silver Cord* being a Sidney Howard play about a young man with a mother-fixation.

Later, after they become lovers, Julian constantly demands that
Hilary kiss him "properly," thus evoking his own fixation at the
oral stage—the earliest level of development in Freud's scale of
sexual growth. And, when the couple makes love for the first time,
Julian is the virgin, not Hilary. Waking the next morning, she observes that her nightgown, her shoulder, and breast are spotted
with blood. Although the flow of blood is from Julian's damagi-
eye, Mary Renault's thematic execution is clear: the psychologically unborn Julian, like the helpless lad on the hospital cot in
Chapter II, still needs Hilary as an energizing source.

The collected evidence shows that Hilary must be a confessor, a
doctor, a midwife, a mother, and a mistress to Julian. How well
suited is she, we must ask, for this enormous responsibility? Mary
Renault dramatizes this problem with the same tough dignity that
colors most of the novel. She never shows her heroine as a passive
sounding-board or as a dim projection of Julian's mind. A person
with her own needs, fears, and values, Hilary is not a fixed object
in anybody's world. She constantly surprises herself and the
reader by her unexpected reactions to Julian. First of all, she cannot help projecting their affair against the backdrop of her blasted
romance with David, which took place ten years before the novel
opens. She comes to understand, no less than Julian and his
mother, that *her* past influences the future of *other* people.

While they were both graduate residents in a hospital, she and
David had a love affair which lasted a year, at which time he was
offered a promotion she herself had coveted. Resourceful, independent, and self-sufficient, David is the direct opposite of Julian.
Like Elaine Fleming, who recoiled from a romantic vision of love-
as-excitement to a tamer, more jaded one of love-as-duty, Hilary
turns from an extremely competitive man to a veritable adolescent. Where David parried her professional and personal energy
with his shrill independence, Julian requires all she can give.
Once sexually competitive, she finds herself, ten years later, ironically attached to an utterly subservient man with no wish to com-
pete. The freedom she had battled for with David finally comes
to her but in starker, grimmer terms than she had ever imagined.
She also learns that her enlightened humanistic ethic proves inad-
equate to deal with Julian's need for self-discovery and self-justification. In his inept boyish way, he persistently courts her: "She
had had two weeks of duty at the Hospital since their first meet-

ing, and during each of them had encountered him there a little
too often, it seemed, for mere coincidence. He always contrived to
leave with her, and to drag out their progress through the garden
as long as possible" (80). Annoyed, magnetized, and baffled in
turn by his awkward advances, she suddenly realizes that she has
grown fond of him. Before the attraction of his good looks has
worn off, he fills a void in her empty life.

In all her fiction, the characters Mary Renault most admires—
like Mic Freeborn, Elsie Lane, and Joe Flint—are the ones that
resist easy classification. Julian's appeal for Hilary falls within this
range. Oscillating between joy and despair, abounding self-
confidence and morose silence, and between suffocating attentiveness to her and wanton neglect, he refuses to be labeled. Hilary
often regrets encouraging his advances, and she finally admits
having fallen in love with him before she knew it. The various
lags between her vision of their relationship and the relationship
itself reveals that, in her own way, she is just as unformed and
unready as Julian.

As the novel progresses, Hilary discovers the necessary limits
within which they must wage their romance. Because of their age
difference, his lack of a job, and his mother's opposition both to
herself and his acting career, Hilary persuades him to wait a year
before marriage. This advice, of course, is sound and prudent.
Yet, ironically, their love only becomes real when it transgresses
such civilized judgments. One of the reasons *Return to Night*
makes such exciting reading is its unified picture of sexual love as
an involuntary adventure in development. Like Vivian Lingard
and Kit Anderson, Hilary learns through loving that she is capable
of deliberate cruelty. Because her resentment toward Julian is ac-
cumulative rather than specific, this knowledge comes as a great
surprise. It reaches its most heightened expression when she discovers he is feigning illness to shirk responsibility: by retreating
into the false security of an imagined case of laryngitis, he avoids
seeing a theatrical producer in London about a stage audition.

The worst feature of Hilary's conduct is that she knows Julian
cannot help punishing himself for his physical beauty. In that he
is behaving as honestly as he possibly can, given his relationship
with his mother, Hilary's reaction is more contemptible than his.
Only a basically moral person would worry about injuring other
people, as Julian does: " 'You can't have a father who's a swine

and a brute, as mine was, without wondering where it's going to come out in you'" (327). Openly disregarding his involuntary limitations, she attacks him where he is most defenseless:

"I've only been working; not handing cups of tea to old ladies and thinking what sort of doctor I'd be if I could only make the effort to be one."

She felt herself go white with anger. "Don't try to put me in the wrong. You know it didn't bore me, as long as I believed in it. If it had the slightest reality, it wouldn't bore me now. You're like a child bragging of what it will do when it's grown-up. Except that a normal child wants to grow up, and you're afraid to." (340)

It is consistent with Mary Renault's personalist ethic that this temperamental flare-up should bring the lovers closer together. Hilary becomes aware of her deep need for Julian precisely because he is able to plumb wild depths of her personality. This merging of their fortunes is managed without any preparations or explanations: "Suddenly they both began to laugh" (346). Their vision of each other at this crucial point is Lawrencian in character. Like Ursula and Birkin in Lawrence's *Women in Love,* they share their most intense moment of intimacy after their fiercest quarrel. By yielding to the authority of the blood, they achieve an understanding that overrides the feeble demands of rational justification.

This new knowledge is genuinely creative: while it places Julian beyond the reach of his mother, it also allows him and Hilary to cope with problems beyond their range of possible knowledge and control. Ironically, their decision to postpone marrying for a year creates an uglier impression than the one they had tried to avoid. Hilary discovers that local gossip has linked Julian romantically not with her, but with Lisa Clare, her married landlady-friend. Although this situation is unpleasant enough, it is aggravated by the fact that Lisa is pregnant. Hilary and Julian see that the only way they can clear Lisa's name is to immediately announce their engagement. As an example of the deft structuring of the novel, this imbroglio occurs right after the scene discussed in the previous paragraph. Thus, by carefully deploying events in sequence, Mary Renault gains the impression of conveying genuine character development. In that Hilary and Julian have just affirmed their love as a vitalizing force, they can now meet the test of an untimely engagement notice.

Lisa and her husband, incidentally, are not major characters; kept discreetly in the background, they contribute economically to the artistry of *Return to Night*. The Clares, it is pieced out, have had a difficult marriage: as a foreign correspondent, Rupert spends very little time at home; and Lisa has already lost two children before birth. Because their marriage finally does overcome tremendous odds, it serves as a working model for Hilary and Julian. The Clares also teach her that the only aids she has are her powers of endurance and love; and, ironically, she has to summon these resources earlier than expected. For another outside pressure she and Julian can do nothing to arrest is already gathering force. Because of the political tensions of the late 1930's, his reserve unit may soon be called to active duty. This unloving stroke of irony places him beyond her control and, accordingly, further from a stage career than he is at the time of the book's opening. On the other hand, she has learned that the readiness is all. She and Julian have already validated their commitment; what remains involves her translating her love to the arena of personal conduct.

Mary Renault ends the novel before a solution is reached. Nevertheless, *Return to Night* contains too much art and moral wisdom for us to discard it—either as a literary conundrum or as a case history. Any critical reconstruction distorts and thus falsifies an artist's use of poetic devices to reinforce and extend surface meaning. Because a critic must explain within twenty pages or so how things like motif and symbolism operate as revealed experience in a four-hundred-page novel, he reduces his novelist's rhythmically orchestrated groundswells to desert terrain. All descriptive criticism, then, benefits the reader at the expense of the writer.

Although I see no way of circumventing this problem, I should like to show how the rhythmically continuous birth motif blends with light-and-dark imagery to augment the theme of *Return to Night*. We have seen that Hilary's ultimate task is to serve Julian as a combination Venus and Madonna figure while retaining her identity as a person. Mary Renault both deepens and extends this question by punctuating the novel with a series of actual births.

Hilary delivers a baby girl in Chapter II which lives only a few days; Lisa Clare, whose fortunes are roughly similar to Hilary's, has already suffered a stillbirth and a miscarriage before the book opens. The healthy baby she does bear is a girl. Yet the one Hilary delivers at the beginning of the last chapter, "which had nearly destroyed the mother to whom it had clung" (404), is a boy.

These instances subtly place the female in sacrificial relation to the male. At the end of the book, Hilary, as well as Julian, awaits life. Also like him, the dawn of her life is now measurably more remote than at any time since their courtship. By the time she teaches him to accept himself, she will probably be past child-bearing and, more grimly, at a stage of life when she may be deserted for a younger woman. Although the idea is never openly stated, the upshot of her sacrifice may be that she has groomed Julian for a rich, mature life, but one that will be enjoyed by someone else:

It was true, she thought; for the second time that night she had lis-tened to the resisting cry of birth. But this time it would cost her more . . . . What she had now was not for her possessing. She was only the Madonna of the Cave, Demeter who fashions living things and sends them out into the light. All she had done, and had still to do, would work to accomplish her own loss; to separate and free him, to make him less a part of her, and more his own . . . . She would never bear a child to him. It would be too long before she could spare for its needs the love of which his own need had never been satisfied; before his mind was ready, her body would be too old. (411–12)

The novel's light-and-dark imagery flows in the same symbolic channels. To underscore the theme of appearance and reality or promise and fulfillment, the book includes several false dawns. When we fuse the running motif of the false dawn with the thick midnight darkness of the closing scene, we can see how skillfully Mary Renault accommodates her moral vision to fictional tech-nique. Hilary and Julian's relationship makes nearly all its major advances in the evening or the night: Julian's scrap with the Lon-don laborer, his performance in the play, his desertion of his mother, and his lovemaking with Hilary all take place in the hours of darkness. He has yet to adapt himself to the secular light of day. He always leaves Hilary before dawn, his explanation that he

has lost his voice takes place on a bright fall afternoon, and more
than once he recoils sharply from sudden bolts of light. On one of
these occasions, artificial electric light, not natural sunlight, blinds
him momentarily, after which he stays away from Hilary for three
weeks.

The profoundest expression of light-and-dark imagery occurs in
the scenes at Mott's Cave, an underground grotto and tourist's
attraction which Hilary and Julian visit twice. Aside from suggesting the dark cave of the womb, the cave in *Return to Night,* like
that of Forster in *A Passage to India,* represents prime experience
stripped of civilized values. Seeing it first through the detached
eyes of a spectator, Hilary notes with surprise the hypnotic effect
it has upon Julian: "His eyes seemed to have deepened and dark-
ened, and in his face was a curious look of remoteness and of rest"
(180). His conduct in the cave partakes of those archetypal acts
and primordial layers of experience beyond causal reasoning.
(Julian's mental construct of Hilary as a female rendering of the
Jungian witch doctor lends credence to this notion.) After descending to the bottom level of the terraced grotto, Hilary feels
helplessly drawn into a timeless mystery:

> It was the place, she thought, the absolute exclusion of familiar
> light and living, the stillness: she understood, for the first time in her
> life, what the phrase "a stony silence" meant. (182)
>
> .   .   .   .
>
> He wanted the impossible. Her emotions, her intelligence, her whole
> adult apparatus rejected it. But behind these, something accepted;
> remembering, from a time which had had no use for tactful regres-
> sions, the bald decencies of the schoolroom. He was intolerable, she
> thought. But he was probably right. (191–92)

The deepest expression of this primordial streak occurs when he
seats her in the Chair, a limestone deposit located at the cave's
lowest point. For him, the Chair symbolizes the concentrated core
of experience, a profound self-exploration that must be conducted
in total darkness. (Oedipus sits in a stone chair in *Oedipus at
Colonus.*) After Hilary innocently sits in the Chair, he subtly keeps
her there. And when, shortly after this incident, the lights in the
cave go out, we feel that Julian over-loaded the electrical circuit
himself. Although this never occurs to Hilary, she does see that
the act of sitting in the Chair is ironically both an enthronement

and an imprisonment. Together she and Julian experience a mystical ecstacy while she rocks him in her arms and strokes his hair. And later, when they become lovers for the first time, he translates her bedroom into the dark, clammy cave:

The light went out and the door closed. She could not see him now, because the moon was in her eyes. For a little while she could not see anything but the moon; she did not know, seeing herself and her surroundings still with the remembering eye of commonplace, how the shadows and straight lines of light had changed it to a dim green cavern, whose walls were broken by slender stalactites of white rock; how dark the red of her hair seemed in the blue light, like the dark-red stains that stripe the walls of the limestone caves; or that her gown had the look of green water flowing in half-transparent streams from her shoulders over her breasts. (251)

This shift in point of view, delicately executed though it may be, breaks the uniformity of the book's narrative focus. Until this point, Mary Renault had staged all of the encounters between Hilary and Julian from Hilary's perspective. It seems reasonable to assume, therefore, that, unless Julian's thoughts at this point were very important, Mary Renault would not have arrantly broken narrative continuity. This break in perspective does, in fact, clarify some major assumptions: aside from conveying the nature of Julian's psychological disorder, it records the distance Hilary must go to meet him on his own terms.

The cave of primordial experience, with all its super-personal ramifications, must be served. In the last chapter of the book, Hilary rushes there to prevent a catastrophe. Having missed Julian's visit due to a hospital emergency, she knows he will interpret her absence as an act of desertion. Like Pip in Dickens' *Great Expectations*, who comes to understand that the substance of his life resides within the hulks and marshes of his childhood home, Julian demonstrates, less consciously perhaps, that the cave frames the conditions of *his* life. Hilary's wild ride to the cave describes the progress she had made since the first night she slept with him: she now understands his nature and has subordinated her own needs to his. And, although the drive through the midnight rain is managed with more theatricality than many readers would accept, the blatant melodrama squares well with Julian's psychological and vocational redemption.

Acting quickly when she sees him about to drown himself in the underground lake, Hilary sits in the Chair before she calls out his name. Her use of the Chair as a place from which she can command him represents both an enlargement of her moral vision and the sacrificial nature of her love. Like a protective mother, she wraps the shivering Julian in her coat while he weeps at her breast. As has been stated, this superfine act of renunciation may well recoil upon her. Any tutorial or parental role is, by definition, limited in duration. Julian is capable of causing Hilary tremendous harm. Should he ever leave her for a younger woman, she will stand in danger of repeating Elaine Fleming's experience of losing not only him but also her moral balance. The roles of natural and of spiritual mother resemble each other more than she understands.

Return to Night may be the best of Mary Renault's English novels. Although the psychological assumptions of the 1930's play too large a part in her portrait of Julian, she nonetheless builds a compelling work around the irony suggested in the title. Is Hilary's self-willed entrance into the cave of Julian's preconscious a regression or a surrender to the forces of darkness? Or does her act suggest a genuine confrontation with profound moral problems at their source? Instead of trying to answer these questions, I should like to quote Laurence Binyon, who provides both the epigraph and the title of *Return to Night*. Binyon's octosyllabic couplets explain how, like Henry James, Mary Renault can construct a profound, vivid work around a fragment or "germ"; what is more important, the following lines also justify the Jamesian credo that art creates a freshness and an order unavailable in raw experience:

> Dawn like a thousand shining spears
>   Terrible in the east appears;
> Hide me, you leaves of lovely gloom
> Where the young dreams like lilies bloom.
>   In vain I turn aside to where
>   Stars made a palace of the air;
>   In vain I hide my face away
> From the too bright invading day.
>
> That which is come requires of me
>   My utter truth and mystery.

> Return you dreams, return to night,
> My lover is the armed light.

II   North Face (*1948*)

North Face begins with Neil Langton walking toward Weir
View, a resort hotel in Devonshire, where he has arranged to spend
a two-week vacation. On this same opening page, Mary Renault
introduces the first of the book's many structural contrasts: the
male versus the female principle. Passing under an arbor of con-
verging trees, Neil observes a scrawny mock-Gothic tower cleav-
ing to the flank of the seaside hotel. Referred to as "a genteel
spinster" (2), Weir View is peopled exclusively by women when
Neil arrives. Aside from Mrs. Kearsey, the owner, we soon meet
four vacationing females—Miss Searle, an Oxford don; Miss
Fisher, a nurse; a Mrs. Winter, and her daughter Lettice, "a natural blonde . . . too evidently aware of her . . . cinematic
charms" (5).

The sham Gothic tower adjoining Weir View both balances this
smug feminine domesticity and, as Neil's private lodging, foreshadows negative elements in his personality: "The tower reared,
sensationally, above the trees. Very naif explorers took if [*sic*] for
part of a ruined castle; the more sophisticated knew it at once for
a Folly of the most extravagantly Gothick kind. Its grey battle-
ments, patched with orange lichen, were flimsy; its ornate windows, with their decaying foliations of wrought iron, had never
contemplated defence against anything but the drab realities of
the Industrial Revolution" (1). This opening fails to live up to its
promising expectations. The day after Neil's appearance at Weir
View, Miss Winter and her long-suffering mother drop out of the
action completely, leaving *North Face* a much different kind of
novel than we had anticipated.

The departure of the Winter family combines with several
other features to give the impression that the book was originally
planned as a long, psychologically involved work incorporating interior monologue techniques and rising to a new kind of social
morality. For the first eighty pages, there is no observable theme
or dramatic conflict. Instead of anchoring personality and theme
in plot development, Mary Renault generates mood; but she does
so for private, rather than novelistic, reasons. The first several
chapters of *North Face* strike us as a veiled self-exploration. Re-

placing tempo, action, and movement is a stylized duel of wills
between Miss Searle and Miss Fisher. As Mary Renault carefully
avoids giving her nurse and her intellectual a first name, they exist
as stunted personalities, divided halves of a single self. Mary Renault's own bifold career as a nurse and a woman of letters tempts
us to approach the book, therefore, as a self-unfolding or ironical
self-inventory. The obvious parallel—both in setting and method
—is *The Sacred Fount.* And, like Henry James, she presents the
give-and-take of normal conversation as a witty, multi-leveled
drama which becomes, at times, a tactical battle:

While Miss Searle's intellect sought a telling rejoinder, her cheeks became faintly pink, and her frame underwent an indefinable softening
of its angles.

.   .   .   .

   Neil thought, obediently, of her examples. Having asserted himself
to his satisfaction, he continued to say anything which would keep the
conversation pleasant, and a going concern.

.   .   .   .

   The external part of all this, as it reached Miss Searle, added up to
a long, intimate look of understanding. When he started to talk again,
she found that she had lost the thread twice, and had to concentrate
urgently in order to have a reply ready in time. (32–3)

The feinting, the maneuvering, the subtle inflectional shadings,
and the discreet understatements are cleverly done. On the other
hand, much of this ledgerdemain is wasted. Although Mary Renault breaks new fictional ground for herself by showing, through
interior monologue, how thoughts are laundered and formulated
for polite discourse, her witty observations are static. They contribute nothing to narrative pace and little more to character development. Whatever merit these Jamesian posturings have as satire or psychology is erased by their withering effect upon the plot.
The first four chapters of *North Face* are highly civilized, but dull
and disjointed. Like the haggard Folly introduced on the first
page, the muffled drama between Miss Searle and Miss Fisher
fails to earn novelistic capital. Mary Renault has more usable
data in the book than she can dramatically command. The sluggish pace diminishes most of the power of her rich effects; in
short, we never feel the force of the novel.
   The beauties and depths of *North Face* are things we ponder in

retrospect rather than participate in actively. One possible explanation for this failure is the book's lack of critical distancing. Mary Renault has not worked as a nurse since the war. The discrepancies between nursing and novel-writing, as ways of life, constituted, therefore, a problem she never resolved. From the flawed scheme of *North Face,* we can also say that she never even expressed it. Because she could not formulate a working perspective from which to reconcile the two disciplines, she was unable to handle the problem artistically. Ironically, nursing and fiction-writing are basically selfless in orientation, demanding absorption in other people. Yet, as everyday facts, they also impose an uncompromising standard of personal dedication. Had Mary Renault seen them as mutually sustaining rather than as mutually exclusive, she probably would have never written *North Face.* The book is her attempt to blend the best features of two ennobling and exacting ways of life. If we find nothing else to admire in the novel, the author's intention merits unreserved admiration.

The educational, emotional, and psychical rift between her nurse and her intellectual cannot be bridged. Regardless of their topic of conversation, Miss Searle and Miss Fisher only succeed in misunderstanding or in offending each other. As this linguistic barrier takes shape, the reader feels that Mary Renault is preparing some major statement about today's divided mentality. Unfortunately, social criticism of this kind is not the subject she works best with. Miss Searle and Miss Fisher drop out of the book for long stretches; and, when they reappear, their collisions differ markedly from the ones that dominated the opening chapters.

Although the Miss Searle-Miss Fisher confrontation sustains little dramatic immediacy, we would be unjust to ignore its value as social philosophy. The book's flawed artistry weakens, but does not wholly negate, the urgency of Mary Renault's arguments. Even after we concede the serious rift between art and governing idea, we can still appreciate the soundness of her moral vision. First of all, she did not need C. P. Snow or Paul Goodman to warn her of the destructive reverberations begotten by specialized education. Although the intellectual (or humanist) and the nurse (or scientist) must practice the same lucid dedication in their respective crafts, the cool, unhurried deliberation encouraged by the one discipline and the quick action demanded by the other foster to-

tally different attitudes. As we have seen, the crafts of Miss Searle
and Miss Fisher erect linguistic and emotional barriers neither
woman can surmount. This contrast is introduced deftly and convincingly:

Miss Fisher's ball of wool rolled off her lap, and over to Miss Searle's
feet. She reached for it as Miss Searle stooped politely. For a moment
their hands met on the ball: the hand of a scholar, meticulous, with
fineness but no strength in the bone, taut veins blue under the thin skin
at the back, the nails ribbed, brittle and flecked here and there with
white; the other broad-palmed and short-fingered, with the aggressive
smooth cleanliness that comes of much scrubbing with antiseptic followed by much compensating cream, the nails filed short and round,
their holiday varnish spruce. Each woman was momentarily aware of
the contrast. (8)

Miss Searle finds nursing "a noble vocation, but, tragically, coars-
ening" (7). But, in spite of her ability to diagnose Miss Fisher's
shortcomings, she is unable to sympathize with them. Instead of
using her humanistic education to gain insight into Miss Fisher's
personality, Miss Searle prefers to humiliate her by splitting
grammatical hairs. She has, in fact, lost her capacity for responding generously to literature itself, as can be seen in Miss Fisher's
reaction to *her* reaction to Chaucer: "She hasn't noticed that it's
about *people*. It's poetry, in a book, with clever rhymes and all
that, by someone who's dead" (23).

Although this disclaimer smacks too obviously of Mary
Renault's own attitude, it is, nonetheless, justified. Driven to com-
pensate for her plain looks by pursuing scholastic honors, Miss
Searle has always sought the safe academic response. Contrary to
Miss Fisher, who finds the mode of others bracing and stimulat-
ing, she chose Weir View for a vacation because of it's obscurity.
The natural beauties of the locale and the presence of other people count less for her than *The Canterbury Tales, Mansfield Park,
Henry Esmond, Dr. Thorne*, and "a new paper on Old French
metrical forms" (7), all of which she assiduously reads rather than
stirring a hundred yards from the hotel grounds. We are not surprised to learn that she is sickly, that she wears thick glasses, and
that she catches colds easily. Having severed herself from the
everyday world, she barely avoids being hit by a car the one time
we see her cross the road from Weir View.

To develop her observations on the gulf between the academic cloister and the operating theater or market place (her terms are not exactly those of Snow), Mary Renault fleshes out Miss Searle's character with historical depth. Consistent with Miss Searle's failure to mature beyond her compulsion to excel scholastically are her sexual experiences and her attitudes toward love. Once again, we see the same graceless tendency to sacrifice the vital and the concrete to the derived and the abstract:

She believed in love, and in preserving a high ideal of it. To confirm her belief, she had herself been in love twice, experiencing on each occasion some years of romantic secret unhappiness. Each time she had realized she was in love shortly after becoming certain that the object, once by a vow of celibacy and once by approaching marriage, was placed forever beyond hope. . . . The only modern novels that found permanent room on her shelves were about women of exquisitely refined sensibility, to whom a dozen unkind or tasteless words, a moment's falling away from perfect tact by a loved one, were lethal, the end of the world. They reinforced her faith that she was herself adjusted only to relationships like this. Her own loneliness had become for her simply the proof of a discrimination to which nothing was tolerable but the best. (104)

If these views are cultured, they are also sterile and non-sharable. Because of her exalted standards, she has buried herself within a membrane of mental concepts no other person can pierce. A second look explains that these standards are a hard protective shell, deriving from a chronic fear of people. The sidelines from which she judges Miss Fisher are cold and comfortless. Whatever dignity Miss Searle briefly preserves is bought at the heavy price of life's awe and wonder. And, when her fragile moral world explodes, it is shattered by her chosen tendency to neglect the human in favor of the mechanical or abstract:

What should she read? She was almost decided on *Mansfield Park*; but to make the final choice she must have her glasses. The case was in her bag; but it was empty. She remembered, now, that she had taken them off . . . and must have left them somewhere downstairs. This showed the advantage of an orderly method; had she discovered this later, if [sic] would have meant going down in her dressing gown. As it was, she had got no further than changing her shoes for her more comfortable moccasins. (224–25)

Standing at the foot of the stairs, she sees in silhouette Ellen Shorland and Neil embracing. This unexpected sight demolishes Miss
Searle's smug self-congratulation and leaves her marooned on the
rocks of her own inadequacy. An unplanned irony of this imbalanced novel is that one of its major characters should be made so
violently aware of her own moral and emotional imbalance.

At the end of the book, Miss Searle conforms brilliantly to the
self-annihilating pattern of the Jamesian trapped spectator. She
has been forced to acknowledge that her lifelong habit of judging
rather than acting has been self-defeating. But her refusal to act
constitutes in itself an insipid form of action, as far as its effect on
her life is concerned. Clearly, the devoted student of humane letters has failed to respond to life with any warmth or humanity.
Like many Jamesian heroines, she has demanded too much and
has received nothing. And although, unlike James's Catherine
Sloper (*Washington Square*), Fleda Vetch (*The Spoils of Poyn-
ton*), and Maisie Farange (*What Maisie Knew*), she is never
given a concrete human challenge which tests her moral energy,
Miss Searle suffers deeply. The discovery of Ellen and Neil drives
her further into loneliness and wrecks her flimsy rampart of subtle
distinctions.

Once she acknowledges the inescapable reality of raw physical
love, she must face her own emptiness. In an anguished letter to a
friend, she says of Ellen and Neil that she has never " 'been con-
fronted, even in College, with a moral decision which weighed
upon [her] more' " (274). Miss Searle's stature declines as the
novel progresses. Living vicariously on the emotions of others, she
unconsciously sinks to slander, resentfulness, and shoddy self-
justification: "One must ask oneself, too, what future happiness
either party could hope for on the foundation of a sin which must,
inevitably, prevent each of them for having any respect for the
other. However there is no real need to burden one's conscience
with such questions, since the ruling of both the Church and of
the civil law is perfectly clear" (275).

Miss Fisher, Miss Searle's anti-self, grows, not shrinks, in personal worth as we learn more about her. Nevertheless, Mary Renault is too careful an artist to dissolve the problem of our split
culture into the reader's growing affection for her stolid nurse. If
Miss Searle has dehumanized herself by trying to reduce life to a
thought process, Miss Fisher is the same kind of existential failure,

but in reverse. Her daily regimen of breakfast trays, inoculations, and bedpans rules out sustained, mature deliberation. Accustomed to executing the orders of her superiors, she cannot think originally or analytically. This plucky working-class woman serves as Mary Renault's example of the stout English yeomanry. Like Moore's Esther Waters and Arnold Bennett's Constance Povey, she often looks ridiculous—as when she casually begins reading *The Miller's Tale* and when she tries to impress Miss Searle with her own intellectual prowess: " 'Ta, after you. Well, hope springs eternal, they say, but I expect it'll be a case of a castle in the air, more senses than one, don't you?' " (10). Regarded by Miss Searle as a "mental slum" (10), this ruddy British gamecock regularly loses the battles of wit she blindly engages in—both with her counterpart and with Neil Langton as well.

On the other hand, she has cultivated a warm solicitude for the welfare of other people. Whereas Neil is locked within his grisly past and Miss Searle must keep herself from judging people uncharitably, the doughty Miss Fisher has the grit to face problems cheerfully. Her act of dressing Neil's injuries after his mountain-climbing accident is a sound other-regarding act with beneficial results. Miss Searle, who can only criticize people from the fake security of her escapist fantasies, would have been helpless in such an emergency. That Neil cannot remember Miss Fisher's name after she sterilizes and bandages his hand reveals that true goodness is self-effacing; it demands nothing for itself, not even recognition.

Aside from ministering to Neil at a critical moment, Miss Fisher also outstrips Miss Searle by conducting a brief romantic escapade during her short stay at Weir View. The reader is never privileged to view this affair; in fact, we never even learn the name of Miss Fisher's friend. As has been mentioned, many of the thoughts of Miss Searle and Miss Fisher are recorded in a chopped, broken manner. What seems to occur, however, is that Miss Fisher casually meets a man, perhaps married, standing in front of a theater in nearby Bridgehead. The next day, the two go to a carnival; and Miss Fisher returns to Weir View with a tumbled look and with her lipstick smeared. About a week later, she reveals that she will not see her unnamed suitor again. Although her act of conversing with a strange man outside a theater is definitely beneath Miss Searle's standards and probably beneath her own, as well, it is at least an affirmative gesture. Miss Fisher comments to herself on this same day, "You can throw your life away . . . sitting around for a miracle to happen" (107). The undramatized relationship which ensues is undignified in origin, but real. Like Eliot's fisher king in *The Waste Land,* Miss Fisher is still searching for value and meaning at the end of the book. Her failure, then, is less complete than that of Miss Searle. Miss Fisher is not a bystander; she knows, furthermore, that she will continue to risk the danger that emotional involvement often carries in its wake.

Mary Renault endorses her outlook; the most important kind of knowledge is human knowledge, and this requires the selfless engagement that all significant personal relationships entail: "One was incurably soft, she thought. Men were a curse: careless, wrapped up in themselves, not giving a damn unless they wanted something, and as blind as bats even then. One had known this for a good fifteen years: and still one of them only had to come along looking a bit under the weather, knocked about through his own silly fault, shiftless and guiltily casual like a kid; and there one went again, soft as tripe" (276).

It is necessary to point out, finally, that although *North Face* is relatively cheerful and good-natured in its moral attitude, Miss Fisher does not embody a romantic solution to the grave social dangers the novel discusses. She does contain the seeds of social rebirth in her psychic chemistry, but these seeds lie in arid, untilled soil. Mary Renault sees modern society too realistically to advance simple romantic formulas. If nursing does not stifle Miss Fisher's humane impulses, it does little to hew them into viable social concepts. She surprises neither her reader nor her author. To remain true to her vision of the essential character of nursing, Mary Renault can do no more than present Miss Fisher as a counterbalance to Miss Searle and as an unmined source of social energy.

In the third chapter, Mary Renault introduces the character of Ellen Shorland as an intended answer to the bifold problem of her own vocational ideals and the cleavage in modern society. The synthesis is never artistically convincing. Several of her fellow vacationers observe that Ellen defies classifications or labels—a sure sign in all of Mary Renault's fiction that a character had retained his vitality by avoiding the rehearsed response: "She was slight, with a fair skin and intermediately coloured hair; neither short nor tall, nor striking in any way" (50). Or: "He took a quick look at her profile, remarking again how a certain delicate strength, integral to its structure, was spoiled by an unfinished look . . ." (119).

Although she sat for the Oxford entrance test, the war forced Ellen to take a job and give up her education. Her dissatisfaction with factory work and an inheritance (at the time of the novel, about 1946, she is twenty-three and both her parents are dead) spurred her to take a secretarial course. The war recently over, she has come to Weir View to relax before looking for a job. Ellen insists several times that her main quarrel with factory work was the need to deal on a daily basis with so many different people. Although she enjoys conversation, she does not like groups or institutionalized relationships. Instead of socializing with her fellow factory workers, she preferred returning to her seedy Belgravian flat where she avidly read medieval literature. Ellen is both learned *and* humane. By having remained close to the life of the common people, she has avoided the plight of Miss Searle; her sensibilities have neither become blunted nor derailed into the airless realm of non-sharable values.

Ellen's unrehearsed, yet cultured, response to life, therefore, is designed as a workable midway zone between the scientific and the humane tempers. These alien elements, however, never blend in Ellen's personality. Her vocational and educational backgrounds are asserted rather than dramatized, and they play a very minor role in her conduct with Neil; accordingly, she neither transforms nor is transformed by Miss Searle or Miss Fisher. Had Mary Renault shown Ellen interacting with them, she could have commented seriously on the important public questions she had introduced; but she misses her chance. Although Ellen has the compassion and wit to stir both women, she has little to do with either of them.

But, even though Ellen's profoundest responses fail to chime with the book's major social theme, they are arresting enough to warrant investigation, especially as they pertain to her relationship with Neil. Shortly after her arrival at Mrs. Kearsey's, Ellen's fellow boarders are struck by the random appearance of Eric Phillips. Only Miss Searle is fooled by the forced casualness of his greeting to Ellen. Called by Neil "an obvious type, like an adver-

tisement for shaving cream" (61), he is also regarded by Miss
Fisher as living proof of Ellen's debased sexual tastes. Although
he mysteriously leaves Weir View the next morning, this judgment is strangely redeemed in the closing scenes. Mary Renault
cheapens her ironical effect, however, by developing it in a rather
tedious personal disclosure in the next-to-last chapter. Like Mrs.
Fleming's lengthy self-justification in *Return to Night,* the position
of Ellen's self-stock-taking invites the criticism that Mary Renault
unjustly withheld important data. This passage is more offensive
than its counterpart in the earlier book: first, because it lacks the
hypocrisy and public relevance of Mrs. Fleming's monologue and,
second, because Mary Renault had used the same device to inform the reader of Neil's troubled past in chapters II and IV.
There, however, the bald exposition is unloaded during two sleep-
less vigils in the gaunt tower adjoining the hotel.

Several times before the next-to-last chapter, Ellen had wist-
fully mentioned Jock, her former fiancé, a mountain climber and
fighter pilot who was killed during combat over the English
Channel. The children of step-sisters, Ellen and Jock had known
each other all their lives. Their engagement had been casually
arranged by their families and cheerfully accepted by the two
young people as an established fact. But, just as this cozy, long-
standing attachment began to grow complicated, Jock was killed.
Hearing the news of his death, Ellen astonished herself by expressing relief instead of sorrow or loss.

Consequently, she showers guilt upon herself. Using reverse
psychology, she planned a debauch with Eric Phillips precisely
because she knew he would offend her and thus enforce her sham
loyalty to Jock's memory. The ruse of summoning Jock's shade as
a barrier to the creative challenge of love collapses, however,
when Neil shrewdly isolates the source of her psychic problem—
that she did love Jock, but fraternally as well as sexually. Unable
to wipe the blot of incest from her mind, she could not resist viewing his death as a reprieve from a terrible mental burden.

Ellen's new understanding of her psychological block frees her
from guilt and enables her to marry Neil. Yet, coming at the end
of the next-to-last chapter, her act is too slickly contrived. What is
worse, it tempts us to interpret her personality simply as a function of psychology. Mary Renault failed to conceive Ellen's character with the same warm insights that she imparted to her study

of Miss Fisher. The stale novelistic ploys used to develop Ellen as a person rob her of human nature. As I stated above, the three novels of Mary Renault's middle period reflect a firmer grasp of male characters. Relying on her intuitive knowledge of women to endow Ellen with depth and agility, Mary Renault, in *North Face*, devotes most of her energy to the more difficult problem of Neil. From the perspective of her entire career, her energy is not wasted; Neil represents a marked advance over her earlier male protagonists. In the process, however, she commits the error of sacrificing Ellen to him. He is so much more powerfully rendered than Ellen that he not only dwarfs her as a character but also raises the disturbing question of her suitability as his wife. Although it will not be our last, this example is one more proof of the blotched, disjointed nature of *North Face*. Neil *does* convince us of his human nature; on the other hand, he creates problems in narrative structure and balance that his creator was not able to resolve.

The first things we learn about Neil are that he came to Weir View to climb the mountains and cliffs of Devonshire, that he takes medinal to help him sleep, and that he relies on cross-word puzzles to escape his problems. Neil, then, like Ellen and Hilary Mansell of *Return to Night*, is chiefly motivated by fending off the horrors of his inner self. Given his sorrowful past, we can easily credit his need to forget. Neil is a former teacher of Classics. At the outbreak of the war, the head of the boys' school where he was teaching discouraged him from enlisting in the army and also pulled political strings to delay his call-up. It was then that Neil met Susan, a junior nurse of twenty-three employed in the school's infirmary. One of the best things about *North Face* is Mary Renault's close authentication of the wartime setting; and, despite its numerous faults, the work does stand firmly as a war novel. Nowhere does the wartime milieu cut into the lives of the characters more deeply than in Susan's courtship with Neil. Had England been at peace, they probably never would have noticed one another. But, after discovering themselves to be practically the only people at the school between the ages of eighteen and sixty, they hastily fall in love and get married.

From the time of their courtship through the birth and early years of their daughter Sally, Neil is plagued by the fact that he is still a civilian. He finally submerges his doubts about Susan's

motherly talents and volunteers for duty. Susan then fulfills his
worst fears: in his absence, she meets and has affairs with several
American soldiers stationed in a nearby camp. Returning to civilian life, Neil is alarmed by Sally's unkept clothing, her penchant
for American slang, and especially Susan's failure to toilet-train
the child. One night, after a teachers' meeting, he returns home to
find Sally fatally burned while Susan was bedded down with an
American soldier. Like Ellen and, to some extent, Miss Searle,
Neil is forced to endure a night of horrors after his crushing discovery. The morning after the fire, he sees that a white stripe has
asserted itself in his hair as an outward sign of his suffering. He is
now at Weir View waiting for his divorce to be adjudicated, after
which Susan will marry the man she was with the night of Sally's
accident.

This turn in the plot, incidentally, forces us to see the war period and the years following the war as a single epoch. Again, it is
worthwhile to observe the war influence at work. Although Susan,
now pregnant, will marry the anonymous American soldier, there
is no reason to think she will be any happier with him than she
was with Neil. Once more, public mood rather than personal commitment forms the basis of her union. After the war mentality and
the impact of Sally's death subside, she will probably repeat the
same acts that wrecked her first marriage.

Ellen and Neil, then, encounter each other at a time of anguish
and loss. Both characters are also guilt-ridden: Neil, because of
the destruction following his tour of service in the army; and
Ellen, because of her obsessive need to chastise herself. Ellen and
Neil prove to be a bracing influence on each other; for, while she
dispels his need for drugs and restores his ambition to become a
writer, he refreshes her blurred vision of the past. This service,
significantly, also operates to Neil's advantage. His own friendship
with Sammy Randall, who, like Jock, was a mountaineer and a
war casualty, gives Neil a rare insight into his own mental state.
The faint homosexual coloring Mary Renault imparts to Neil's
friendship with Sammy and the temperamental affinities shared
by Sammy and Jock have the redemptive force of enabling Neil
to see Ellen's conflict clearly.

Before learning of Jock's influence, he had feared the creative task of responding to Ellen as a unique person with her own private needs and emotional tensions:

> This continual sense of a need as great as his own reaching towards him and beaten back by forces he only half understood, the morbid inescapable jealousy against which there was no weapon and which he was ashamed to own, got under his practised self-protection, and roused a sensual reaction against which, sometimes, he could throw up no defence at all (220).
>
> . . . .
>
> He had not thought the thing out so clearly as to know that the picture had grown on him with her elusiveness, that he wanted her in a kind of vacuum, in order without interference to explore and possess her. (234)

Symbolic of her bondage to the past is Jock's flyer's insignia that she wears on a chain around her neck. Yet, even after she removes the medal, Neil understands maturely that her blighted relationship with Jock is a fact he must accept. Unlike Miss Searle, Ellen and Neil progress together from an absolutist attitude to a sunnier, more relativistic awareness of themselves and others. This operation is carefully executed in stages, all of which are both psychologically valid and faithful to the suffering that nearly always accompanies moral growth.

On the same morning of Eric Phillips's spectacular leave-taking, Neil spies Ellen trapped on a shelf of rock. Forced to rescue and comfort her, he finds himself more vitally absorbed in her life than he had planned. The most important thing about his conduct, though, is that he readily accepts the accidental and unstaged episode. The next day he and Ellen arrange an informal outing at the seaside, where they discover a meteorite and then the rotting corpse of a flyer. This twin discovery forms the dramatic underpinning of one of the book's most important points. Contemporary British society, in Mary Renault's opinion, had not, in 1948, recovered from the social changes engendered by the war.

Today's society is still collectivist and bureaucratic in orientation. Mary Renault anticipates the mentality that dominated both government and business in the 1950's by suggesting as early as 1948 that individuals have more value today as parts of a group than they do as persons in their own right. (In her Author's Note

to *The King Must Die,* she refers disparagingly to "the levelling
fashion of our day" [333].) The meteorite, then, as a collection or
aggregate of fused substances detached from the flaming, swirling
mass which gave it life, symbolizes our dead bureaucratic society.
Conversely, the flyer's corpse represents naked individuality in
its starkest, most irreducible form—death. The swimming party in
Chapter VII, although casually undertaken, surprisingly becomes
a mutual drowning into life. The blunt, unanswerable fact of
death quickens both Ellen and Neil into a heightened awareness
of the richness of life.

Also included in the scene is an archetypal foreshadowing of
Neil's routing the withering psychic presence of Jock: "Neil came
over. . . . His next step fell on a loose stone; he stumbled, and
pitched forward almost on top of the thing" (115). Neil already
knows that Ellen has drawn a mental parallel between the dead
airman and Jock. (Jock, as has been mentioned, was also a flyer
whose dead body suffered a horrid sea change.) That Neil barely
misses trampling upon Ellen's mental surrogate of Jock is widely
suggestive. Besides indicating the status of his relationship with
her at this point, Neil's act also charts the path he must follow to
purge her greatest self-doubts.

Although this episode reflects an interest in universal truths,
Mary Renault is more actively concerned with society today. The
barrier between Miss Searle and Miss Fisher represents one major
accent of this theme. Another may be found in the running contrast developed between the medieval and the modern world-
view. Ellen drenches herself in medieval culture to offset the institutionalized working conditions at the aircraft factory. Neil
formulates the contrast when he says that people in the Middle
Ages faced their horrors directly. If they were capable of great
cruelty, Chaucer's contemporaries never buried the person within
the group. Contrary to the opinion of Miss Searle, the real worth
of *The Canterbury Tales* is not in its syntax or its metrical patterns; Chaucer's lesson to us is his insistence upon the uniqueness
of persons.

This theme merges with several others in the visit Ellen and
Neil make to a medieval castle. Arriving at the Norman keep the
day after their outing at the lake, they find that their expedition
has been spoiled by a touring party of children. Given the medieval context, the castle is an experience they would rather enjoy in

relative privacy. Accordingly, they return that evening after dinner and several drinks. Their hearts buoyed up by liquor, they notice that the tree-lined avenue leading to the castle is thickly populated by lovers. Neil behaves skittishly when he finds the castle-gate locked. Becoming the braggart soldier of medieval and Renaissance drama, he climbs the outer rampart of the keep with Ellen and then tries to break into the keep itself: "Not to put too fine a point on it, he wanted to show off. He had not altogether stood out today for practical efficiency; now, under the influence of the lane, the moonlight, emotion, and several drinks, he wanted to compensate for this, not by being practically efficient but by some lawless defiance of circumstance and fate" (163).

Neil's posturing is a natural reaction from his lean, athletic puritanism. (We think of Auden's obsessively disciplined mountaineers.) Once inside the walls of the castle, he and Ellen undergo a mystical experience. Aside from achieving a dynamic sexual awareness of each other, they gain a sense of continuity with medieval life—its brutality, its overcharged heroism, and its indestructible romantic idealism. It does not matter that the caretaker ejects them from the castle grounds. Although their illegal entry inside the ramparts violates a local ordinance, they have already declared themselves lawbreakers by mingling with the creative spirit of medieval romance. Having forgotten their repressions, they are now able to join the ranks of the faceless lovers along the walk. As an additional comment on modern life, everything in the chapter defies logic and structure: a prophetic gipsy Ellen and Neil accidentally encounter, a missed bus connection, the sudden materialization of a remote acquaintance of Neil's, and the powerful surge of feeling engendered by the Norman castle. Ellen and Neil are not so modern as Miss Searle. Breaking from the rigidly organized patterns of modern life, they define themselves as living people. By joining the lovers ranged along the walk, Ellen and Neil both affirm the power of love and take their place in the human community they had previously shunned.

Neil's changing attitude toward mountain climbing follows in the same fertile channels. Early in the book, he welcomes the rigors of mountain climbing as a release from introspection: "Always when he had come to the hills happy in himself, which was good, they had freed him from himself, which was better" (27). His engagement with mountain climbing, then, is admittedly a denial of life. Although adventurous and exacting, it is remote from the valley or shoreland of human frailties. (This pun, incidentally, is worth mentioning because it is only one of several word-plays in the book: the weird collective mentality of Weir View; the necessity for Neil to humble himself, or kneel, reverantly before Ellen; the name of Miss Fisher and her status as a good-willed quester for humane values.) Mary Renault depicts mountain climbing as a kind of death more than once. Not only has Neil been dead since his daughter's death, but the two other mountain climbers in the book, Jock and Sammy Randall, are also dead. Ellen is right when she decries the discipline as snobbish, defensive, and heartless in its severe exactitude: "What is it but the cream of snobbery, to risk your life over years, perfecting an art that has no audience, unless it's one or two fellow-artists whose standards are as strict as your own?" (210).

Mary Renault conveys Neil's final acceptance of relative human values through the medium of mountain climbing. Neil climbs his last mountain after a hot argument with Ellen. His final break from the past can be seen in his willingness to undertake the climb without adequate equipment or preparation. His neglect of the academic formalities of mountain climbing, then, operates directly with his growth as a person. Mary Renault uses weather imagery here to signify that the heated argument with Ellen is a natural phase of the relationship rather than a deadlock. As the swollen, festering skies erupt into a storm, Neil sees that he is going to fall. But, before he slides down the rocky scree, he understands the depth of his need for Ellen. Only a very powerful motive—the fear that he has lost her love—could have provoked his impromptu climb during foul weather. Like Michael Ransom of *The Ascent of F6*, he learns something urgently fundamental about himself at the end of his perilous climb:

Not in search of death, but of life, he had gone to the rock; to be measured in seconds perhaps, perhaps to be bought with death as soon as realised; life, and reality, none the less . . . . Desire, a condition inevitable but secondary, had fogged the issue. Her need, her conflict, her muted life, had drawn him like an unclimbed face which promises difficulty and exposure at every pitch; but at the summit the realisation of oneself and of the mountain, union and release, a sky whose spaces humble, but no longer humiliate or appal. (249)

Neil's torn hands, the rain, and the humble meal he shares with some local cottagers all contribute to the idea of his rebirth. The attention bestowed upon him by Miss Fisher when he returns to Weir View is still another expression of the idea that the spirit of love, or the Holy Ghost, is still abroad. Neil's ability to ask for help forms the final stage of his regeneration. After discovering the uniqueness and the preciousness of life, he reaches a more balanced understanding of himself in the total human picture.

Mary Renault does not dissolve all the tensions she had introduced. As in *Promise of Love* and *Return to Night,* she leaves the reader shortly before her two main characters are about to marry. But this device does not necessarily reflect a waning of interest or a shrinking from subject matter beyond her novelistic grasp. The approaching marriage of Ellen and Neil, with its age barrier of fifteen years, will require great caution and self-control. All the demons have not been routed. The book concludes honestly on a tentative note. If the reader is justified in thinking that the conflicts in Ellen and Neil's relationship have only been temporarily lulled, he is also right to wonder whether new ones will take their place.

North Face is an intelligent but badly managed novel about obstacles to personal freedom and happiness. Mary Renault develops this theme by oscillating subtly between social and psychological events. Any verdict on the artistic stature of the book must acknowledge its wealth of data, and we have already mentioned some of this rich panoply. Equally significant is the abundance of mountain-climbing lore used to authenticate atmosphere. Most of the chapter titles are technical terms familiar to mountain climbers. The entries in Neil's notebook and passages like the following make *North Face* a treatise and an evocation, like Turgenev's *Sportsman's Notebook,* Conrad's *The Mirror of the Sea,* and Hemingway's *Death in the Afternoon.* No less than these sensitively perceived works, *North Face* both celebrates and renders cannily the working principles of an unfamiliar discipline:

The buttress ended as an extension of the ledge itself; but as soon as he got his head over, he saw he must work round to another point. From the buttress-top to the face, there was nothing but a long steep tongue of scree; not, like that of the first ledge, a thin coating over rock, but thick, indefinite, based loosely on dry earth. There was no sign of a handhold, and he had no time to waste on digging about for one. Leaving the buttress, he made his way with some trouble to the tapered end of the ledge. The other end would have been better, but that way there were no holds. (243–44)

Stabilizing the novel's many ideas is an elaborate network of balances, contrasts, and doubling motifs. These function at many levels and include Miss Searle and Miss Fisher; the tunnel of leaves leading to Weir View; Ellen's broken engagement and Neil's broken marriage; the experience shared by Ellen and Neil of having lost an intimate friend in the war; and, finally, Mrs. Winter, an overly solicitous mother, and Susan Langton, a neglectful one. Unfortunately, many of these structural devices do not bite into its thematic substance. *North Face* is a crowded book. It contains more material than can be comfortably absorbed into its two hundred and eighty pages. Perhaps the root of the problem lies in the impression that the book gives of changing course at the third or fourth chapter. One specific example of this is its failure to strike a common chord embracing the love story and the Miss Searle-Miss Fisher cleavage. The Jamesian shadow-boxing involving the two women extends no farther than the tea-table and the hotel veranda. Whereas interior monologue techniques figure largely in developing this relationship, Mary Renault creates a glaring imbalance by executing her love story as a more conventional narrative.

In spite of these faults, we should not discard *North Face* as a misbegotten, lumpish novel. Although the book has an uneven texture, it displays a keen social vision along with an aptitude to structure philosophically many different kinds of subject matter. It is certainly a more distinguished failure than *Kind Are Her Answers* or *The Middle Mist*, and it is especially rewarding to the serious student of Mary Renault's fiction. The hindsight afforded by the mastery of her later works allows us to conclude our estimate of *North Face* by quoting the excellent words of Gilbert Ryle. Ryle is addressing the question of trends in modern British philosophy; but his judgment has the authority and wit to refresh us with its surprising range of application: "The sophistication of the virtuoso does not make him a master. Yet sophistication, though not sufficient, is still necessary for progress." [2]

III   The Charioteer (1953)

Mary Renault's frank treatment of homosexuality in *The Chari-oteer* delayed the book's American publication for six years (1959); had her next two books not enjoyed such great success in the United States, we might have been deprived altogether of the wisdom and beauty of *The Charioteer*. The publisher's squeamishness, or marketing instinct, in this case is amusing. Although *The Charioteer* does contain a good deal of unorthodox subject matter, it is by no means Mary Renault's first "gay" novel. Homosexuality formed a muted undercurrent in both *Promise of Love* and *The Middle Mist;* less obviously, but more integrally, it recurred in *Return to Night,* with either Hilary or Julian dressed "in drag" for the occasion.

This judgment is not so far-fetched as it sounds: the sexual dynamics of the Hilary-Julian affair are the same ones that pertain in *Promise of Love, The Charioteer, The Last of the Wine,* and in Lysias's cynical letter in Plato's *Phaedrus.* Each of these works describes an older, more worldly person extending a protective, quasi-parental sexual animus toward his youthful beloved. This brittle relationship is often marred by jealousy, insecurity, and sexual possessiveness on the part of the older person as he sees his beloved growing away from him. (The ending of *Return to Night* anticipates Julian's sexual rebellion from Hilary, his aging wife or "drag king.") These conditions are woven into *The Charioteer,* down to the book's minor details. The affair of Ralph Lanyon and Alec Deacon, which takes place off stage, fails because both men contend for the tutorial role. As short-lived and insecure as homosexual friendships are, the more successful ones usually incorporate fixed attitudes and stances as prima facie ingredients.

The human problems dramatized in *The Charioteer* are almost uniquely homosexual; homosexual love is uniformly shown as less free, less mobile, and less durable than the ordinary sort. On the other hand, the author's compassion rules out our studying *The Charioteer* strictly as a homosexual novel. Mary Renault agrees whole-heartedly with one of her character's judgments of homosexuality: "'It's not what one is, it's what one does with it'" (131). The performance matters more than the tendency. Laurie Odell, the book's major figure, conveys the important truth that, despite inherent obstacles, dignified love can flourish within a homosexual frame. Trammeled by a shattered knee, an ungainly limp, and an uncertain future, he is warmly characterized as a modern Hephaestus, or maimed artist, who clings tenaciously to a love ideal in the face of tremendous odds. His is an entirely attractive character portrait. Regardless of one's personal reaction to homosexuality as a literary theme or way of life (Mary Renault is unmistakably addressing a heterosexual audience), Laurie's effort to create something lasting and beautiful within a sharply limited context compels the reader's admiration.

The first two chapters foreshadow historically and psychologically Laurie's effort to win the love of Andrew Raynes. Starting with the third chapter, the action is confined to the fall of 1940 and, largely, to the West Country setting where Andrew and Laurie meet. This fourteen-chapter segment could stand firmly as a novel in itself: it develops a moral issue through a personal relationship and shows how both the relationship and the issue are affected by society. The first two chapters, however, contribute depth, clarity, and also some essential background data that could not have been included in any more economical way. By showing us Laurie at the age of four, shortly before his father's death, and again at the age of sixteen, as a public school student, Mary Renault conveys his life as a progressive event.

The values and the responses he evokes in the opening sections color practically all of his later conduct. By protesting his father's banishment from home and, later, Ralph Lanyon's explusion from school, Laurie defines himself early as a champion of lost male causes. The bitterness and loss attending both these departures establish men for him as martyrs to authority. Even though Michael Odell's drunken promiscuity and Ralph's admitted homosexual debauch with a younger student both warrant disgrace, they provoke a psychological father-search that mingles with the tales of rough male adventure told to Laurie as a child. His favorite boy's story is that of St. George; brought up without a man in his home, he has nothing to temper or civilize this chivalric view of men. The world of male heroics gathers to mystery and glamor in his impressionable mind. His father, a hard-drinking Irish journalist, and Ralph, the knightly prefect of Laurie's dormitory, clothe Laurie's inflated imagination with saintlike human substance—but, significantly, either *in absentia* or in a highly stylized, transitional setting, where boyish awe often overlaps with sexual impulse.

The scene in Ralph's room, just after the news of his expulsion becomes public, is one of the best in the book. Included here is a critical awareness of the imbalances traditional British education blindly fosters. The fag system, the absence of girls, and a sanctioned hierarchy that extends to all social and academic relations in boarding schools taint Laurie for the rest of his life. Nor can his fractured home life correct this imbalance. Having lived alone with his mother since the age of four, he is involuntarily drawn to senior students, and he courts this same hero worship for himself in the younger boys. Ralph summons him to his room after learning that Laurie has planned a schoolwide protest of the expulsion decree to the Board of Governors. Disciplined, athletic, and whiplike in his austerity, Ralph censures Laurie severely for his lawlessness. This respect for authority and stoical indifference to his own fortunes place the nineteen-year-old Ralph in the airy company of the gods: "[Laurie's] admiration for Lanyon had soared to the point of worship. This is the happy warrior, this is he whom every man in arms would wish to be" (27).

Although Ralph allows the formal tone of the interview to break down, he sacrifices none of his knightly valor. After suggesting his own affection for Laurie by giving him his copy of the *Phaedrus,* he vanishes romantically into the British Merchant Service. Seven years later, at their next meeting, Laurie acknowledges Ralph as a forceful psychic presence; Ralph has merged with Laurie's father to form a composite mental picture of a proud, suffering father-figure: "Now he felt strands and fibers of Lanyon twitching in his mind where he had not recognized them before, and realized the source of those standards which had supplemented his mother's in those parts of his life where she could not go" (114).

If Ralph emerges as a powerful father-figure whose approval Laurie seeks and whom he tries to emulate, the context can only be sexual. Imagining himself as "wholly his mother's child" (15), Laurie has only the female role and the female response to identify with. Once again, it is important to insist that homosexuality in itself need not preclude dignity or happiness. What Mary Renault objects to is the regimented alignment of lover and beloved that homosexuality encourages. Instead of blithely encouraging homosexuals to develop heterosexual values, she realistically places the burden of selfhood where it belongs: on the person involved. Homosexual friendships will be brittle and painful so long as they remain classifiable. What is needed is a dignified sub-structure of love rather than the prevailing one of vanity, sexual appetite, and assignable roles.

Without this human groundwork, Mary Renault claims, homo-sexual love can never gain the status of a genuine human relation-ship. The persons involved can expect no aid from others. In fact, the general public attitude is so hostile that homosexuals are forced to seek acceptance wherever they can find it. Just as diffi-cult to combat are the deeply ingrained habits and values that first conditioned the homosexual response, for homosexuality is not an overnight development. In Laurie's case, we see the pattern emerging and hardening in the first two chapters:

> His father was packing . . . . As Laurie looked, he took a file of papers out of a drawer, flipped it through, took out a few sheets, and tore up everything else the file contained. The pieces he threw down in a corner, on the floor, and simply left them there. Laurie had never in his life seen a grown person do this. (10–11)

. . . .

> The wastepaper basket [in Ralph Lanyon's room] was full. It would have been overflowing if the contents had not been rammed down. The mass of torn papers stirred in his mind some dimly remembered sense of dread. (26)

Accordingly, the objects Laurie cherishes most in his early life are a pen-cap given him by his father and Ralph's *Phaedrus*. When he succeeds Ralph as head prefect and moves into his room, Laurie's composite sexual ideal has already assumed definite contours, which are being promoted and reinforced by school tradition.

Before investigating the connection between Laurie's idea of maleness and his being his widowed mother's only child, we must establish clearly that *The Charioteer* is not a mere case study; it is a profound novel about human beings struggling to be human. As Mary Renault becomes a more skilled artist, we see an increasing trend in her work to authenticate milieu both through detail and shrewdly angled point of view. The fields of force generated by Laurie's solitary life with his mother until age sixteen provide an excellent example of Mary Renault's growing artistic powers. The only male in his mother's world for many years, he mentally assumes the prerogatives of brother, protector, and lover, in addition to those of a son. Although his epiphany is unabashedly contrived, Laurie's involuntary recollection of the old ballad, *Childe Maurice*, the day before his mother's wedding, harmonizes with both his cordial dislike of his new step-father and his childhood fantasies: "He had known *Childe Maurice* by heart for years. The tale of this young outlaw, the hidden love-child whom his stepfather murdered, taking him for the lover instead of the son, had always gripped Laurie's imagination. He had never wondered why" (269–70).

Laurie's more settled reaction to his mother is two-pronged. First, his image of himself as his mother's lover provokes a guilt akin to that of Ellen Shorland in *North Face*. Like Ellen, he cannot sunder sexual love from family devotion and, therefore, fends off further remorse by avoiding girls altogether. This mental block becomes even more formidable when played against his being the only son of a deserted widow. Beside fearing the male role as a many-sided challenge beyond his powers, he disavows heterosexuality as treacherous to his mother. Mary Renault convinces us that, by age twenty-three, Laurie has trained himself to ignore girls. The battery of mental gymnastics and pangs of moral guilt he has foisted upon himself for his mother's sake justify fully his view of the female principle as cozy, familiar, lulling, and faintly stagnant. He refers to the night nurse at the hospital as "a comfortable person" (36), and he has even come to equate his mother with "stability and rest" (64).

The Charioteer offers a harsher moral prognosis than *North Face*. The good-natured, somewhat cheerful relativism of the earlier book does not apply to Laurie. Even when he is most vigilant and dutiful, forces enter his life and disrupt his moral stability. For, in spite of his astringent self-discipline, he has overlooked the throbbing, singing masculine world that will inevitably burn through the thin membrane of his emotional vacuum.

The novel takes both its title and its governing metaphor from the *Phaedrus*. As the foregoing discussion suggests, *The Charioteer* embodies the rigorous rhetorical standards advanced by Sokrates in the last part of the dialogue. The novel is a close investigation, or anatomy, of homosexuality; at the same time, it weaves the various fibers of Laurie's life into a rich human tapestry. Much of the work's warm intelligence originates in Sokrates's denial that a person in love is too unsound and self-indulgent to be trusted. Along with Sokrates, Mary Renault believes that human love can be the greatest of rewards. Although love entails abandon, or madness, the madness is often divinely inspired. The individual himself must see that he uses his inspiration as a force for the highest good. In order to develop the existential ramifications of love, the author builds her drama around the celebrated myth of the charioteer.

According to Plato, the soul is a charioteer pulled by two horses. While one of the horses aspires to the heavens, the other gravitates earthward. The metaphorical task of the charioteer is to prevent the darker, vicious horse from weighing down the chariot:

> We formerly distinguished the soul into three parts, two of them resembling horses, the third a charioteer. One of these horses we said was good, the other vicious. The better of the two is an upright noble animal, a lover of honour, sensible to shame, and obeying the word of the driver without the lash. The other is crooked, headlong, fiery. . . . Now, when the driver is inflamed by love and desire for some beautiful human being, the tractable horse holds himself back, and restrains himself all he can from attempting any sensual enjoyment of the beloved object, but the other, setting whip and rein at defiance, struggles on . . . to unchaste intercourse.[3]

Mary Renault applies this myth to Laurie by developing his capacity for love as a force that includes, but eclipses, raw physical lust: the brute energy symbolized by the darker horse must be subordinated to honor and reason but may never be totally negated. Although Laurie does kiss Andrew Raynes, his act is not one of lust. The Platonic argument that there are degrees of perfection both humanizes Laurie and makes his attraction to Andrew more credible to the modern reader. The unrehearsed kiss does not destroy Laurie's dignity; it reveals him as a human being. By mingling appetite with his nobler impulses, he proves that he is trying to locate the ideal in the real; for Andrew is no projection of his fantasies. Although the emotional circuit generated between the two men can be traced, its basically human character is never sentimentalized or abstracted.

Mary Renault balances her adaptation of Plato's myth by using Laurie's own copy of the *Phaedrus* as a symbolic record of his emotional adventure. Laurie is graced with noble ideals which take root in the sensible world, but he is kept from exercising them. Shortly after his term in the hospital begins, we learn that he has carried Ralph's gift with him through the entire war. Now frayed, whitened by salt water, and stained with blood, the book is a charm that has endured, along with Laurie, the rigors and dangers of warfare. Within the next few months, however, the *Phaedrus* describes his lost hopes. The cherished gift of his boyhood idol, it ridicules his failure to outgrow his adolescent father-quest. While the physical state of the book reflects his years of suffering, the book's content spells out the ideal he has never realized. Nothing in his experience conveys the substance of his being more fully and more accurately than this copy of the *Phaedrus*. Both as material fact and as human ambition, the battered, third-hand dialogue describes Laurie on every page. His giving of the book to Andrew is both a final act of love and a tragic recognition of his own despair. Faced by a bleak future, he is content to bestow symbolically upon Andrew the only surviving fragments of his broken wings.

Laurie and Andrew meet in a hospital. As an example of Mary Renault's virtuosity with hospital settings, it is worth pointing out that the hospital in *The Charioteer* is a military one and that the point of view is that of a patient. After the hospital's maids resign in a group they are replaced by conscientious objectors. Laurie's own military experience and the blatant scorn most of his fellow patients extend to the pacifists do not keep Laurie from falling in love with Andrew. The quintessence of Andrew's charm can be best described as a combination of clarity, brightness, and boyish sweetness; but, aside from being strongly moved by Andrew's manner and appearance, Laurie is driven to admire his friend's moral courage.

Just as Andrew once refused to acquiesce in his family's tradition of attending military academy, his strong pacifist principles rule out active service as an adult. The terms of this refusal to serve reflect a gritty self-honesty: " 'What I finally stuck at was surrendering my moral choice to men I'd never met, about whose standards I knew nothing whatever' " (76). Although Laurie regards this decision as publicly irresponsible, he admires Andrew's

stern personal conviction. Andrew chose the more difficult road
and has abided by his choice. As a Quaker, he guides his life by
the precepts of love and harmony, even to the point of social derision. Shortly, however, his religious beliefs sow unexpected harvest. Andrew proves, just as Laurie did, that prime impulse cannot be cloaked by a private sense of duty. But his self-denial is
more ironically immediate. As a man who must, by principle, extend love to everybody, Andrew unknowingly stimulates his
friend sexually. His sincerity and his innocence prove much more
disarming than the seasoned advances of any practiced seducer.
The sexual basis of his affection for Laurie prompts him to remove
his shirt on one occasion, to make the boldest blank-faced sugges-
tions, and to respond without disgust to Laurie's kiss. Actions like
these force Laurie to practice a watchful self-control far beyond
his expectations.

The self-deprivation Laurie inflicts upon himself in order to
preserve Andrew's innocence allows him to progress morally. As
his friendship with Andrew blossoms, he seems about to achieve
the dynamic harmony between head and heart, impulse and ideal,
suggested in the *Phaedrus*. He cheerfully accepts his lameness,
because, had he not been wounded in combat, he would never
have met Andrew. When other losses and inconveniences besiege
Laurie, he again subordinates them to his higher purpose. In spite
of his ever-shrinking world, he keeps his ruling principle untarnished. Before Andrew's appearance at the hospital, Laurie
used to enjoy visiting the garden of a middle-aged fundamentalist
widow named Mrs. Chivers. One day Andrew follows him there,
infusing the garden with a freshness and innocence Laurie had
never experienced before. Andrew calls the garden Laurie's "'private Eden'" (73), and the two friends actually eat apples together before Mrs. Chivers banishes Andrew because of his refusal to fight in the war.

The next setting for Laurie and Andrew's idyllic afternoons is
nicknamed Limbo, "'a sort of eternal consolation prize'" (82).
After partaking of the beauty and innocence of Eden, Laurie settles gladly for this lesser lot: by his standards, Limbo with Andrew is infinitely preferable to Eden alone. Later, when the
oncoming winter drives them from Limbo, they resort to meeting
in the kitchen of the hospital ward late at night. Here the context
of their love is not only diminished; it is also cheapened and sub-

jected to pressures beyond Laurie's control. By conducting his nightly vigils with Andrew after the other patients have presumably gone to sleep, he invites the worst kind of slander.

Knowing that the rumors surrounding these midnight meetings range hotly from unpatriotism to debauchery, Laurie again chooses the more difficult, more creative, line of action: "Over his bacon and tea, Laurie felt that the only comfort would be found in full-time, party-line, nondeviationist hatred. One could warm oneself with a good thick hate by shutting all the windows and doors; but he knew, unfortunately, beforehand, that the snugness would not last, and the fog would drive him out into the cold again, gasping for air" (90).

Mary Renault sharpens Laurie's resistance to the prevailing herd morality in several ways. We learn that "he received infinite consolation and joy merely from the contemplation of Andrew's being" (93). Yet, once again, the reader never feels that Laurie has sentimentalized his beloved into an abstraction or a puff of smoke; the sacrifices he makes and the pain he willingly undergoes insure Andrew's solidity as a concrete person. As has also been mentioned, Andrew cannot see further than the Christian tenets that govern his life. Laurie's public school experiences and his skirmishes with Charles Fosticue's homosexual sub-culture at Oxford give him a keener insight. One of the main themes of *The Charioteer* is the Platonic argument that the good, not the bad or the ordinary, is the enemy of the best. Laurie persists in his ironical courtship of Andrew in accord with the best possible moral standards.

Because Laurie fears that Andrew cannot face being a homosexual, he never hints that their relation partakes of anything but innocent comradeship. What he cherishes most in his nightly meetings with Andrew is, in fact, their innocence and their resistance to pattern or classification. These brief sessions in the kitchen are untarnished by the shrill jealousies and the female posturings of his other homosexual experiences. Laurie is too forthright to encourage a liaison that could bring shame and guilt to his friend; it is with a high sense of mission that he shields him from the encroaching world of debased sexuality. Thus he is flooded with benign protectiveness when he kisses Andrew. We observe here that the stock homosexual pattern of roles has unconsciously emerged, but there is an important difference. Regardless of his later failure, the protective coloring of Laurie's love shows that he has advanced measurably from the recessive, submissive role of his earlier years.

As has been stated, Mary Renault seems to feel that tutorial zeal and youthful adulation dominate homosexual unions. She also suggests, though, that even within this circumscribed format there is room for freedom and growth. Postponing for the moment the major question of Ralph Lanyon's re-emergence into Laurie's life, we can see that Andrew, whose name begins with the first letter of the alphabet, represents a genuine starting point. Mary Renault does, in fact, indicate that, in the larger view, Andrew might not be the end of Laurie's quest for identity. By assuming, for the first time, the unfamiliar male role, Laurie has learned to love in a new way. He could achieve, thereby, the psychic balance and self-acceptance to enjoy heterosexual love, a more distant goal, at a later time. In line with his preference for a free alliance rather than a stock homosexual debauch, Laurie defies definitions and labels. Were he anything less than a person, he would have fallen in love with an older man, not with the colt-like Andrew.

Ironically, at this very time, another "A," or promise of freshness and renewal, enters Laurie's life in the person of Nurse Adrian. First, her naïveté and nursely attentiveness affirm his commanding advantage in any relationship they may share. Second, because he has dutifully kept secret his attachment to Andrew, he need not worry about offending him. Nurse Adrian's offered love seems on all counts to provide an opportunity for a new life. Laurie clearly enjoys her kiss enough to repeat it. Curiously, his rejection of her, in this same scene, enhances his dignity. Mary Renault forces us to see his act as heroic and even as tragic. Had Laurie's idealistic love for Andrew been blunted by expediency, selfishness, or conventionality, he would have welcomed Nurse Adrian's declaration of love. Her embrace constitutes one of those rare chances that can change the entire substance and direction of one's life.

But, instead of rejoicing in his heterosexuality or promoting it, Laurie clings to the sanctity of his prior commitment: "What's the matter with me? he thought. At first he wouldn't admit to himself that it was happening. . . . Then suddenly he felt delighted with himself. After this . . . one's limitations would never seem quite so irrevocably fixed. At this moment she linked her arms around his neck and for the first time kissed him of her own accord. He saw her face; it brought him down to earth with a jolt. He remembered now who it was that was paying for all this" (250).

Regardless of the context, only a person of rare moral fiber could have reacted so unselfishly. Laurie's love for Andrew is reduced, disguised, and socially prohibited; but, as a sharable, renewable fact, it merits all of Laurie's energies. Laurie is sorely tempted on several different occasions, but he has the character to convert his temptations into an affirmation of his principles. Perhaps the most creative, and also the most ironical, aspect of his choice is that, so long as their relation flourishes, Andrew must never learn of Laurie's sacrifice or the motives behind it.

While Laurie is becoming a new person through his discovery of Andrew, he meets his former hero, Ralph Lanyon. During an air raid, Laurie finds himself sheltered in a church with Sandy Reid, a young "medic" who had already declared his homosexual bent several times at the hospital. Parts of their conversation are worth quoting for their economy in describing the difference between Laurie's friendship with Andrew and the cheap maneuvering characteristic of most homosexual alliances:

Sandy's face had fallen, but not despairingly. He had probably had some practice in distinguishing between ignorance and reserve. "Oh, you're from Oxford . . . . Then you know Charles Fosticue, I expect."

"Only by name," said Laurie with prompt firmness. He gave thanks to his own instincts of self-preservation. "I used to see a good deal of Pat Dean; do you know him? He married a girl from Somerset last year."

Stalemate had now been reached . . . .

"Not," Sandy was saying (he had evidently decided to resurvey the terrain), "that I ever knew Charlie Fosticue at all well. I just mentioned him because he's the sort of type everyone meets once. I've run into Vic Tamley now and again. Rather a pleasant person, I thought."

"Yes, I heard someone say so, I forget who."

"I thought you might know him, he seemed rather your type. Drink up . . . ."

"Thanks, but I shall really have to get cracking to catch the bus."

"Oh, hell, no, you've only been here five minutes. Don't forget I saved you from rubbing knees with sixty-five typists in the shelter." (112–13)

In spite of Laurie's disgust, he nevertheless accepts Sandy's invitation to a party when he hears that Ralph will be there. This reunion takes place in the next chapter, where Laurie also has his first sustained view of homosexuals at their leisure. This extremely long chapter (forty-nine pages) is a drunken mixture of crude distortions and painful home truths. The feigned vocal inflections, the vulgar passes, the vain gossip, and the shrieking possessiveness culminate aptly with a suicide attempt by Sandy Reid after his other paroxysms of jealousy fail to arouse attention. At one point, Laurie is asked if he is Hazell, the young flagellant who caused Ralph's expulsion from school seven years before—a question surprising only to Laurie. Because of their closed society, most of the guests at the drinking bout have either lived together at one time or become party to one another's secrets through gossip.

The gathering is, therefore, an abstract of homosexual life in England. Laurie observes in all these people a blind eagerness to forsake privacy, decency, and responsibility. They have become so narrowly conventional within their own sphere that they have no life apart from being homosexuals: "They were specialists. They had not merely accepted their limitations, as Laurie was ready to accept his, loyal to his humanity if not to his sex. . . . They had identified themselves with their limitations; they were making a career of them. They had turned from all other reality, and curled up in them snugly, as in a womb" (132).

This inside view of England's homosexuals sharpens to a shrill focus in Chapter VIII. After discovering a pair of man's pajamas in Ralph's room, Laurie meets their owner, Ralph's downstairs neighbor, Bunny. Bunny, who expresses broadly both his sexual attraction to Laurie and his waning interest in Ralph, heartlessly doctors Ralph's drinks in order to drive Laurie back to the hospital himself. Mary Renault counterpoints Bunny's private outrage against Ralph by introducing a public one in the form of an air raid. This intense moment acts as a personal test to the characters involved. Not only does Bunny blithely abandon Ralph sleeping in his chair; he also handles Ralph's car disrespectfully and even refuses to take Laurie home when his advances are rebuffed. Yet Laurie stands up to him—both by challenging his conduct toward Ralph and by insisting on being driven to the hospital. Also to his credit is his conversion of this awkward escapade into an affirmation. Mary Renault performs here the difficult job of forcing us to see him as not only brave, but manly:

He got back to the ward within seven minutes of the time limit; but Andrew, he found, had finished his work and left.

He had got to see Andrew. He felt a need more imperative than any he had experienced in the keenest crisis of personal love. He wanted to recover his belief in the human status. (208)

Laurie's passing reference to H. G. Wells's short novel, *The Country of the Blind* (1911), is more apt than he realizes. He encounters personally an isolated community where all the inhabitants permit a single malfunction to rule their lives. Like the people in Wells's Latin American society, Sandy Reid and his friends arrogantly insist that their mode of life is the only authentic one. The parallel between *The Charioteer* and Wells's tale has even further application: Laurie finds himself engulfed by people who do not know how near destruction their abnormality has brought them. After sundering himself from the group, he tries, like Wells's Nunez, to climb toward the light; but, again like Nunez, his failure contains elements of victory. When a roving band of explorers spy Nunez's broken corpse along a pile of rocks, they see that he died smiling. Laurie, too, may boast in defeat that he has glimpsed his ideal and strived energetically toward it.

Like all good tragedies, *The Charioteer* endorses man's perfectibility. Shining through Laurie's failure is a warm declaration of man's ability to overcome himself and society's laws in order to join with a transcendent ideal. But Mary Renault's artistic integrity and social vision keep *The Charioteer* from dwindling into sentimental overstatement. Man does enough to sacrifice comfort and stability in the name of a higher truth; he need not look spectacular in the bargain. Laurie squanders much of his newly won maturity after he meets Ralph at the party.

In the seven years since their last meeting, Ralph has been even more of a force in Laurie's life than the younger man understands.

For, in addition to standing as a direction for Laurie's psychic energies, Ralph captained the ship that brought Laurie from Dunkirk to England. Now a sharply hewn twenty-six, Ralph looks like the model ship's officer. He evokes metaphors of swords, ships, and military drills; and, in Laurie's mind, his taut Nordic austerity blends perfectly with the rich blues and golds of a naval officer's uniform. Soon, however, Laurie's association with Andrew enables him to perceive the dross in Ralph's character. The narrow house Ralph lives in symbolizes his existence as one of the walking dead. Having lost his command when his ship sank, he has chosen a dwelling similar to a seaman's quarters. Ralph adds weight to Conrad's dictum that shore life ruins sailors. A member of Sandy Reid's sub-culture, he has become corrupt. (In two chapters alone, we meet three of his former love-mates.) Despite its magnetic authority, the love he offers Laurie is tainted by physical possession, a martyr complex, and a compulsive drive to power. Allusions to Sinbad, the Flying Dutchman, and the Ancient Mariner help develop Ralph's character. At the time we meet him, he is a land-locked sailor, a man without a job or a person to love. Ralph's energy, decisiveness, and professional skill have lifted him above his homosexual animus; but, because he had half of a hand destroyed in combat, he is no longer eligible for a command post. A man without a future, he is now fighting a tendency to indulge his self-pity in drink and in sordid relationships.

Ralph's shattered hand is widely suggestive. From one standpoint, it represents his weakening grip upon Laurie since the emergence of Andrew. The mutilated claw is also valid, however, as a dual symbol of Ralph's clutching need for Laurie and the sinister love he offers him. (As a neo-Ancient Mariner, Ralph not only detains Laurie in his pursuit of Andrew; he also materializes in church as a guest during Laurie's mother's wedding.) Before long, Laurie sees that the meek, retiring Andrew is more tough-minded than Ralph. Shortly after their reunion, Ralph arranges to get Laurie transferred from the hospital where Andrew is working. Although Ralph later admits that he behaved hastily and unjustly, his act defines him as the mawkish schoolboy of seven years before. His habit of calling Laurie by his boyhood name, "Spuddy," and the authority he casually arrogates encourages a deadening compliance. So long as he allows Ralph to manage him, Laurie can never be a responsible adult.

Laurie's predicament soon swells, therefore, to a question of being. A rejection of Ralph's offer to live together becomes, then, the ritualistic killing of the king necessary to Laurie's own personal sovereignty. More than once, Laurie seems close to performing this self-liberating act. Ralph's willingness to allow Laurie as much time as he wants with Andrew proves both magnanimous and offensive. By trying to make Laurie's choice easier, Ralph postpones it. Laurie *must* love someone who gives endlessly while asking nothing in return. On the other hand, he owes Andrew his entire devotion. His love for Andrew resides on a higher moral plane than Ralph can understand. Unlike Laurie's conduct, Ralph's is motivated by the immediate dictates of expediency and physicality and can be measured by individual acts:

"You'll have plenty of time for the other, Spud, without all this butchery. We'll be separated enough before this war's over, with me still in the navy and you in a job. Let's take what we can, God knows we can't afford to waste it. You don't know how little there is in a world of what we can give each other." (315)

. . . .

Laurie realized now that, from the moment when Ralph had learned that this was a love without physical bond, he had thought of it as something not quite real . . . . Laurie remembered how he always said "this boy," on a certain inflection, faintly indulgent; it would have been patronage in someone a little less kind. As far as he was concerned, Andrew was someone by whom Laurie had been refused. (297–98)

Laurie's existential drama is projected against the often mentioned, yet rarely discussed, fact that a person can love two people simultaneously. Although Andrew's boyish purity has transformed Laurie's life, the mystery and glamor spun by Ralph for the past seven years generates a tremendous counterforce. Laurie finds it easy to judge Ralph objectively; his real test occurs when he tries to act in keeping with his judgments. He simply cannot resist the tendency to be mastered. By yielding to a sense of boyish fair play instead of pursuing his adult preference for Andrew, he shackles himself to a past he has already outgrown.

Although Laurie achieves the Sokratic ideal of reaching for beauty and truth as soon as he is made aware of them, his human limitations reflect the non-Sokratic lapse between judgment and act. The death of his dog, the experience of reading his school scrapbook, the presence of his favorite aunt, and the loss of his mother demolish his composure. By legal arrangement, Laurie assumes ownership of the family estate (and its dead memories) as soon as his mother remarries. Whereas she elects new life, Laurie inherits death. The past, it seems, cannot be happily resurrected. Laurie and Ralph return to the house after the wedding and become lovers for the first time, thus conducting their own nuptial rite. Laurie's act of giving Ralph a sword once used in a school play becomes an ironical wedding gift. Aside from betokening a surrender of the male prerogative, the sword fixes a schoolboy context for their future together. After the night in the galvanized setting of his childhood home, Laurie forfeits the self-mastery associated with Plato's intrepid charioteer.

The residue of his friendship with Andrew trickles away in a manner consistent with Laurie's sentimentality. By surrendering personal choice, Laurie exposes Andrew to the choices of others. His absence obliges Andrew to face his homosexuality in exactly the abrupt, violent manner Laurie had worked so hard to avoid. Masquerading as Ralph, Bunny drives to the hospital and scourges Andrew for alienating Laurie's love. By answering Bunny's lewd accusations with a punch on the jaw, Andrew violates in a moment all his religious scruples. He then leaves the hospital and retreats to a bombed-out sector of London, where, amid rubble and mess, he hopes to regain his self-respect. Laurie goes to Ralph's room after learning that Ralph has accepted the guilt for Bunny's crime.

At this point, Laurie's cycle is complete. Whereas discharge from the army means freedom and opportunity to others, it means entrapment to Laurie. To avoid additional loss, he resorts to self-preservation and expediency. In an inevitable act, he lies to Ralph and also deceives himself in order to salvage something from the scraphead of his frayed emotions. He and Ralph will live together as two mutilated soldiers. Although neither will allude to the fact, both know their intimacy to be grounded in deprivation and despair. Perhaps the saddest part of Laurie's comet-like path, suggested in the Platonic envoi to the novel, is that, although he sees

Ralph's love as second-rate, his only choice is to promote it for all he is worth:

Quietly, as night shuts down the uncertain prospect of the road ahead, the wheels sink to stillness in the dust of the halting place, and the reins drop from the driver's loosened hands. Staying each his hunger on what pasture the place affords them, neither the white horse nor the black reproaches his fellow for drawing their master out of the way. They are far, both of them, from home, and lonely, and lengthened by their strife the way has been hard. Now their heads droop side by side till their long manes mingle; and when the voice of the charioteer falls silent they are reconciled for a night in sleep. (347)

To do justice to the astutely orchestrated structure of *The Charioteer*, we must comment on the ironical tensions established between Laurie and his society. The cliques of Charles Fosticue and Sandy Reid only make up a dwarfed half of this picture. Balancing the homosexual society is the roistering atmosphere of the hospital where Laurie is a patient. Although Laurie works, jokes, cries, and commiserates with the other wounded soldiers, he must always be on his guard. His best friend among the patients is Reg Barker. A thoroughly likable ex-navvy, whose unfaithful wife is retarding his recovery, Reg serves a bifold purpose in the book. His rough, comradely affection for Laurie, which Mary Renault discreetly develops before introducing Andrew, encourages the reader's sympathy and trust. We are meant, first of all, to like Reg Barker, just as Reg is meant to like Laurie. Second, by avoiding Laurie when he discovers his homosexuality, Reg underscores the littleness of the homosexual's social range. Wounded in the same Dunkirk campaign, Laurie and Reg overcome class barriers to create a genuine friendship. They confide in each other, they help each other perform chores around the hospital, and they drink beer together.

Reg's unselfish concern for his friend's reputation and Laurie's willingness to risk a court-martial for Reg bespeak the depth of their gentle-tough intimacy. Yet, Laurie is right when he senses that he cannot confide in Reg. Reg respects Laurie too much to reject him out of hand. It is to the credit of both men that Reg continues to be kind and generous to his chum after discovering Laurie's affection for Andrew. But a strict limit has been imposed; after Reg recognizes Laurie as a homosexual, all of his responses to him are conditioned by this single fact. He is still as kind as he can possibly be—but to a homosexual, not to a normal person. Reg now undresses privately, and his wife's casual references to homosexuality make for restraint whenever the three are together. In short, Laurie and Reg can no longer be friends, a loss that Laurie feels sharply and with deep personal regret: "He was overcome by a sudden, stifling claustrophobia. Charles's and Sandy's friends had tried to lock the door on him from inside. Now Reg was doing it from out in the street. There was a difference: he liked Reg much better" (212). Laurie's transfer to a different hospital carries no release from these tensions. He cannot rescue a boy of nine or ten from falling out of bed without worrying whether the nurses will interpret his act as one of seduction. Laurie knows he is being talked about; he also knows that most normal people will not respond to a homosexual as tolerantly as Reg. If the best Reg can do for Laurie is to withdraw from him awkwardly, Laurie must live in constant terror of his other non-homosexual acquaintances.

The Charioteer rises to a high note of social morality in its treatment of this problem. For, to avoid the derision of the normally sexed world, Laurie must sink himself progressively deeper in shame, secrecy, and the fear of being unmasked. Mary Renault's major representative of the smug heterosexual world is the Reverend Mr. Straike, Laurie's mother's second husband. As his name suggests, this fleshly, judicious minister both rakes and strafes his new stepson's shaky moral defenses. The fact that Straike is both a fixture in Laurie's family and a classmate of the House Master who expelled Ralph from school solidifies Straike's menacing presence as a social fact. A final chord of thematic unity is sounded by his profession; for Straike's pompous conventionality, like the intolerance of Mrs. Chivers, the fundamentalist zealot who orders Andrew from her garden, expresses boldly the failure of organized religion to address itself to the homosexual problem. This failure, furthermore, is self-defeating: their ousting of Andrew, the only authentic Christian in the novel, deprives Mrs. Chivers and Straike of a living source of the charity so lacking in their own sham theology.

The Charioteer is a relentless book that presents in a driving, yet globular, fashion several abrasive moral questions. Although I have been firm in my praise of it, I should like to mention some of its faults before concluding. The most damaging of these is Mary Renault's characterization of Andrew as a private person apart from Laurie. Andrew's appearances in the book are so rare and brief that we cannot understand Laurie's powerful attraction to him. Mary Renault's failure to dramatize Andrew's basic goodness as a force beyond sexuality is not one of flawed execution but of omission. His dramatic presence does not square with his thematic function: Andrew is simply too minor a character to carry the moral weight of the narrative, and his scrappy appearances never attain the force to stir the imagination. In the last analysis, we cannot detach Andrew from Laurie's reaction to him; he exists, therefore, only as a phase of Laurie and, what is worse, as a prop to the book rather than a character *in* it.

A second fault in *The Charioteer*, less damaging than the first, is the author's bold use of coincidence to dislodge herself from a taut encounter; farcical entrances of minor characters after Laurie kisses Andrew and again after Laurie censures his mother for killing his dog signal an inability to sustain moral comment within the fabric of scenic immediacy. On the other hand, Mary Renault dwells too long on Ralph and Laurie's discussions of homosexuality. These passages have the solid merit of bringing in background material, and they do this important job more smoothly and naturally than the monologues in *Return to Night* and in *North Face*. But they move very slowly, undermining the novel's crisp tempo. In a larger sense, these sections, which are loosely styled upon Platonic dialogue, irritate; for, when the reader wants to learn more about the immediate problems of Laurie and Andrew, he must slog through long lectures on the origins and social ramifications of theoretical homosexuality.

In spite of these disclaimers, however, the final judgment of *The Charioteer* must be warmly positive. Although the subject matter of the book makes it a chafing experience, its probing honesty awakens our moral responsibility to an urgent social problem. Had Mary Renault designed her novel as easy-going popular fiction, she would have sacrificed its grating persistence. The nature of Laurie Odell's commitment and the inevitable loss of his human ideal may well encourage posterity to praise *The Charioteer* as her finest work.

CHAPTER 4

From Wine to Vinegar

*T*he *Last of the Wine* is neither a historical narrative nor a
plotted novel in the familiar sense. Set in Athens, c. 415–
399, B.C., the book is written as a rambling autobiographical
memoir. Although it descends from works like Robert Graves's
Claudius books and Thornton Wilder's *The Ides of March*—in its
use of both Classical setting and the first-person narrator—*The
Last of the Wine* represents a major artistic advance for Mary
Renault. It may even come to be regarded as one of several novels
that will eventually disprove a critical tendency to see all fiction
since *Finnegans Wake* as an echo or a footnote. Along with books
like Barth's *The Sot-Weed Factor*, Durrell's *Alexandria Quartet*,
Doris Lessing's *The Golden Notebook*, and Merrill's *The Diblos
Notebook*, *The Last of the Wine* enlarges both narrative form and
the scope of imaginatively perceived experience residing between
reader and writer.

I   The Last of the Wine (*1956*)

Perhaps the force prompting this dual advance in *The Last of
the Wine* is the Athenian political ideal and its slow, but inevitable, death during the years of the Peloponnesian War, 431–404. At
no other time in history has the individual citizen felt such a warm
interchange between himself and his surroundings as in the Athens of Perikles, Pheidias, Aristophanes, and Sokrates. Her antique
setting, therefore, allows Mary Renault to develop the private fortunes of her characters in direct ratio to her public theme. In this
respect, *The Last of the Wine* stands closer technically to Tolstoi's *War and Peace* than it does to Hugo's *Les Misérables*,
where the historical sections color the human drama but do
not intersect dramatically with it.

But, as a post-Jamesian novel, *The Last of the Wine* surpasses
even Tolstoi's great work in the advantages it takes of the first-

person narrative. The book is written by an Athenian called Alexias. His retrospective memoir includes the solid merits of historical
perspective and point of view. In an apparently casual reference
to current politics or to his personal affairs as a middle-aged man,
Alexias can etch a surprisingly sharp contrast between Athenian
life before and after the collapse of the Periklean ideal. At the
same time, the loosely constructed personal reminiscence creates a
mood of confidential intimacy and historical urgency which gives
the point of view a working framework. Alexias's natural limitations as an interpreter suggest analogies and inferences only
hinted at in the narrative. Although he occasionally startles us
with his acuity, the adroitly angled point of view grants jarring
insights into Greek politics and also into his own mind. Many of
these ironies take root in the memoir form itself: *The Last of the
Wine* is not designed for any auditor or reader; for as a memoirist,
Alexias is unravelling the past for his own private satisfaction
alone. Precisely because he seeks justification in nobody's eyes but
his own, his oversights and moral lapses strike us with tart immediacy. A person who is trying to understand himself within the
frayed embroidery of Athenian history, he clothes himself in the
same rich humanity as he does the events he records.

The literary model for *The Last of the Wine* is the historical
method of Herodotus. Rather than using the more austere, sober,
and highly factual technique of Thukydides, Mary Renault prefers to convey history through personality. Without reducing historical fiction to a category of biography, she builds a cultural
epoch by examining the daily lives of a few representative Athenians. Once again, the governing idea of the Greek polis or life-
giving communality must be stressed; Alexias's growth and personal development take the form of accepting responsibility
within the discipline of his city-state.

Here is Mary Renault in *The Lion in the Gateway* (1964), a
children's account of Greek military history, interpreting the ideal
of historical writing as she sees it reflected in Herodotus. Bearing
in mind the Athenian political milieu, her description coincides
neatly with her subject matter: "He thought that character is destiny. He never writes about human beings as if they were economic units, statistics or lines on a graph. He is full of stories
which show what men are made of and how they behave in the
great crises of their lives. This makes him the most interesting of

all historians. His people are alive for us after two and a half thousand years" (174).

In the novel's hard-hitting first paragraph, Mary Renault immediately plunges us into the moral and physical reality of Classical Athens: "When I was a young boy, if I was sick or in trouble, or had been beaten at school, I used to remember that on the day I was born my father had wanted to kill me." The following paragraph continues confidently in the same vein, but with a surprising split between idea and tone: "You will say there is nothing out of the way in this" (1). Mary Renault sustains the mood of this trenchant opening—both through style and through her masterly grasp of the Athenian spirit.

And the firmness of her soldierly, measured cadences gain a magnetized impact when she recreates the many-colored luster of cosmopolitan Athens: "The cheering began in the City. . . . Then it roared through Piraeus; one could hear the music coming, and shield clashing on corselet to the beat. Now you could see between the Walls the helmet-crests moving, a river of them, a long snake bright with his new scales in springtime, bronze and gold, purple and red. Sparks of light seemed to dance above it, the early sun catching the points of many thousand spears; the dust-cloud shone like powdered gold" (39).

As the passage indicates, to read *The Last of the Wine* is to taste the charged metallic flavor of Athenian life. The motion, the sensation, and the energy of Athenian routine are a delight and an education; but they are also the quintessence of diligent study. Mary Renault's command of her subject matter drenches everything in the novel in the same golden fire. Her mastery in presenting manners of dress, styles in sculpture and architecture, political developments, and techniques of warfare is so uniformly smooth that we tend to overlook the enormous research that went into the composition of the book. Any artist must rework his finished artifact thoroughly in order to gain the quality of fluidity and grace; and, barring the question of language, *The Last of the Wine* could have easily been written by an educated Athenian gifted with a highly pictorial imagination.

The following excerpt shows how totally Mary Renault has immersed herself in the life of the Classical period; for the sharp detail with which she documents the naval practices of the time reflects an undeniable genius for scholarship in the most creative sense: "Meantime the pilot and some of the hands had got the great sail lowered over-side, and were frapping it over the breach with hawsers run below the keel. It stanched the wound of the ram, and though it was clear she was making water all over her hull, the baling did begin to gain a little" (270). To capture the magnificent range and scope of *The Last of the Wine*, we must allude to the wide-screen film spectacular (or, at least, to its artistic possibilities). The battle scenes, the geographical and historical sweep, and the colorful panoply of life along the harbors and farms of Athens provide ideal substance for a technicolor epic.

And the cast of characters is epical. Mary Renault introduces prominent, obscure, and imaginary figures to create the Athenian mood. Among the more notable contemporaries, Timon is mentioned; Euripedes has a brief walk-on role; Kriton and Lysander, the indomitable Spartan general, are given small speaking parts; Plato appears several times, first as a burly young wrestler and finally as a disillusioned aristocrat; Sokrates, portrayed uniformly as a rock of sound judgment, serves as an unchanging standard of excellence against which Mary Renault measures the collapse of Athenian tradition. Kebes and Simmias, two Thebans who appear in Plato's *Phaedo*, enter the action at Phylae, the place from which the Athenian patriots mounted their offensive against the Oligarchs (the Thirty Tyrants) in 403.

Other contemporary Greeks enrich the prevailing Athenian temper, Mary Renault again describing through character portrayal and concrete incident the fall of a way of life. The life of Phaedo, for instance, is historically undocumented in many crucial areas; but, in spite of these factual obscurities, including Phaedo's birthplace, Mary Renault conveys a thoroughly convincing character portrait. Whether Phaedo was a Melian or an Elian, and whether he was rescued from his degrading job as a male prostitute by Kebes, Alkibiades, or Kriton, matter far less than his later becoming Greece's outstanding exponent, after Sokrates, of the negative elenchos. Phaedo's ability to maintain intellectual freedom in spite of physical enslavement constitutes a shining affirmation of Athenian excellence.

Mary Renault's characterization of Xenophon, as well, may offend scholarly accuracy; at any rate, the Xenophon of *The Last of the Wine* is much more Spartan in temperament than either Edith Hamilton's in *The Greek Way* or Stringfellow Barr's in *The*

Will of Zeus. But Xenophon, too, serves a creative purpose within
the structure of the book. As a practical, sensible extrovert, he is
easily the sort of person who could lead a fifteen-hundred-mile
expedition from Babylon to Sardis in addition to writing tracts on
hunting, house management, and educating a wife. This reverence for order and disciplined routine might have also attracted
him to the Spartan ethic of obedience, even to the point of leaguing with the Thirty Tyrants, the insurgent puppet regime that
ruled Athens after the Spartan occupation of 404.

Within the dramatic contours of the novel, Xenophon, the practical man of goodwill, occupies an opposite pole from the brood-
ing, introverted Plato. Yet, Mary Renault's Xenophon never violates historical probability for the sake of narrative plotting. Like
Alkibiades, who stands throughout the book as the magnetic and
inconstant darling of Athenian society, he is a private person
whose public acts add to the social tragedy that throbs at the
heart of the novel.

In the only full-length scholarly article devoted to Mary Renault, Landon C. Burns, Jr., says that the wine mentioned in the
title, *The Last of the Wine*, symbolizes love and "the specter of
change and death and loss which is inevitably the concomitant of
love." [1] Burns's aptly phrased judgment, although basically sound,
overlooks the novel's historical theme. Both the physical setting
and the time scheme of *The Last of the Wine* compel our studying
the work as an evocation of Athens's last years of greatness. Before we investigate this process of social erosion, several historical
facts must be stated. First of all, Athenian greatness must be fixed
in the spirit of the times. Moral and political philosophy begins in
Western civilization with Sokrates. This emphasis also marks the
thought of Plato, who, together with his master, saw the human
soul, and not the physical universe, as the center of philosophical
inquiry. We cannot overstate the point that this human-centered
mode of thought fostered a mode of statecraft that has not been
matched in Western civilization. (William Morris's ill-fated Guild
Socialism is probably the closest parallel.)

The political ideal of life-as-dialogue, or of civil law as the fruit
of a conversational give-and-take between citizens, yielded a democracy of brilliant amateurs. In the Athens of Perikles, every
citizen enjoyed equal political status. Citizenship was the only

qualification for voting, for membership in the sovereign assembly, and even for participation in public debates. The citizen created, revised, and protected the social code that defined his freedom. Although this political ethic has no counterpart today, we can nonetheless appreciate academically M. I. Finley's summary comment on the nature of the Athenian polis: "it was the source of all rights and obligations and its authority reached into every sphere of human behavior without exception." [2] Because of the free interchange between self and state, polis was also a way of life. H. D. F. Kitto has captured the vitality bred by this dynamic interplay of private and public impulse. It is instructive to note, in passing, how closely the singing golden balance of Perikles resembles the literary creed of the Auden circle during the 1930's: "The Mean did not imply the absence of tension and lack of passion, but the correct tension which gives out the true and clear note." [3]

If this working and workable ideal permeated many layers of Athenian life, its ruin had equally powerful reverberations. The twenty-seven-year war with Sparta ended Athens's reign as the cultural, mercantile, and maritime ruler of the eastern Mediterranean; accordingly, two plagues between 430–426 resulted in the loss of a third of the Athenian population.[4] These raw statistics symptomize a deeper malaise which I intend to discuss later; yet it is not premature to explain the attrition as an outgrowth of Athens's split vision of herself as an empire and as a democracy. By attacking Plataea and Melos, Athens pridefully overreached herself, submitting, in the words of Kitto, "to the philosophy of naked force." [5] Mary Renault interprets the wisdom of Apollo, in *The Lion in the Gateway,* in the following words: " 'Know yourself. A man is only a man. Nothing too much' " (150). In *The Last of the Wine,* she applies the oracle's words to Athens itself. As John Stuart Mill wisely insisted, a community, no less than a person, must resist smugness if it wants to insure growth and development from within.

The final chapter in the painful drama of Athens, depicted in Plato's *Euthyphro, Apology, Phaedo,* and *Crito,* treats the last days of Sokrates. Soldier, stonemason, and philosopher, Sokrates is the distillation of Athenian excellence; never having written a line, he stands as the supreme exemplar of the ethic of life-as-dialogue; and his execution marks the formal death of the Golden Mean. The author's ending *The Last of the Wine* shortly before his trial may offend some readers; nowhere does Athenian hubris manifest itself more vividly than in this self-defeating act. On the other hand, Mary Renault's novelistic strategy has the positive merits of artistic symmetry and balance. The book ends with a highly wrought encounter that points directly toward Sokrates's trial and execution in 399. This final outrage upon justice, harmony, and wholeness lodges itself in our minds; we ourselves recreate imaginatively the horror that spelled the end of a way of life; and, because of our participation in the drama, the loss becomes ours.

Athens never regained her lost status. Mary Renault carefully describes the decay as a cancerous erosion rather than an overnight change. After Perikles, the new type of political leader was the demagogue: rabble-rousing oligarchs (Kritias) and even democrats (Anytos) inflamed audiences with sentimental trumpery instead of appealing to the traditional Athenian virtues of justice, reason, and honor. In the theater, the comedy that flourished after the Peloponnesian War was markedly less pungent and topical than the kind associated with Aristophanes; Menander and his fourth-century contemporaries wrote respectable comedies of manner that feature stock character-types and tepid moralizing.

This same passive neglect of living standards of excellence is also mirrored in the statuary of the time. Mary Renault brings out in the later scenes of her novel the general tendency of sculptors toward the end of the century to subordinate the ideal to the individual or the voguish. When Alexias takes a job as a sculptor's model during the last hungry days of the war, he is disgusted with the attitudes and postures he must assume to satisfy the new public taste. If the difference between fifth-century and fourth-century Athens may be metaphorically compared to the difference between wine and water, Alexias himself often provides a fresh insight into the breakdown of the older mortality:

Even now, though the rising generation seems to think nothing of it, I cannot bear to see a runner gone all to legs, looking as if he would be fit for nothing, when off the track, except to get away from a battlefield faster than anyone else. (29)

. . . .

Later I learned that my father had . . . punished me for my disrespect, as any father would. I have never beaten my own boys so hard; but for all I know, they are the worse for it. (53)

The fifth-century Athenian sought simplicity and wholeness in all his endeavors. Ignoring the avenues of thought that led later generations to such impasses as Cartesian dualism, the survival of the fittest, or Marx's dialectical materialism, he sought to make his life a fully globed organic activity. The Palaestra, an academy for wrestling and other sports, may serve as our model of the prevailing Athenian ideal of wholeness and balance. The practice of spending a few hours each day exercising at the Palaestra was a matter of course to the young Athenian. To educate oneself in history, music, and philosophy at the neglect of physical training was not only unthinkable; it was barbaric. Without a sound, well-kept body, the Athenian could not see himself as an integrated human being. It is not surprising to learn that Sokrates conducted some of his liveliest arguments at the Palaestra. There was no split between athletics and academics; after a young man had taken his turn with the discus or javelin, he would often relax by joining his friends in an informal polemical debate.

This practice vanished in the fourth century, when professionalism, specialization, and a tendency to brood on theoretical imponderables severed the organic link between mind and body. Kitto provides a summary comment on the radical shift in being that occurred in Athens at the turn of the century: "What we meet in the fourth century is a permanent change in the temper of the people: it is the emergence of a different attitude to life. In the fourth century there is more individualism. We can see it wherever we look—in art, in philosophy, in life. Sculpture for instance begins to be introspective, to concern itself with individual traits, with passing moods, instead of trying to express the ideal or universal. In fact, it begins to portray men, not Man." [6]

The index, or reference point, for all the developments in *The Last of the Wine* is the narrator, Alexias. An only son of a wealthy landowner, Alexias becomes an ephebe, a prize-winning runner, a cavalry soldier, and a naval lieutenant before the book ends. As a person who derives his meaning and function in life from the state, he traces a downward course that mirrors the sorry fortunes of his society. Alexias is linked with death and destruction since birth: before his first birthday, Perikles dies; the war begins; and his mother, brother, and aunt die of the plague. In spite of his efforts, Alexias cannot avoid corruption, sorrow, or loss. The first major event in his life is his homosexual friendship with Lysis, a sculptor's model, soldier, and wrestler eight years his senior. Regarded with envy and admiration throughout the city, the union of the two youths promises to be the outstanding event of the Palaestra circle. Bearing in mind the generous Athenian attitude toward homosexuality, the relationship of Alexias and Lysis is not only socially orthodox; it is also morally promoted. Myron, Alexias's patrician father, explicitly warns his seventeen-year-old son against consorting with women. But he cordially welcomes Alexias's chance to learn valor, honor, and military prowess from a young officer of the warrior class. The theoretical scaffolding of this unfamiliar homosexual ideal is found in the *Phaedrus*, where Sokrates says that an army of lovers would be invincible: rather than inviting disgrace in one another's eyes, the soldier-lovers would go to the direst extremes of bravery and courage.

But, even though Lysis and Alexias do fight, drink, and study together, their relationship sours. Burns's judgment that Alexias achieves manhood and maturity[7] is only marginally true; he never rises above the submissive role in any of his relationships. At least twice, during the time when his friendship with Lysis grows more blatantly sexual, Alexias goes to brothels, but cannot remember or declines to say what he did. The single affair he does acknowledge is with a woman named Euphro, the mother of a sixteen-year-old son, now dead. Yet again, he does not allow us to see this mother-son sexual relationship develop. When he marries, he selects Thalia, Lysis's widow, for a wife. But his typical evasiveness about sex elicits only the most conventional praise of her wifely merits.

Like Laurie Odell, Alexias never outgrows the masculine ideal of his youth. After absorbing "the worst beating of [his] life" (52) from his father, he experiences his first heightened sexual reaction to Lysis. Lysis, moreover, is the same age as Arete, Myron's second wife, whom Alexias calls "the pattern of all mothers" (25). When Alexias learns, at the age of fifteen or so, that Arete is pregnant, he is resentful. The following passage reveals the frankly sexual context of his resentment: "I said to myself that my grief was absurd; yet it filled my heart and even hurt my body. It seemed to me that my mother had betrayed me; having taken me up when I was wanted by no one, now she had leagued herself with my father to put another in my place. I hated him for it, though I knew it was impiety towards the gods" (51).

Alexias's first act of defiance against Myron occurs when he disregards his father's wish to expose Charis, his baby half-sister. Hereafter, he not only sees Myron as his rival in love and battle; he comes to exalt himself as Charis's true father or giver of life. Once more, he unconsciously connects this new self-concept with his muted passion for Arete. When Myron staggers home three years after the disastrous Athenian campaign at Sicily, where he had been numbered as a fatality, Alexias's reaction is even more bitterly complex. Impressment on a Phoenician galley has changed the former beloved of Alkibiades and the brave soldier who was once called Myron the Beautiful into a twisted wreck of running sores. The glorious Athenian past, then, survives only as a whipped, battered husk; the wine has turned to vinegar.

Myron's leaguing with the Oligarchs offends Alexias politically; but even more grating are the harsh reasons for his father's choice: "My father's foot had healed; he was beginning to get about the City again, and to pick up his old friendships, together with some new ones that dismayed me. All his moderation was gone; I heard him express himself against the democrats with such bitterness as I had scarcely heard within the walls of our house before" (198).

Myron's intrusion is most deeply felt, however, in the change he creates in his family's domestic harmony. His cruelty to his servants and his wife earn him the scorn of everyone in the home. And Alexias resents deeply the time and attention Arete must now devote to him. (The word, *arete*, means *excellence* in Classical Greek; Myron's homecoming may be seen, therefore, as a wall between Alexias and his oedipal standard of womanly excellence.) Charis's open preference for Alexias soon stings Myron so deeply that he accuses Alexias of being her natural father. At this point, all of the pain caused by Myron's homecoming explodes in Alexias's mind. The bitter accusation forces him to admit inwardly the sin of desiring sexual union with his step-mother. He then plummets headlong into the dark underworld of his irrational self. Haunted by the furies as he races dizzily along the mountainside, he finally faints under the strain of his psychological burden: "Their faces and their feet were blue like the night; their garments were without substance, sometimes showing their dark limbs, sometimes the ground behind them. With a shout of horror I leaped to my feet, and fled; and now I knew that what I had

taken only for the noise of my laboring breath, had been the hiss
of the snakes that twined and darted in my hair" (204–05).

The benign, elderly priest who restores him to health owns,
ironically, a marble statue of Myron as a youth carved by Pheidias. Wherever Alexias turns he cannot escape his father. The
son's failure to live according to his lights, hideous though they
may be, becomes clear to him here. The later chapters of the
novel describe him as having accepted his subservience to Myron
and a second-rate existence in general. He begins to drink, to indulge in debauchery, to fall prey to political demagoguery. When
recurring physical pains end his career as a runner, he gives up
all ambitions to excel. This willingness to stand back reflects in
miniature the decay of his society's morality of life-as-dialogue.
Such an ethic can only flourish in a milieu which perceives individuals as coordinate, not super- or subordinate. Alexias and his
city-state both come to grief for this reason; but, where Athens
overextended herself, Alexias commits the inverse error of not
reaching far enough.

The Last of the Wine is an epic in reverse. Epics traditionally
celebrate the founding of a civilization or way of life. The sharply
detailed battle scenes, the indirect invocation of the epical theme
in the novel's first paragraph, the mediocrity of the central character, and the descent into the naked, lawless self comprise an elaborate epical machinery directed to Mary Renault's commanding
theme of a civilization's destruction. The swoon Alexias falls into
symbolizes, together with his father's homecoming, the fall of
Athenian man. His failure to act maturely and decisively mirrors
his society's failure to shun the temptations of imperial violence.

All of the key issues in the novel merge in Chapter XVII, in
which Lysis and Alexias represent Athens in the Isthmian Games,
a bi-annual pageant celebrated by all Hellenic city-states. By fix-
ing the date for the Games in 412, Mary Renault fuses the fall of
Athens with that of Alexias. The year 412 saw the revolt of the
Athenian allies and the escalation of Sparta's attacks on Athens,
thanks to Persian gold. When Lysis and Alexias climb the Acro-
corinth, a mountain-shrine of Aphrodite, they notice Spartan ships
moving across the Isthmus to the Aegean. This mobilization violates the sacred truce all Hellas traditionally observes during the
Games. The overland passage of the ships and the lookout from
which Lysis and Alexias view the event make Sparta's treacherous

act a sin against both nature and religion. It becomes inescapably present at this moment that Grecian honor and tradition are empty political catchwords.

While Alexias prepares for his race, he again learns that everything in Greece comes with a price tag. Disgruntled by the presence of touts, gamblers, and hucksters at the practice sessions before the Games, he is bribed to lose the race in which he is entered. Like Athens herself, he cannot fend off the reality of material gain. After the fear of disbelief and discredit persuades him not to report the bribe, he wins his race—but at a terrible cost. Not only does he compromise his honor by keeping the bribe a secret; he also incurs an ailment during the race which, as has been mentioned, disqualifies him from running again. As an emblem of the times, the Isthmian Games describe Greek affairs as having reached an insoluble crisis.

The fate of Lysis at Corinth is even more calamitous than that of Alexias. In the final round of the Pankration, defined in *The Lion in the Gateway* as "an all-in of wrestling and boxing mixed" (45), Lysis is matched against an opponent called Sostratos. The decline from the Classical ideal of grace, agility, and proportion is dramatized no more forcefully than in Alexias's description of him: "At first I could not trust my eyes. . . . Two or three times, indeed, I had seen this monstrous creature, going about the fair. I had not doubted he was some travelling mountebank, whose act consisted of raising boulders or bending iron bars. . . . Now here he stood, a mountain of gross flesh, great muscles like twisted oakwood gnarling his body and arms; a neck like a bull's; his legs, though they were thick and knotty, seemed bowed by the weight of his ungainly trunk" (178).

This barbaric tendency toward overspecialization—which strikes an embarrassing parallel with our own age—also typifies the violence so characteristic of the times. Lysis's defeat in the punishing, unscientific brawl with Sostratos signals a flaw in the nature of things and forces Alexias to see the golden Mean as a weary anachronism. His impression is fortified by the crowd's reaction to the fight; the onlookers themselves reflect the same blood lust and worship of raw animal strength as Sostratos:

This man had sold grace and swiftness, and the honour of a soldier in the field, not caring at all to be beautiful in the eyes of the gods,

but only caring to be crowned. And yet to him the victory had been
given. (183)

. . . .

Just then Lysis came uppermost for a moment . . . . But as Sostratos rushed upon him, he threw up his foot and swung the man right
over so that he crashed to the earth instead. The noise was so great
that I could hardly hear myself cheer. But there was something new
in it. I had not noticed it at first, but it was growing. In those days,
the pankration was a contest for fighting men. I suppose there had
always been a few slave-minded ones who had got another sort of
pleasure from it; but they had known enough to keep it to themselves.
Now, like ghosts who get strength from drinking blood, they came out
into the light and one heard their voice. (180)

The friendship of Lysis and Alexias begins immediately to erode;
for Lysis, basely defeated, irretrievably loses some of his luster for
Alexias. This change is vaguely sensed by Lysis. The men grow
secretive, more inclined to jealousy, and can only drown their
temperamental outbursts toward each other in long drafts of
wine. Before long, when the wine of Athenian life runs dry, Lysis'
marriage and the suffering caused by Spartan raids force the men
to fend largely for themselves. The elation they temporarily feel
when they league together during the patriots' offensive at Mu-
nychia is burst by Lysis' death.

Alexias does develop to a degree: he becomes a skilled naval
lieutenant; he acknowledges without resentment Phaedo and
Plato as his intellectual superiors; and he tactfully compliments
his father when he is given Myron's armor to wear in battle. He
pays for this development, however, with enormous psychological
hardship. His passive endorsement of mob violence at Samos, his
marriage to Lysis' widow, and his apparent failure as a parent all
undercut any uneasy compromise he may have made with himself. But, as a mirror of both his society and his era, Alexias cannot
enjoy success. To show him attaining a creative dignity in a setting where dignity and honor have become obsolete would violate
artistic symmetry. The Mary Renault of *The Last of the Wine* was
too much of a scholar and an artist to commit such a blunder.
Alexias's ability to live within a set of radically revised personal
standards does signal some kind of victory; in this sense, his life
goes on somewhat smoothly and even comfortably. But to deny
his failure to achieve his youthful promise is to distort the novel.

Alexias's passivity makes him the typical Mary Renault hero whose acts are largely determined by others. His refusal to embrace suffering in a suffering world deprives him of transcending the collapse of the golden Mean.

The first historical event Mary Renault dramatizes in depth is the mutilation of the statues of Hermes, or Mercury, in June, 415. Posterity still cannot name the men who, on the eve of Athens's naval expedition to Sicily, destroyed these sacred monuments; but Mary Renault makes both historical and artistic capital of the event. Aside from building a public drama around the gossip and rumors engendered by the mysterious felony, she juxtaposes the Herm-breaking in Chapter III with Alexias's first awareness of his sexuality—the context for his gravest personal failures. The care taken by the felons to break the erect phalli of the Herms aptly symbolizes the mutilation of the creative principle nourishing Athenian life. Lysis's defeat in the Isthmian Games also defines the Herm-breaking as a symbolic foreshadowing of the death of agility, harmony, and even communication (Hermes being a messenger).

As a phrase in a festering social drama, the Herm-breaking is pivotal—standing midway between the start of the Peloponnesian War in 431 and Sokrates's execution in 399. The Herm-breaking delayed the Sicilian campaign at least a month and removed Alkibiades from command in favor of the aged, infirm Nikias, whose hesitancy allowed for Sparta's intervention in Sicily in 414, the major cause of Athens's defeat. Like Myron, who returns bent and broken from the campaign, the Athenian fleet never recovered the humiliation of Sicily. For the scholarly background to the moral and political malaise which erupted in the Herm-breaking incident, we have the comments of Edith Hamilton and Stringfellow Barr:

The real cause of the war was not this or that trivial disturbance . . . . The motive power was greed, that strange passion for power and possession which no power and possession satisfy. Power . . . or its equivalent, wealth, created the desire for more power, more wealth.[8]
. . . .
If a subject polis claimed it suffered from injustice, such as Athens' doubling the tribute in 425, the only court it could carry its grievance to would be a court in Athens. Was this freedom?[9]

Just before Myron leaves for Sicily, he voices the novel's key statement about Athens's wanton imperialism: " 'The gods punish hubris in men. . . . So why should we think they praise it in cities?' " (45). In a passage slanted wryly to the policies of certain congressional inquiries during the 1950's (we think too of the Reichstag trials and the Moscow purges in the late 1930's), Mary Renault suggests the remorseless chaos that follows the loss of rational control in a public body. The collective trials and the use of hired bullies and informers by the Oligarchs strike the same sour note as the conviction of Sokrates.

Mary Renault never suggests a causal link between Athenian morality and the breaking of the Herms; but already in 415, we can see the self-defeating events of 404 inflaming the Athenian temper: "A public award had now been offered to informers, and a board appointed to hear them. Soon information was coming in not about the Herm-breaking, but about anyone who might be supposed to have done, or said, or thought, something sacrilegious. My father said to anyone who would listen that this was bribing scum to come to the top, and that Perikles would have sickened at it" (36).

This moral groundswell erupts into the Sicilian disaster. The event is reported to the Athenians at home by a Phrygian barber, whom Mary Renault describes in this manner: "Short, smooth and paunchy, with a ruby in his ear, and a black beard crimped to display his art. Having come some way in a hurry, he was sweating like a pig from his hair down into his beard; he looked the kind of little man who gets a roar in a comedy by pretending to have dirtied himself with fright" (139).

The Athenians suffer justly for their rapacity. Because they neglected the warnings of Perikles, they must listen to the barber. Even more grotesque in appearance than the barber, however, is the drunken survivor who reports Athens's defeat at the battle of Goat's Creek, or Aegospotami, in 405. Like the barber and the courtesan who later mourns the death of Alkibiades, this unnamed person only appears once in the novel. The three characters reflect, thereby, an important aspect of Mary Renault's blending of history and art. Their lowly social stations performs the choric function of marking Athens's enormous decline from the standpoint of an outsider who is also an inferior.

If the athletic phase of this drama reaches its zenith at Corinth, the political phase at Athens during the Oligarchs' reign of terror, and the philosophical phase at Sokrates's unreported execution, the collapse of military excellence occurs at Arginsuae in 406. Mary Renault plays the battle against both the Sicilian campaign and the Herm-breaking. The refusal of the Athenian generals, especially Tydeus, to heed Alkibiades's advice on the deployment of their troops at Arginsuae led to one of the most disgraceful defeats in military history. Nikias's poor health, his superstitition, and his ignorance of military tactics permitted the Spartan ambush that destroyed the Athenian forces at Sicily.

Arginsuae was even more corrosive in its effects upon Athens. Without cover, fire power, or a line of retreat, the Athenian garrison was thrashed so decisively that high-ranking officers, as well as soldiers, joined the enemy ranks during the battle. This desertion is no mere weakening of military discipline. Like the closing scenes in Tennyson's *Idylls of the King*, Alexias's account of the Arginsuae disaster includes an upheaval of rational, and even natural, order. The colossal blunder of the generals and the patriots' inability to distinguish friends from foes justify the defilement of the Periklean Mean as an internal corruption. At the end of the fight, the disorder, the incongruity, and the isolation marking the encounter gain a fine moment of Conradian absurdity: "All around me in the sea was shouting and crying; I heard someone calling again and again, 'Tell Krates not to sell the land! Not to sell the land!' till his voice was cut off in the middle. My ears roared with water . . ." (273).

Various kinds of disorder, then, bruise one another in the closing chapters. Within the chronology of the book, the cancerous movement is from the physical to the political and finally to the philosophical realm. A few striking similarities with Isherwood's *Berlin Stories* suggests that *The Last of the Wine* forms an exciting development in the formulation of a new novelistic genre— the inverse epic. Both Isherwood and Mary Renault control narrative tempo so that dramatic pace and personal hardship build with increasing momentum and force. Besides infusing this technique of *progression d'effet* into their epic machinery, both writers are also fond of introducing historical detail in an explosive summary passage:

Berlin was in a state of civil war. Hate exploded suddenly, without warning, out of nowhere; at street corners, in restaurants, cinemas, dance halls, swimming-baths; at midnight, after breakfast, in the middle of the afternoon. Knives were whipped out, blows were dealt with spiked rings, beer-mugs, chair-legs or leaded clubs . . . . In the middle of a crowded street a young man would be attacked, stripped, thrashed and left bleeding on the pavement; in fifteen seconds it was all over and the assailants had disappeared.[10]

It was not for some weeks that people began to die. At first it was the very poor, the very old, and those who were sick already. As things got scarcer prices got higher . . . every day the army of the poor was growing, and when people had been poor for long enough, they died. (299)

Another persistent note in both writers is the idea that any unjust government sooner or later turns ordinary people into beasts. As the Nazis gain power in *The Last of Mr. Norris* and *Goodbye to Berlin,* the jungle mentality informing all German life in the 1930's grows more overt. Chapter XXVI of *The Last of the Wine* describes the subject Athenians outstripping their Spartan captors in wickedness. Sparta's respect for Hellenic tradition kept her from enslaving Athens, even while her fierce general, Lysander, was overthrowing other democracies all around the Aegean. Conversely, Mary Renault depicts the Athenians killing their own fellows in order to win Spartan favor. These events are historically warranted: the mass arrests, the closed trials, and the confiscation of property by the Thirty Tyrants—actual occurrences in Athens during the waning years of the Fifth Century—create a milieu in which a man like Myron could be driven from his century-old family estate and then attacked from behind.

Mary Renault's *progression d'effet* is no less effective than Isherwood's. When Lysander blockades the port of Piraeus, life becomes as much a matter of animal cunning and survival to the Athenians as it did to Isherwood's Germans after the blackshirted stormtroopers assumed power. (The abortive attempt of Theramenes to settle for terms with Sparta during the occupation, incidentally, brings to mind Chamberlain's appeasement flight to Munich in 1938.) High-born Athenians begin eating donkeys, dogs, and rats; poverty forces Alexias to expose his new-born brother on the mountainside after Arete dies in childbirth; Lysis' bride, Thalia, aged fourteen, tries to become a prostitute. This parallel with Otto Nowak, Isherwood's bisexual sixteen-year-old male prostitute in *Goodbye to Berlin,* describes how deeply political corruption can strike into the daily lives of any people; even innocence and youth cannot escape the contagion of power and violence.

A final similarity linking Isherwood and Mary Renault pertains to their comparable method of artistic selection. Plato's visit to Kritias, his uncle and the cruel leader of the Thirty Tyrants, after the Tyrants openly threaten Sokrates, is deliberately undramatized. As in Lysis' death and several major events in Isherwood's book, the device of the hasty summary or indirect account has satirical force. By refusing to develop an event dramatically, a writer stresses the triviality of that event within a larger design. The truncated, or played-down, acts in *The Last of the Wine* are noble and heroic; therefore, the sting of Mary Renault's satire recoils upon Athens herself, where, once again, virtues like nobility have become a dead letter: "What passed that day between Plato and his kinsman, none of us knew. If you ask how a man of twenty-four could put shame into one of five-and-forty, when Sokrates himself could not, I have nothing to say, except that Sokrates defied the Thirty, and lived" (345–46).

The single flicker of hope during the entire epoch proves disarmingly false. With great mastery, Mary Renault first builds up the patriots' offensive at the old, wealthy city of Samos and then exposes it as just another case of Athenian dry-rot. The overthrow of the Samian oligarchs in 411 made Samos a democratic stronghold and rallying-point from which to oppose Kritias. Called a "new, democratic Polis-in-exile" [11] by Barr, Samos strengthened even the most idealistic patriots: "I have never felt less like an exile. It was we who were the City now, a free Athens beyond the sea. We carried her sword too and her armour; it was the Navy, not the government at home, which levied the island tribute to finance the war. The sun shone; the sea like hammered silver flashed below us; we felt we were making a new thing on the earth" (240).

Yet filth and greed can only beget more of the same. Mary Renault's shrewd angling of Alexias's narrative explains the entire Samian campaign as impure long before Alexias admits the fact. The Athenians, no less than the Spartans, are insurrectionists foisting laws upon a foreign country on her own soil. An unjust, meddling democracy has no moral or practical advantages over a dictatorship. The street fighting, the mass slaughter, and the zeal with which the patriots embrace mob psychology show a total collapse of the morality Alexias and his friends are allegedly fighting to protect: "People were still taking up the cry of 'Death to the tyrants!' But now I heard a different note in it. There was a huddle of men in the corner of the square; and as I looked, a face rose up from the midst, with blood on it, and the eyes wide, staring about. Someone was being mobbed there. This is a thing that you do not see in war; it was like filth flung on my exultation" (234).

The excesses of democratic rule sound the final jarring chord of *The Last of the Wine*. Again, loss of reason shifts the political climate of Athens to an extreme as unhealthy as the one of the Thirty Oligarchs. No less than under Kritias, the new Athenian democracy has sacrificed the individual citizen to a mechanical abstraction—in this case, the People. By a careful blend of history, social psychology, and narrative art, Mary Renault bodies forth the dangers latent in any democracy. A prideful scorn of excellence and a tendency to reduce political standards to the lowest social level are just as imminent in a democracy as the fatuity of gaining selfhood within the life of a master race is in a dictatorship. What is missing in both political doctrines is the free exchange of ideas and the sensitivity to individual needs insisted upon by Perikles. Mary Renault's description of Anytos, a democratic zealot who was the most influential of Sokrates's detractors, and of his alcoholic son, Anthemion (375, 377), create a believable context for the mechanized mediocrity so characteristic of the fourth, and perhaps of our own, century.

Like the death of Sokrates, the Bomb has introduced an age of commonness and collective impersonality which has all but ruled out any dignified search for transcendent values. Mary Renault returns to this problem with renewed vigor in her three latest novels.

II   The Mask of Apollo (*1966*)

The Mask of Apollo is a worthy sequel to *The Last of the Wine*. By portraying various changes in Greek life in the half-century following Sokrates's death, it is both autopsy and prophecy. Although the peripheries of *The Mask of Apollo* extend from 388 to 342 B.C., most of the action takes place in the years between the deaths of Dionysios I, Archon of Syracuse, in 367 and Dion, Syracuse's first constitutional monarch, in 354. Athens has not regained her eminence. Most of the notable public men are either Sicilian or Macedonian, while Syracuse, mirroring the bewildered, dissolute temper of the times, furnishes the physical and moral setting for most of the novel. The theater has degenerated to slapstick and political propaganda; accordingly, audiences now prefer engineering tricks to dramatic art; and actors talk about portraying the scabrous Thersites as a sympathetic character.

The Athenian spirit does burn brightly in the persons of Plato, Dion, and Nikeratos, or Niko, a professional tragic actor and the narrator of the novel. Plato, who has tried to make his life a paean to Sokrates, sees in Dion, his former pupil, an opportunity to test his ideal of the philosopher-king. But the application of kingly principles to concrete situations brings bitterness and loss. Although Plato and Dion act honorably, they invariably find themselves blocked by expediency, ambiguity, and greed. The death of Athenian leadership has robbed fourth-century politics of any unifying principle: city-states all over the Aegean and Adriatic are now bickering; governments function without constitutions; commerce, banking, and trade have fallen into the hands of financial buccaneers. As we might expect, all confidence and stability have disappeared; nobody can afford to be sure of anything. Like the anti-right-wing legislators of the 1930's, Plato and Dion learn quickly that they can only fight evil with a lesser evil.

The complexity of the age explains the need for this indirection and uneasy compromise. Son of a Sicilian donkey-driver, the tough, self-made Dionysios I has for years been the most powerful ruler in Hellas. After his tragedy, *Hector's Ransoming*, wins first prize in an Athenian dramatic contest, the former pillager of temples takes sick and dies. Fearing a political rival in his later years, Dionysios had avoided training his son and namesake in matters of government. The job of educating the pampered, lethargic young Archon after his father's death falls to his brother-in-law, Dion. Convinced that Dionysios II could be trained to rule Syracuse honorably and justly, Dion invites Plato to the royal court.

But Dionysios's political education is undermined by a faction of older courtiers, political hangers-on who oppose public reform out of self-interest. Leaguing behind Philistos, the former adviser of Dionysios I, these men persuade the young ruler to disgrace

Dion by banishing him. This folly spreads like brush-fire. For Syracuse's traditional foe, Carthage, has raised its hackles: distrusting Philistos and despising Dionysios the Younger, Carthage will only conduct its diplomacy with the powerless Dion. Its inept cub of a ruler is leading Syracuse to moral and military death.

To avoid tipping the scales, the structure of *The Mask of Apollo* dispels much of this bleakness. Chapter I, with its strong, hopeful ending, strikes a note that peals brightly through the mists of misgovernment. While acting the role of Apollo, Niko frightens a mob of oligarchs who storm the theater at Phigeleia. Niko's act takes on monumental import when we understand that any stage production in Classical times was regarded as a religious festival. Niko's impromptu performance reaffirms the power of dramatic art and preserves the sanctity of the theater. The outlook is hopeful. All of the novel's creative energies have aligned to serve piety, justice, and imaginative beauty. Insurrection is averted; Niko's acting career is given a boost; artistic excellence—Apollo's timeless wisdom asserting itself mightily at the ceremony of Dionysos —has touched and blessed human life. Niko's later decision to remain in politically torn Syracuse is another attempt at this union of politics and philosophy, religion and art.

But by the end of Chapter II, the vapors have gathered and thickened. Although Niko meets Dion, his model of manly excellence, Dion asks him to act *Hector's Ransoming*, the prizewinning tragedy of Dionysios I, whose politics Niko detests. Life has become so complex that Niko cannot even choose good over evil any more. Victory and defeat again look alike when Niko's convictions drive him to support Plato, who has just pronounced his edict on the closing of the theaters. Wherever Niko turns, he must sacrifice, compromise, or cheapen. Unable to serve both Plato and Dionysios—reason and emotion, respectively—he reflects his self-divided society; both Niko and his contemporaries discover that the golden culture of Hellas has become so tarnished and scored that it no longer recognizes beauty or wisdom. Everything is conditioned by greed.

Although Niko insists that the drama must be kept pure, partisan politics creep into the theater. This sullying of Niko's purism is foreshadowed early in the book: "There were still nearly as many wars going on as dramatic festivals, and all of them needed extras" (30). Niko cannot escape the confusion of art and strongarm politics. Owing to the absence of mass communications, political leaders often used the stage for purposes of propaganda. Twice, political hirelings tamper with stage properties to change the meaning of a play Niko is acting in; he carries secret messages between cities; he loses an outstanding role when Dionysios's death stops the production of *Hector's Ransoming* in Syracuse. His greatest public success also occurs as a result of Dionysios's death, when Niko is asked to speak the funeral address. The act that radically changes Niko's fortunes twice within a few days carries the added irony of boosting his career at the expense of his talent; for it is as an orator, not as a dramatic actor, that Niko becomes popular. Even success is taken out of his hands and clad in an unfamiliar garb.

Niko has the credentials to recount faithfully and fully his era's lost opportunities. The son of a leading Athenian actor, he combines family pride with a theatrical tradition. His training in basic techniques of stage-acting allows him to see himself as a craftsman, a poet, and a priest. His acting success he credits to divine visitation; for Niko says he is able to act his roles with such power because the god enters his soul and possesses it during the sacred ritual of the play. This profound sensitivity makes him one of the renowned tragic actors of his day and, owing to the exalted station of prize-winning actors, enables him to meet many of his celebrated contemporaries.

His emotional friendship with the noble Dion imparts exciting crosscurrents to the political drama. To Niko, Dion embodies the dramatic ideal of kingship; Dion's knowledge of political theory, together with his silver personal example, teach Niko how to portray royalty on the stage. An Athenian, a democrat, and a descendant of the theater of Euripedes, Sophokles, and Aischylos, Niko joins his fortunes with those of Dion. Not only professionally and politically, but also emotionally, Niko maintains an ever-heightening stake in Dion; but the interchange of selves is imperfect. Whereas the younger man enriches his art with political lore, Dion never acquires the supple personality necessary to both actor and politician; and Dion's failure engulfs and drowns Niko's success. Before they understand what has happened, Niko and Dion fire the public disaster standing at the novel's center.

The metaphor of the stage, which dominates *The Mask of Apollo*, defines the calamity. Everyone in public life finds himself wrapped in a role he either dislikes or mishandles. Niko, whose resilient, unclassifiable personality allows him to remain uncorrupted by the roles *he* plays, becomes as much of a tragic hero as Dion and Plato. What all three men aim at in their heated discussions of poetic drama is a universal working ethic which ratifies a free interchange between theory and practice. The disagreements, blunders, and oversights of the three men signify less than their initial working premise of man's perfectibility. That Plato, Dion, and Niko can struggle toward a transcendent morality in a ragged, corrupt world constitutes in itself the stuff of heroism.

The toil of uniting principle and practice falls upon Dion. Austere, stately, and refined, he recalls the Athenian ideal at its best; Niko calls him "an old athlete from those days of the gentleman amateur they talk about" (53). Mary Renault often likens him to other tragic heroes trapped by their greatness of soul: Shakespeare's Brutus, Othello, and Coriolanus. Dion's downfall impinges on the Sokratic imperative of correcting shoddy thinking. Sokrates affirmed that once men were shown the best, they would automatically embrace it; and Dion comes to grief, ironically, because he follows his master's dictum so faithfully. By being unflaggingly moderate, sober, and reasonable, he parodies the Apollonian credo of moderation, sobriety, and reason. Unremitting reason, it seems, is not only unreasonable but deadly; for Mary Renault mentions in her Author's Note that "the deep political disillusion of the time expressed itself intellectually in a search for ideal systems" (369). The chiselled, puritanical Dion embodies this bleak search. An alloy of dross would have made him one of antiquity's greatest rulers; but the historical Dion was too close-grained and brittle to make Syracuse anything but a cauldron of havoc.

The gods are not mocked. When Dion compromises, as he must, everybody suffers. Syracuse undergoes a decade of insurrection, bloodshed, and depopulation. Dion fails on every score: as a parent, when his dissolute son commits suicide; as a leader, when he employs spies and then murders his political rival, Herakleides, "for the sake of the city" (344); and as a man. His brief period of office ages him tremendously; and, when he dies—suitably, at the hand of one of his own paid spies—his death is viewed as a blessing. The title of the novel describes him with loveless accuracy. As both a grotesque replica of the Apollonian ideal and a frozen still-life, he shows that even virtue and honor can be death-dealing. The agony caused by his puritanical stiffness is Hawthornesque in intensity.

Like the literal mask—a stage property Niko inherits from his father—Dion is at first an inspiration and then a reproach to his fellows. As has been suggested, the tragedy in *The Mask of Apollo* is social and cultural as well as personal. The golden Macedonian prince, Alexander, who appears at the very end of the novel, reverses the weary intellectual absolutism of the Academy. Youthful, dynamic, and temperamental, Alexander is Dion's foil. Because Hellas could not rise to Dion, it must succumb to a spellbinder whose bag of tricks includes imperial expansion, demagoguery and the cult of personality.

The closest literary parallel to *The Mask of Apollo* is *The Bacchae* of Euripedes. Both works pay homage to the anarchy in man's nature; both also represent the same drastic change in their authors' attitudes toward moderation and proportion. *The Bacchae* is actually staged in *The Mask of Apollo*. During the production, Dion is mocked by his enemies through the character of Pentheus, the stiff, wooden king of Thebes. The similarity between the two men is more striking than Dion's enemies realize. After Pentheus fails to kill Dionysos or Bacchus, who has impudently materialized as a heifer, the forces of riot kill the Theban king. Because Pentheus and Dion both negate brute energy, they must suffer. The moral contexts of Euripedes's play and Mary Renault's novel are interchangeable. Although the aristocratic mask of Apollo, like the conch in Golding's *Lord of the Flies,* represents a standard of civilized excellence, Apollo's power to interpret the will of Zeus expresses itself only in the theater—Dionysos' festival. The oracle resides, then, in the house of malice, lust, and greed; and it derives its very being from these implacable forces of fury.

The Mask of Apollo is the strangest and perhaps the most modern of all Mary Renault's works. Gone are the high tones, the flowing colors, and the heroic cadences of *The Last of the Wine* and the two Theseus novels. Mary Renault cannot be faulted on her knowledge of the Classical theater; she writes about fourth-century techniques of acting and staging, production and management, with her usual authority and point. But these passages convey no lyrical magic; the entire effect of *The Mask of Apollo* is one of harshness and severity. Matching the novel's astringent theme is an equally stern narrative execution. The final sentence of the book summarizes a painfully disconnected world: "No one will ever make a tragedy—and that is well, for one could not bear it—whose grief is that the principals have never met" (366).

Despite Niko's disclaimer, *The Mask of Apollo* is this tragedy; and the tragedy is all the more terrifying for its vast cultural scope. Mary Renault has given us a century and a civilization out of joint with itself. This disunity calls for a fictional method equally discontinuous and broken. Niko, therefore, risks his life to carry a secret message to Plato in Tarentum—to discover that the substance of his communique is already public knowledge. Mary Renault seems to create exciting scenes and situations only to flatten them, and she sternly disallows us to touch the knurls and bosswork on her soldiers' armor; neither do we feel the seaspray lashing up from a trireme's swift prow. In fact, we only learn of the heroic events of the time long after they take place and usually at second- or thirdhand.

As has been stated, *The Mask of Apollo* passes muster as a sequel to *The Last of the Wine*. A major theme in both novels is the loss of communication. Its hasty summaries, abrupt transitions, and ironical character deployment make the later book an even grittier experience than its predecessor. The prophecy of Yeats's "The Second Coming" has been fulfilled: life is so chipped and disillusioned that nothing can resist the encroaching jungle. *The Mask of Apollo* is both a novel and an anti-novel: a novel, because it portrays justly and accurately the spirit of an age; an anti-novel, by virtue of the disjointedness between event and character. Either label captures the tense unity of an impersonal method voicing an equally impersonal, stripped theme.

CHAPTER 5

The Mainland Savage

MARY RENAULT's Theseus is a splendid anachronism. As Northrop Frye demonstrates in *Anatomy of Criticism*, the fictional hero in Western literature has descended over the centuries from godlike majesty to a subhuman, subterranean level.[1] A hasty contrast between the gods or god-gotten heroes of Homer and fictional protagonists like Dostoevski's underground man, Beckett's bums, and Arthur Miller's salesman bear out Frye's argument. Recent literary characters reflect an increasing tendency to exist either marginally or below society. Unlike the people in Dickens, Thackeray, or Trollope, they are displaced, deracinated, and incapable of changing themselves or anybody else. Mary Renault's reason for opposing this trend is to restore drama and adventure to contemporary life.

Theseus's suitability as a vehicle of social criticism is verified by legend. Instead of embracing futility or remaining transfixed by doubt, he changes circumstances to suit his purposes. The Theseus novels are better than *The Last of the Wine* because of his mighty presence. Theseus is the only self-acting protagonist in the entire Renault canon. Whereas Alexias and Niko mirrored the virtues and the faults of their culture, Theseus is a shaper of social values. A tireless wrecker who constantly purges evil, he destroys for the purpose of creating order. Thus he kills sadistic bandits like Skyros, Sinis Pinebender, and Prokrustes not wantonly, but to domesticate the wild country along the Corinthian Isthmus. He is everywhere a creator of values: in his various functions as enemy, originator, and, finally, enforcer of his society's moral code, he channels all his energies into the unprecedented feat of unifying Hellas under a single rule.

Although posterity cannot separate hearsay from fact in what has been preserved of Theseus's deeds—he is the earliest figure studied by Plutarch—Mary Renault organizes her mythical data with great originality. As in *The Last of the Wine* and in *The Mask of Apollo*, her dramatic intention is never buried under a shaft of scholarly detail. Artistic control and sound judgment allow her to create a unified portrait of a man and his age that stands with the best historical novels of the century. The complex narrative flows richly and confidently, unravelling itself with all of the tragic inevitability of the myth it conveys. Especially in *The King Must Die*, the abundant source material never obscures plot or character development.

Her treatment of the diverse accounts of Theseus's origin describes vividly this spontaneous feeling for myth: Theseus survives the wreckage and distortions of thirty centuries as the great national hero of Attic legend, which claims him as the son of Aigeus, king of Athens, and of Aithra, daughter of the king of Troizen. The older legend of Troizen, however, while agreeing on Theseus's royal ancestry, makes him the son of Poseidon. Instead of wrestling with lineage, Mary Renault makes Poseidon Theseus's patron deity and weaves this motif into a complex father-search; but none of Theseus's luster is diminished by his mortality. That he is a vessel of Poseidon's wisdom bespeaks, prima facie, his exceptional nature; for as Kitto points out, using Achilles as his example, the gods only reveal themselves to extraordinary men.[2] Descending from the house of Erechtheus on his father's side and from the house of Pelops on his mother's, Theseus contains within himself the lyrical grace of Athens and the soldierly resolve of Sparta. This combination justifies his ascendancy as the first ruler of Greece. The best of Hellenic culture mingles in his blood. To reinforce this idea, Mary Renault infuses in her archetypal Greek hero the proud defiance of Achilles and the restless cunning of Ulysses. Historically, politically, and spiritually, Theseus serves as an ancestral reservoir for the glories and the ravages of Classical culture.

Theseus is, in fact, a priest king, a monarch who regularly consults and sacrifices to his patron deity before any major undertaking. His father-search—joining the twin themes of killing the earthly father, or father-surrogate, and embracing the spiritual father—is an extended religious act. The structure of the Olympian pantheon reveals Mary Renault's sound artistry in validating both Theseus's kinship to Poseidon and his centrality in an unfolding world drama. After the death of Kronos, the world was divided into three parts. Zeus, the most honored of the Olympians, ruled the sky and the earth; Hades, the underworld; Poseidon, the sea. Poseidon, who kept a team of white chariot horses in the stables of the sea, is said to have created the horse. Possessed "of a surly, quarrelsome nature," [3] the "Earth-Shaker," or "Wave-Gatherer," was also the patron deity of bulls. Testy and pugnacious himself, Theseus discovers that his personal destiny is largely conditioned by bulls, horses, and the sea. An excellent swimmer whose blue eyes parallel Poseidon's sea-blue hair, he has a natural affinity to water. His father rises out of the sea to greet his mother the night Theseus is conceived; Theseus's best friend, Pirithoos, descends from a tribe of master horsemen; Theseus even marries the sea symbolically before his conquest of the Minotaur—another bull-like being—in Crete; finally, his son, Hippolytos, is killed in an angry sea-squall that throws a bull into the path of his horse-drawn chariot.

The quality that knits Theseus's personal fortunes, his kingly attributes, and the divine will is *moira*. Mary Renault dramatizes *moira* as an active putting-to-work of one's total energies. Both a privilege and a duty, it comprises the limits, direction, and focus of a person's resources. Pittheus, who is Theseus's grandfather and the wisest man of his times, defines *moira* in *The King Must Die* as "'The finished shape of our fate, the line drawn round it. It is the task the gods allot us, and the share they allow; the limits we must not pass; and our appointed end'" (15–16). In *The Bull from the Sea,* Theseus discusses the dynamics of *moira*: "'Men could be more than they are. . . . There is a faith, there is a pride, which has to be acted first and grows by doing'" (44). Both Theseus and his sage grandfather agree that *moira* is a divine gift of which they must prove themselves worthy. The responsibility rests with the individual's capacity to act. On the one hand, he must observe the Apollonian credo of temperance and moderation. One's end is contained in one's beginning, as can be seen in the presence of the sea, bulls, or horses at each crucial stage of Theseus's life. What must be avoided is the prideful excess of overreaching oneself; and, by arrogating godlike powers to himself, Theseus turns the inescapable conditions of his life to self-destruction. But, just as urgent is the need to move forward, to realize self without any supernatural guarantees.

As the existentialists insist, man's potential talents require a

strong exercise of will to attain concrete performance; but, in
Mary Renault's view, the unknown quantity of a divine plan is
another factor. Even if man's limited vision often confuses self-
overreaching with self-overcoming, this important difference is always ascertainable to the gods. Burns has captured the essence of
the difficult theological rift between divine foreknowledge and
predestination or determinism. Once again, we shall see that the
burden of self-attainment falls squarely on the individual; even if
certain conditions of a person's life are fixed, the person himself is
totally in charge of them: "*Moira* is to be distinguished from predestination in that within the bounds of his *moira* a man has complete freedom—freedom even to refuse to accept his *moira.*" [4]

The divine and the human also mix in the various religious
ceremonies described in the books. The union of Aigeus and
Aithra is a case in point. A high priestess of Troizen orders Aithra
to sacrifice her maidenhead to Diana, who has visited the land
with drought. At this same time, Aigeus, who lacks the male heir
that will stabilize his harried kingdom, stops at Troizen on the
way home from the Delphic oracle. He and Pittheus then arrange
a sexual union for their mutual benefit. Yet, as blatantly expedient
as the ensuing sexuality is, it should not be condemned as a blas-
phemous act. The measure of politics involved in Theseus's beget-
ting provides a human touch together with satisfying a public
need; for all religion, politics, and history must include human
imperfection in order to have human relevance.

That Theseus's birth is a direct result of political maneuvering
proves that the divine will not only accepts but operates within
the tissue of social necessity. Theseus's doubtful paternity is grist
to the same economy. First of all, his uncertain origin—like that of
Romulus, Alkibiades, Robin Hood, and King Arthur—reaffirms
the archetype of the miraculous birth of the hero.[5] Second, the
disgrace of being a bastard compels Theseus to undertake bold,
dangerous acts. Mary Renault uses creatively the various tensions
surrounding his birth: although he is endowed with kingly attributes, he must enact his *moira* by exercising them. His defensiveness and sense of shame, then, allow him to earn his kingship.
This union of opposites is bridged by public need and personal
resolve. As Theseus overcomes his limitations by performing dangerous acts, these acts prepare him to regenerate Greek culture.

Mary Renault reveals this same merging of opposites in Theseus's military undertakings. For archaic man, there were no specific, isolated acts. The numerous repeated experiences in the companion novels affirm cosmic rebirth through similar events. Certain human acts or patterns of action recur because of their importance in a supervening design. Nothing is wasted in the divine economy. The prefabricated harmony of the universe employs archetypes as a way of reinforcing the metaphysical oneness of things. Leibniz's interlocking network of monads attempted to justify the universe as a conscious operating unit. The movement in all idealist philosophy is from chaos, or diversity, to order. Theseus is a Hegelian hero, an actor in a timeless world drama who executes the will of the divine intelligence. As Eliade often states in *Cosmos and History,* the transformation of chaos to order repeats the divine act of creation. The act is both specific, as a strenuous personal event, and paradigmatic, as a phase or category of the divine economy.

Regardless of whether Theseus founds a new civilization or destroys an older culture, he always acts in the name of public reform and organization. Hegel's phenomenology allows us to interpret his conduct from both the human and the cosmic points of view. Hegel insisted that, because any civil code is an expression of the divine will, the law cannot arbitrarily be broken. On the other hand, public law must be tested to fend off the dead hand of stagnation. Creation, therefore, is affirmed within destruction whenever the law is broken or amended. All of Theseus's acts are parts of one timeless act: while Mary Renault's highly graphic style and the soaring energy of her central character insure dramatic immediacy, the entire sequence of Theseus's efforts occur instantaneously within the eye of the god. The inability of any mortal to know the divine will reinforces narrative urgency. Both Theseus's indomitable spirit and the inevitable rift between the human and the divine keep the novels from hardening into a schematic formula.

Mary Renault has handworked the amorphous Theseus legend to energize this two-pronged theme of timelessness and immediacy. In several cases she humanizes the myth to make it more acceptable to the modern reader. Thus Skyron, whom Theseus kills near Megara on the Isthmus road, neither lands on a tortoise nor becomes one after falling from a high cliff; more credibly, he lands on a tortoise-shaped rock. Later, after Theseus presents himself to his father in Athens, Medea mesmerizes him and disappears. Although Mary Renault retains this note of improbability, she resists having Medea escape from the Akropolis in a magical cloud.

The Kentaurs in *The Bull from the Sea* are even more readily explainable by natural law. For the sake of reader response, Mary Renault retains the awesome character of Chiron; but she humanizes the anatomy of his tribe. Whatever temporary loss she suffers by deflating the Kentaur myth, she quickly regains—both in the primitive mountain simplicity of the Kentaurs' racial character and in Theseus's shock when he first sees them: "At the next turn, I saw a sight made me nearly jump from the saddle: a beast with four legs and two arms, for all the world like a rough-coated pony with a shock-haired boy growing up from its shoulders. So it seemed, first seen. Coming near, I saw how the pony grazed head down, and the child sitting up bareback had tucked his brown dirty feet into the shaggy pelt" (73).

Occasionally, Mary Renault omits a major section of the legend to tighten her plot. Thus we hear nothing of the four years Theseus supposedly spent in the underworld after abducting Helen of Troy. These four years are accounted for in *The Bull from the Sea* by an illness and a slow recovery, during which Theseus indulges in a lengthy private inventory. The episode, as short as it is, serves as the epic hero's descent into the underworld. Just as Mary Renault avoided narrative clumsiness by ignoring the love affair of Theseus and Perigune, the daughter of Sinis Pinebender, she emphasizes Theseus's rapid decline after the death of Hippolytos by omitting the bulky machinery of an actual descent to Hades's kingdom. Artistic selection and narrative pacing probably also explain Mary Renault's glossing over of the civic strife that took place in Athens during Theseus's fall from public power.

A seasoned veteran, Mary Renault rarely misses a chance to infuse freshness and excitement into the Theseus myth. Robert Graves explains that, upon his arrival in Crete, Theseus was challenged by King Minos to prove his kinship to Poseidon. After Minos threw his signet ring into the sea and ordered him to fetch it, Theseus was led by a school of dolphins to the palace of the Nereids where he found not only the ring, but also the sacred crown of Thetis. Gide's Theseus, a much more cunning rascal, removed some jewels from a hidden pouch while swimming underwater and offered these to Minos as proof of his divine origin.[6] Mary Renault's rendition of the event, like Graves's, certifies both Theseus' divinity and his aplomb under pressure; in addition, it ignites the major dramatic conflict of *The King Must Die*. The Minotaur, here a treacherous pretender to the Cretan throne rather than a half-man, half-bull, throws the ring into the sea. After reclaiming it with Poseidon's help, Theseus tosses it back into the water. To avenge himself, Minotauros tries several times to crush Theseus' spirit under the heel of his political power. The carefully modulated series of events takes on a mythical dimension when Ariadne later reveals that Theseus's defiant act constituted the symbolic marriage to the sea all Cretan rulers must perform. Once more, then, Mary Renault affirms the archetypal drama of kingship as an end contained in a beginning. The scene at the wharf is consistent with Theseus's birth and his supreme act of uniting the Grecian mainland with the scattered island states. But just as noteworthy is her ironically withholding from Theseus and the reader the significance of the conflict at the wharf. Theseus is never the passive receptacle of divine power and wisdom; he must prove himself worthy of his *moira* through acts of skill and daring. The only inevitability inherent in his rise is the force generated by his self-elected deeds.

Several other revisions of the myth occur when Theseus leaves Troizen at the age of seventeen to make the difficult overland journey to Athens. According to Plutarch, Theseus kills Skyron, Kerkyon, Prokrustes, Sinis Pinebender, and the ferocious she-boar Phaia on this trip.[7] Mary Renault shuffles chronology to make Theseus less of a picaro and to connect the various killings with the major themes of his life. At the novel's outset, she uses picaresque elements to convey Theseus's moral growth; but she underplays them at her earliest opportunity to avoid a clash in texture between an episodic structure in the first half of *The King Must Die* and the much longer, closely sustained, drama at Crete. Theseus's fight with Kerkyon, whom Graves calls a trouble-maker who challenged passers-by along the Isthmus road to wrestle with him,[8] becomes part of a longer episode which smooths the novel's broken surface. Instead of including the fight within a chain of fatal skirmishes, Mary Renault makes Kerkyon the year king of Eleusis. Burns mentions her adroit use of material outside the Theseus myth, like the Eleusinian mysteries and the pre-

Olympian fertility legends, in this phase of her hero's life.[9] Theseus's opposition to the female-centered social structure of Eleusis
validates Mary Renault's delaying his slaughter of Phaia. This
story is framed within his wild reign as Eleusis's year king. By
having him kill Phaia after he has already challenged Eleusis's
matriarchal ethic, Mary Renault unifies symbolically the female
destruction that marks Theseus's entire stay at the court of
Persephone.

Our final example of Mary Renault's refurbishing of source material refers to those cases where she deliberately adds to the legend. Her endowing Theseus with "the earthquake-aura" (334),
the gift of foretelling earthquakes, is factually improbable. Yet it
performs the solid services of strengthening Theseus's tie with
earth-shaking Poseidon and of illuminating the novel with an
awesome glow. This same color brightens the exciting drama at
the Palace of Knossos in Crete. Plutarch, Bulfinch, and Graves say
little about Theseus's Cretan adventure; Gide follows suit by hastily summarizing Theseus's career as a bull-leaper: "Myself about
to conquer the Minotaur, I learned a good deal from watching the
feints and passes that might help me to baffle and tire the bull." [10]
Mary Renault, on the other hand, reconstructs from recent archeological discoveries the mystery and weighty pomp of the ancient
Minoan culture. The fourth book of *The King Must Die*, which
takes place in Crete, is both the longest and the most powerful of
the nine sections that make up the two Theseus novels.

The foregoing survey suggests how far Mary Renault has advanced artistically. Although her development follows no clear
line, the Theseus novels affirm her status as a scholar, a storyteller,
a mythographer, and a social moralist. By shrewdly excising, re-
shuffling, and augmenting the difficult Theseus myth, she presents
a vision of life that deserves serious attention. Although practically all major post-Victorian writers have insisted that man cannot be the author of himself, Mary Renault strikes lavish sparks
out of the tired soil of our age. Theseus's fierce actions and his
equally fierce commitment to eternal values fuse in a bi-levelled
narrative that refreshes our imaginations. His effect on our imaginations is, in fact, his great achievement; for, even when he fails,
as he must, he does so on the grand scale. There is nothing stale,
shabby, or furtive about him. Poised without being slick, learned

without being pretentious, Mary Renault dares to portray life as romantic destiny. Even though *The Bull from the Sea* is inferior to its predecessor, what emerges from both books is an exemplary man who proves that life can be vigorously lived—both as bold social comedy and as tragedy in the finest classical sense.

I The King Must Die (1958)

Mary Renault's concept of kingship strongly resembles Carlyle's in *On Heroes and Hero-Worship*. The king in both writers is the ablest, the wisest, and the most powerful man in his community; he is a natural aristocrat. Although Mary Renault uses modern psychological techniques to undercut Theseus's majesty, she follows Carlyle by endorsing dramatically the etymology of the word *king*. Old English *cunnen* and *cyng* and Modern German *können* and *König*, each of which belongs to the same word-family as our Modern English *king*, postulate the superlative nature of the ruler. The king rules because of his personal merit or excellence, and he gains his office because he is better qualified for it than anybody else. Ideally and etymologically speaking, he is the outstanding contender for the throne. This Platonic idea is combined with the tragic drama of kingship in Theseus's first remembered event. At the age of six, when Theseus watches the annual slaying of the king horse of Troizen, his reaction to the ceremony foreshadows the rich complexity of his own future: he identifies emotionally with the slain horse while accepting the necessity of the death. As a deeply felt experience, the regicide embodies the explosive union of opposites—in this case, birth and death. Just as the religious structure of Troizen is revitalized by the death, Theseus finds himself both stricken and renewed by the painful event:

That blood seemed to tear the soul out of my breast, as if my own heart had shed it.
As the newborn babe, who has been rocked day and night in his soft cave knowing no other, is thrust forth where the harsh air pierces him and the fierce light stabs his eyes, so it was with me. (11)

The episodic structure of Book I of *The King Must Die* gains unity through the unfolding mythical theme, the figure of Theseus, and the urgency generated by the exciting events that take place. Theseus is constantly in danger as a young boy—taunting a wild boar, scaling cliffs to steal an eagle's eggs, and playing with bees' nests. The shame surrounding both his birth and his diminutive stature impel him to take up fearless acts, many of which he repeats on a grander scale later in life. This driving need to prove himself also squares with the wild sexual and political exploits of his adulthood. Although his political victories all impart a strong aura of sexuality, the opening chapters of The King Must Die disallow a tidy Freudian reading of his life.

Mary Renault mentions Napoleon in her Author's Note together with the "overcompensation" natural to "a small assertive man" (333) who is trying to offset some basic handicap. Theseus hungers after all kinds of success, but his need to excel chimes better with Adler's doctrine of masculine protest than with anything in Freud. Yet even Adler does not exhaust Theseus's rage to overcome. Although self-inadequacy does quicken and spur Theseus's competitive instincts, his centrality in a universal drama transcends matters of psychological case study. As soon as he accepts his shortness, for instance, he learns skills such as speed, timing, and nimbleness, in which shortness is no handicap. These skills serve him later as a national leader. So, while he becomes the best wrestler in Troizen, he is simultaneously preparing himself as an agent of the cosmic will.

The great test that all of the earlier tests in Troizen foreshadow is the lifting of the stone in the grove of Zeus. This challenge, like the Gordian Knot and the Sword Excalibur later in Western history, constitutes both the test of kingship and the formal initiation of a king. Before Aigeus left Troizen, he buried a sword and a pair of sandals—symbols of royalty—under a large boulder; and he ordered Aithra to ask their son to lift the boulder when he reached the age of sixteen. Because of Theseus's size, she delayed a year before testing him—a detail absent from every other mythological account, so far as I can tell. Plutarch, Bulfinch, and Graves, also report Theseus as first succeeding on his first try.[11] Mary Renault's second innovation of having him fail and then doggedly return to the grove with a lever denotes her spontaneous feeling for the man and the myth. As Burns explains, the initial failure humanizes Theseus;[12] but equally important are Theseus's guile and his persistence. His use of the lever establishes wit and cunning as the principles of his future reign. The distance between the wrestling pit and the throne is thereby greatly reduced. Theseus triumphs as a soldier by summoning the same imagination and mental stamina he had evinced as a wrestler. We are forced to mention Carlyle again: for Mary Renault structures all of Theseus's conquests around the commanding idea that human inventiveness will invariably win over mere physical brawn and inert, sluggish matter.

She strengthens her hero's complex father-search by embellishing the received account of his trip to Athens. His intrepid male pride compels him to take the dangerous overland route across the craggy, robber-infested Isthmus instead of travelling by ship. As the ship is Cretan, his act is an indirect slur to Minos and adumbrates his later revolt in Minos's kingdom. The overland journey proves that Theseus cherishes the means to his kingly end as much as he does the throne itself. By travelling on foot, he keeps his promise to his countrymen; he prays dutifully to Poseidon before each of his tests; and his picaresque adventure stresses the ordeal. Although the progression is by no means schematic, his ordeals are first physical, then emotional, and, finally, spiritual, or mythical, in character.

These sections of the novel form a masterful web of cross-references and overlapping motifs. After his joyous-sad union with Aigeus in Athens, Theseus seems to cross his father on every possible occasion: he leaves Athens to return temporarily to Eleusis and then volunteers for King Minos's tribute of fourteen Athenian lads and maidens. A long-range view discovers here the same compression of opposites that operates elsewhere in the novels. By rebuffing his natural father, Theseus turns his father-quest into a pulsing rhythm of death and birth. His defiance of Aigeus looks ahead to his killing of two other father-kings: Minos and Oedipus (in *The Bull from the Sea*). These deaths, like that of the king horse and the Eleusinian year king (we might want to add Hippolyta, a mother-queen), take on cosmic scope. While each regicide fosters greater political harmony, the deaths fuse with Theseus's expanding father-search. Again, the energy flows from the personal or subjective, through the collective, to the universal. Acting under the compulsion of his spiritual father, Theseus ousts his natural father and other father-kings in order to forge the identity of his fatherland.

As has been stated, the picaresque journey from Troizen to Athens is broken by an interlude of several months at Eleusis, the seat of Demeter's temple and the Hall of Mysteries. Eleusis is one of those archaic cultures that worships Diana, the earth-mother, as the source of all wisdom and power. Graves explains that "queendoms . . . preceded kingdoms throughout the Greek-speaking area." [13] These queendoms were matrilineal and matriarchal; for all honors, titles, and privileges descended through the female line: "The women were heads of families [Theseus notices to his amazement shortly after his arrival in Eleusis]; they came about land disputes, or taxes, or marriage portions. Fathers were nobody in Eleusis, and could not choose wives for their own sons, or leave them a name, let alone property. The men stood at the back till the women had been heard . . ." (78).

Mary Renault wastes no time sounding the clash between Theseus, an adherent of the Olympian Sky Gods, and the antique matriarchy of Eleusis. Theseus arrives in Persephone's realm on the very day the year king is to be sacrificed. His bifold role as Kerkyon's slayer and successor has already been mentioned; but before we can appreciate the changes Theseus brings about in Eleusis, we must rehearse the convention of the year king. Ancient man believed that the welfare of any people was closely joined to the person of the king or royal consort. If he fell ill, the whole nation would be threatened; the king's physical corruption, it was feared, would automatically afflict the weather, the crops, and the health of the people. Since the national well-being had to be protected from such a calamity, the afflicted king was, in many cases, put to death before his powers gave signs of failing. An elaborate ceremony usually followed his death, during which the fragments of his corpse were churned into the soil. This two-part ritual in no way discredited the king; for, by conferring upon his person the power to destroy the community, his followers affirmed his divinity; accordingly, their plowing his flesh into the soil was believed to fertilize the crops. Had he been regarded as an ordinary mortal, no need would have arisen to draw such a tight net around his movements or to feed his physical remains to the fields.

Theseus drove this barbaric practice from the Greek mainland.

At first he is puzzled and amused by his new role as Persephone's consort. The darling of Eleusinian society, he is always accompanied by the Companions, a royal escort whose duty is to protect him. Their excursions through the castle and town bring the warmest greetings and cheers: "Nothing is good enough at Eleusis for a new-made King. They drown his days in honey. . . .

Young girls sighing; the King is everyone's beloved. Old women cooing; he is everybody's son. And among the Companions . . . it seemed too that I was everybody's brother" (76–77).

Before long, however, Theseus's restless spirit chafes against the leisure, the luxury, and the rigid bounds attending his position. Like Tennyson's Ulysses, Theseus requires activity; he can only shine in use. The tie-in with that other great Homeric hero, Achilles, is managed in his angry defiance of the laws of Eleusis. Showing the bold pride of a divinely descended warrior-king, he is offended by his lack of freedom. But his great desire to greet Aigeus in Athens wearing the robes and armor of a royal conqueror precludes his leaving Eleusis as a political fugitive. He achieves his goal by becoming an enemy of the state, an arrant lawbreaker. His first attack upon the Eleusinian morality consists of teaching the Companions manliness, national honor, and the craft of war.

The genius for organization and *esprit de corps* he manifests at Eleusis forms still another trial or apprenticeship that fuses with his mythical function: "I have never loved better any warriors serving under me than these, my first command. They were men of another country, of different blood; at first we had barely known each other's language, and now we no longer needed it; we knew each other's mind as brothers do for whom a look or a laugh is enough. In the year of the Games, when I make the sacrifice, I remember always that my life from that day forward has been their gift" (102).

The dramatic bridge between Theseus's mainland and island adventures is Lukos, the captain of the Cretan ship which collects King Minos's tribute of the fourteen young Athenians. Bored, impersonal, and cranky, Lukos is a paradigm of the modern civil administrator who wants to do his tiresome job as effortlessly as he can. Theseus, on the other hand, is all energy, purpose, and self-reliance. By volunteering for the tribute, he joins his personal fortunes with those of the Athenian people. Having received the omen that his *moira* is to become king of Athens, he readily accepts the indirection of the divine will. Naturally, he regrets having exchanged his princedom for the lot of a slave; but he soon converts his decline into a strenuous ascent. Because he is not yet qualified for the duties of kingship, he must perform the phoenix-like act of self-renewing by means of a sudden plunge.

As a phase of the Absolute, his social descent and his kingly rebirth are two halves of the same cosmological act. Theseus demonstrates, while captain of the Athenian bull-dancing team, the Cranes, that a natural leader does not need a large kingdom. He overcomes disgrace by discovering freedom and creativity within his slave society of fourteen people. And again, wit, rather than physical prowess, helps him master the unforeseen. He overcomes adversity by establishing skill as the only criterion of merit for a bull-dancer. Yeats's image of the dance in "Among School Children," an ideal working blend of fluid form and substance, characterizes the smooth dancelike harmony of the Cranes.[14] But the goal is dearly bought. The Cranes cannot hope to survive the ordeal of the bull-ring until they learn to subordinate all other values—race, nationality, personal vanity, and even sex—to the needs of the team. Thus the individual members of the Cranes gain greater selfhood by sinking the self. Each self, meanwhile, as a necessary part of a surgically honed working unit, transforms every other self on the team. Death, once more, becomes life.

An instance of a new order rising from the ashes of an old occurs when Amyntor achieves his *moira* by forsaking personal ambitions for the welfare of the team: "Amyntor . . . had the courage of lions. I have never done a harder thing than tell him, as I had to, that he must let the bull-leaping alone. He was too big for it . . . and too slow; it would have ended in someone's death. He took it like a gentleman, but very hard. Yet, after, he proved the best catcher I ever saw, the steadiest and most daring. I myself, and every Crane who did the bull-leap, owed him our lives over and over" (223).

The group, then, transcends the sum of its members by accepting discipline, organization, and selflessness as guidelines for its life. The personal and collective freedom that the Cranes create is made more impressive by taking place within the dangerous context of the bull-ring. Directing this sternly waged operation is Theseus himself; and as leader of the Cranes, he must exercise judgment, imagination, and self-control. In this regard, Mary Renault's portrait of Theseus coincides well with several earlier ones. Although Gide omits the drama of the bull-dance, he builds his characterization of Theseus along the same basic contours as Mary Renault. Gide's Knossos, the Cretan citadel, is a madhouse; and everyone Theseus meets there is hamstrung—either by theoretical abstractions or by sexual lust. Theseus is Gide's example of pragmatic individualistic man: his single-minded dedication to public service stabilizes him while those around him fall captive to insoluble academic or sexual games. Both Gide's and Mary Renault's Theseus practice restraint and moderation: the need to sacrifice immediate values to a higher, less tangible, goal occurs in both writers—especially in their presentations of the Ariadne-Theseus relationship. Gide and Mary Renault fully appreciate the importance of moral balance. While presenting Theseus as uniting Greece under a refined and reconstituted Athenian rule, they also fix the Court of Knossos as the proving ground for the Apollonian features of his reign.

The dramatic contrast between the Cranes and their Cretan overlords turns on the moral contrast of squandered versus restrained emotions. Mary Renault's Crete is an ancient society in its dying phase. Not only are the timeserving courtiers in the royal palace less free than the enslaved Cranes; the jewelled, heavily scented Cretans betray moral decadence in all areas of life. The satire takes on a Restoration sparkle in Mary Renault's descriptions of the dainty, twittering Cretans holding their lapdogs and flaunting their sexuality in the grandstand of the bull-ring. When Theseus and the Cranes convert the hard, sinewy practicality of the bull-ring into political rebellion, their victory is dramatically valid.

In fact, Mary Renault's imaginative reconstruction of Minoan Crete is the great glory of *The King Must Die*. Besides compressing a mythical world-drama into the political intrigues at Knossos, she recreates the exhaustion of the entire Minoan civilization. Manners, morals, military stratagems, and religious rites parade vividly through the tremendous breadth of Minos's palace. Mary Renault outstrips both Gide and Graves by incorporating into her novel the lavish archeological findings that took place in Crete from around 1889 to 1932. Heinrich Schliemann's excavations in Troy, Mykenai, and Tiryns inspired an Englishman, Sir Arthur Evans, to dig in Crete. Before Evans's heroic undertaking, Homer was virtually our only source of information on the Minoan culture and on the late Bronze Age. Evans's excavations widened this area of learning astronomically; to him we owe practically all our knowledge of Minoan worship, commerce, plumbing, writing, styles of dress, and sport. The artistry of *The King Must Die*

repays Mary Renault's great debt to this scholarship. The following excerpt from Leonard Cottrell's *The Bull of Minos* reflects the
new light cast by Evans's discoveries upon the sport of bull-leaping and its relation to the Minotaur legend:

> Later came the most remarkable of all the discoveries made at
> Knossos: the remains of a spirited fresco depicting, without a shadow
> of a doubt, a young man in the act of *somersaulting over the back
> of a charging bull*, while a young girl, similarly dressed in "toreador's"
> costume, waited behind the animal's flank to catch him . . . . Soon
> other examples of the same scene came to light, proving that among
> these ancient people there had undoubtedly existed a form of sport
> in which the bull played a prominent part. In none of these scenes
> was any contestant shown carrying a weapon, nor was the bull killed.
> . . . Had there been, after all, some kind of ritual sacrifice? Were
> these young men and girls the Athenian hostages who, according to
> tradition, were sent each year as tribute to the Minotaur? [15]

Cottrell also mentions that the underground maze where Minos
kept the Minotaur may have been an elaborate drainage system.[16]
Mary Renault, however, is too much of a natural storyteller to
depress the fabled labyrinth to a sewer. She shrewdly resurrects
the legend of Ariadne's leading Theseus through the complex network of corridors, dungeons, and vaults by means of a spool of
thread. These nocturnal scenes exemplify several features of good
narrative art. While instilling a fine Gothic *frisson* into the novel
by means of lighting and shading, Mary Renault also conveys the
great palace's immensity and savage grandeur as Theseus spirals
downward through the dank underground passage. The snakes,
frogs, mice, and cobwebs he encounters symbolize the terror he
must purge as Minos's successor. Here is truly ancient night. The
state's vast evil is mirrored in Minos himself, an aging homosexual slowly dying of leprosy. As Theseus kills him, he hears the cry
of an infant. Like the other regicides in the book, this highly
charged act telescopes renewal and affirmation with a violent
death. But it does not mislead Theseus into thinking that his work
at Knossos is finished. King Minos was a natural aristocrat. Although his political greed led him to imperialistic crimes, he was
guilty only of intemperance: any king is obliged to enlarge his
country's bounty and power. But the crimes of Minos's children,
Ariadne and Minotauros, are much less forgivable since they

bring death to the state. Ariadne performs the holy office of Goddess-on-Earth without having been divinely chosen. Even the exalted fertility rite she conducts is a fraud since the fangs have been drawn from the sacred snakes. The rotten mooring of Crete is also disclosed by Asterion, or Minotauros, Ariadne's hated half-brother. Theseus is aghast when he learns that Asterion plans to rule Crete without divine sanction: not only would he bring misfortune to his followers but his political ambitions would also besmirch the kingly office. Called "'a beast that thinks'" (188), Asterion is the bastard son of Queen Pasiphaë and an Assyrian bull-dancer. The inherited curse of Pasiphaë's sexual depravity, therefore, is not lost, even though she herself never appears in the book. Minos, Pasiphaë, Ariadne, and, later, Phaedra, comprise a deepening evil that dovetails with the mythical plot.

Evans's excavations have enabled us to speculate confidently on the destruction of the fabulous Cretan palace. Agnes Carr Vaughan explains that "It is now accepted as a fact that about 1400 B.C., a severe earthquake occurred and that Knossos was attacked and overthrown at approximately the same time." [17] Mary Renault seizes upon this double event and channels it into her main dramatic conflict: the clash between Theseus and Asterion. The conflict begins at the Cretan wharf when Theseus remarks too loudly that Asterion lacks the regal bearing of a king. After Asterion drugs the Cranes' bull in order to remove Theseus as a political rival, the bitter personal conflict grows rapidly. Mary Renault employs elements of the film-thriller as she shows Asterion racing against time to muster his forces against Theseus and the Cranes. The inevitable fight-to-the-death between the two men takes place in the citadel's lowest and deepest point—the sacred throne room. Theseus uses techniques of bull-dancing to kill the wicked Minotauros, who, appropriately, wears the sacred bull-mask during the fight:

I danced about him . . . . And it seemed wrong to me that either of us should be armed, save he with his long horns, which presently I must grasp and vault on, while the gamblers called the odds, and the people shouted in the painted stands.

. . . .

Then we two were alone in our little bull pit, as in the days of the primal sacrifice, the armed beast and the naked man. (306)

The earthquake Poseidon unleashes upon Knossos resolves poeti-
cally all the major tensions of the book: Asterion dies for his
treachery; a more equable union of ruler and state comes to
being; and Theseus renews his centrality in a divine plan.

The Cranes' stopover in Naxos, the largest island of the Cycla-
des, on their homeward voyage, is not an anti-climax, even though
it follows the explosive Cretan episode. Naxos is the third state
Theseus collides with that worships the pre-Olympian female deities. A country famous for its vineyards, Naxos strikes a pleasing
balance with the soil-tilling Eleusis and the nautical Crete. The
interlude also has the dramatic merit of redefining several of the
main themes in Theseus's career. His ship docks in Naxos at the
precise time the Naxian year king is to be slain. The contrast between the docile, young year king and the intrepid conqueror of
Crete asserts Theseus's great moral superiority. Like his victories
in Eleusis and Crete, the annual ritual in Naxos contributes to the
author's portrait of Theseus as a ruler whose force of will elevates
him above circumstances. His *moira* enables him to proclaim his
kingly dignity both within and above patterns of repeated experience.

Like the timorous Naxian year king, Ariadne also proves herself
too weak to overcome imposed cultural conditions. Her fiery romance with Theseus ends suddenly at Naxos because of her indis-
cretion. At Crete, Mary Renault developed an inverse relationship
between Theseus's rise from slave to king and Ariadne's descent
from goddess to mortal. At Naxos, the setting for the last step in
her decline, the daughter of Pasiphaë reaches her moral nadir
when, during the Dionysan fertility rites, she grows frantic. Theseus is revolted when he discovers her after the wild revels lying
unconscious, covered with blood, and holding the phallus of the
slaughtered king in her hand.

The fact that Dionysos, or Pano or Bacchus, the god of vegetation and wine, is often depicted as a bull [18] provides the final justification for Ariadne's swift plunge; for, while Theseus bends
ancestral patterns of experiences to his own ends, the ancestral
corruption of the Minoan spirit crushes Ariadne. She sinks to the
madness of eating the raw flesh of the year king and thereby sen-
tences herself to spend the rest of her life in Naxos, for Theseus
wisely sails to Athens without her. The sense of loss and regret he
experiences at leaving her in Naxos anticipates the final event of

the book—King Aigeus's death, another compressed end-and-beginning.

The panic at Naxos teaches Theseus a lesson that qualifies him still further to inherit his father's kingdom: the need for sobriety and restraint in celebration as well as in war. As has been suggested, this Apollonian chord is sounded most sharply by Ariadne's madness, the echoes of which resound from Minoan Crete to Naxos. Although Theseus regrets her misconduct, his acquired self-control refreshes his moral balance. By subordinating his sentimental regrets to his god-appointed task, he evokes the moral clarity and objectivity that allow him to enact his romantic destiny. At nineteen, he is ready to rule Athens.

Myth and romance both endorse man's perfectibility, the oneness of creation, and the ruling presence of an abiding world-spirit; and their epistemology is also in agreement. By insisting that the world-spirit directs the operation of the universe, they both rely heavily upon the metaphysical necessity of spiritual values. Theseus, a romantic and a mythical hero, moves steadily toward wholeness, objectivity, and cosmic order precisely because he accepts the operating universe as a consciously active process. We must reject, therefore, Kevin Herbert's disclaimer in the *Classical Journal* that *The King Must Die* is "popular historical fiction" —a commercialized contrivance of sex and bloated adventure set in a romantic environment.[19] Mary Renault's Theseus books are remarkably organized, and Burns shows convincingly how each of the nine sections in the companion novels contains either a literal or symbolic death of a king, a major challenge to Theseus, and some sort of rebirth.[20]

As we have seen, Theseus does develop by discernible stages. The pace of *The King Must Die* captures the growing complexity of his ordeals as he advances vigorously toward his *moira*. His experiences are sharply specified. While learning self-reliance and independence, he gains either a new skill or a new self-insight; and, because the secular world is part of a unified system, each step in his personal growth touches both Greek political life and the character of Western civilization. At the same time, an unlooked-for event in each of the nine major sections shows him that he is neither so wise nor so strong as he thought he was. Thus he keeps renewing himself in an infinitely renewable world. Only when his rashness costs him his faith in a divinely sponsored universe does he jar the prefabricated harmony by arrogating godlike powers to himself.

The recurring technical problem of the lengthy expositional passage does not cause trouble in *The King Must Die*. Although the early chapters are dominated by tales, the story-telling situation characterizes the Hellenic folk-spirit. Pittheus's long accounts of Greek cultural history and of Theseus's parentage rest securely on the legend that Pittheus was the wisest man of his era. We welcome his voice; in fact, were he not allowed to speak magisterially, the reader might regret the omission. The three-part tale delivered by the Thracian bard (who is probably Orpheus) has this same power and authority. The bard speaks eloquently in Chapter III of female vengeance, the arduous journey or quest, and the raising of a sanctuary—three elements which foreshadow the major events in Theseus's life.

The various tales tighten the thematic structure of Book I without any slackening of dramatic tempo. Although Theseus is feckless and obdurate, he nevertheless learns from them. The tales of Orpheus and Pittheus arm him with the data he needs to begin his travels. Further on in the novel, the tale is managed somewhat differently. A deft raconteur, Mary Renault satisfies reader expectation when she conveys on the Cretan ship certain historical details of the Minoan bull-fight; but she avoids reporting these facts summarily as Theseus hears them from Lukos. Instead, she dramatizes the account by using Theseus to convey the information. The questions and exclamations which interrupt the tale make the scene realistic and lifelike. Mary Renault's strategy produces a perfect artistic illusion; the reader, The Cranes, and Theseus himself discover the Cretan bull-ring together within the tissue of lived experience.

No evaluation of *The King Must Die* can be accurate without a discussion of style. Burns's remarks on Mary Renault's language in the novel are excellent. He begins by praising the lyric simplicity of the first-person narrative. The rich fluid tone justifies the speaker as an aristocrat of language as well as a great national hero. The novel's "slightly stilted diction," its "Homeric phraseology," and its "stately rhythm" [21] create a resonant, fully globed texture that mirrors the amplitude of its sublime theme. As in *The Last of the Wine,* her colorful, highly concrete style blends with her exhaustive scholarship to generate a mood of high excitement; for Mary Renault knows thoroughly the topography, the artifacts, and the military conventions of the late Bronze Age. Her accounts of hand-to-hand combat are unrivalled in recent fiction for their knowledge of the dynamics of human anatomy; accordingly, her descriptions of the vegetation, the rock formations, and the fretwork and inlays on various shields, weapons, and chariots flow with all the rippling muscularity of the period.

As in her other work, Mary Renault's favorite figure of speech, and the one she uses best, is the simile: "The King Horse was so near that I could see the lashes of his dark eyes. His forelock fell between them like a white waterfall between shining stones," (4–5); or "Her deep breasts looked gold and rosy, bloomed like the cheeks of peaches, and her red hair glowed" (69). Yet her highly graphic language and her expert command of syntax also permit her to create complex meanings stylistically. In the following excerpt, we see her combining a parallel construction, a Homeric epithet, and a striking metaphor to capture, within an archaic context, a great man's reaction to a gripping event: "Once more I stood in a ship of Crete, looking at the wine-dark restless sea, and seeing the towering yellow cliffs stand with their feet in foam" (312). Or as in the next passage, she uses a winding sentence rhythm to describe the slow, gyrating action it reports. The periodic construction, the simile, and the two participial phrases flanking the suspended verb release a dark meaning that unfurls simultaneously with Theseus's emotional response. Within these hypnotic verbal coils lurks hideous evil: "The music shrilled. . . . And in the midst of the maze, strung along the crooked path of scoured white marble, hair and skirts and jewels swinging, arms entwined and slim waists swaying to the beat, was the wreath of women, weaving and twisting and turning on itself, like the house snake who sloughs his winter skin and is made new again" (312).

This last quotation, describing Theseus's final glimpse of Crete, has all the sonority of the epical roll call. The closing sentence sinks rhythmically under the sheer mass of the items it catalogues, restoring Theseus to the secular world and washing down forever the wreckage of a stricken empire into the immortal, rolling sea:

Half the island was clean gone, sheared from the hilltops straight down into the sea; and in place of the smoking mountain there was nothing. The god had carried it all away, all that great height of rock and earth and forest, the goat pastures and the olive groves and the orchards and the vineyards, the sheep pens and the houses, gone, all gone; nothing was there but water, a great curved bay below huge sheer cliffs, where wreckage floated; and outside the bay, by itself on a horn of land, a little mound pouring out smoke, all that was left of Hephaistos' lofty chimney. (313)

II   The Bull from the Sea (1962)

Excluding the false love-triangle of Phaedra, Theseus, and Hippolytos, Theseus's life after his conquest of Minoan Crete is not well documented. To make up for this lack and for her own excisions from the legend, Mary Renault sometimes violates chronology. Theseus's adventures with Prokrustes and Podargos, an escaped Cretan bull, are examples of her redistributing thematically the events of her hero's life. Dealing with imponderables like statecraft, marriage, and parenthood, *The Bull from the Sea* is more complex than *The King Must Die;* and it requires event to convey its inwardness. But heroic episodes function differently in the later book: the ruler of a powerful colonial empire, Theseus quickly learns that his adult problems are no longer soluble in physical movement and immediate action. The new human terrain contains dangers he had not expected, and, suddenly and without warning, Theseus becomes a stranger and a misfit. While he yearns for the robust athletic simplicity of his days as a bull-dancer, he finds himself, like his father before him, sinking progressively deeper into domestic and state cares. Many of his problems he does not understand well enough to solve; and, again like his father, he finds the office of king an extremely wearing, lonely experience. *The Bull from the Sea* is a record of his failures; although the novel has the same high color and taut drama of *The King Must Die,* its sour opening remains its dominant mood throughout: King Aigeus's death, the failure of Theseus's countrymen to recognize him, the dissolution of the Cranes, and the sacrificial calf that seems to reproach Theseus during his father's funeral rites strike a sharp negative chord that his bold acts never quite dispel.

The novel is divided into four parts. The first, after setting the grim tone of Theseus's unhappy reign, then describes his journeys, his later conquests, and his meetings with Oedipus, Pirithoos the

Lapith prince, and the Kentaurs. The second and third parts recount (although not so schematically as I suggest) his destructive relationships with Hippolyta, the beautiful Amazon "king" he tames and brings to Athens, and their son, Hippolytos. Book IV deals with his final exile and death.

Whereas *The King Must Die* featured Southern civilizations—Crete and Naxos—its sequel shows Theseus journeying to primitive Northern cultures, like Pontos, Thessaly, Scythia, and Skyros. These northern voyages parallel Theseus's explorations of his glacial consciousness. In each foray, he enjoys a brief peace or victory, only to have his success overturned. The event that bridges his triumphs in *The King Must Die* and his failures in *The Bull from the Sea* is the death of his father. According to an agreement made by the two men when Theseus shipped to Crete, the son would hoist white sails as he neared the port of Athens to signal his safe return home. The hoisting of black sails, on the other hand, would mean death. But, just as Theseus's victorious ship approaches Athens, he orders the helmsman to take down the white sails and run up black ones in their place. This act can scarcely be called an oversight or a misjudgment. In *The King Must Die*, Theseus disguises his treachery by feigning confusion: "He [Aigeus] was a man grown weary. How could one guess his mind?" (331); "I saw for my father a little sorrow, and then joy unlooked-for. How could I guess he would so reproach himself; that he would not even wait till the ship reached harbor, to see if the sail told true?" (331–32).

This willful ignorance turns into special pleading, distorted vengeance, and spiritual pride in *The Bull from the Sea*. When his ship anchors in port, he hypocritically asks the Athenian greeting party to inform King Aigeus of his safe return. Later, at Aigeus's funeral, he does not weep. His need to defend himself to Mykale, an aged soothsayer at the Akropolis, also suggests an uneasy conscience rather than bereavement. Theseus's alleged reasons for killing his father are too numerous and too unrelated to pass his own personal muster. He mentions Aigeus's nearly poisoning him at Medea's instigation years before; at times, he speaks disparagingly of Aigeus's failure to answer his request for arms against Minotauros; at other times, he claims that he simply forgot the agreement about the sails. This desperate inconsistency violates the Classic simplicity of Greek logic and esthetic form.

Another contrast to his self-defeating search for motives resides in the cosmic drama itself. The many repeated events in *The King Must Die* and *The Bull from the Sea* show the tautness of the supernatural economy. The archetypal nature of these events proves, within the novels, the conscious order of things: certain divinely sanctioned acts recur periodically precisely because they join the secular to the divine. A helpful analogue to this idea is the rule of Occam's razor. William of Occam (c.1300–1349) enjoined his fellow Schoolmen to strip their arguments to the smallest possible apparatus; since reducing a proof to its barest essentials diminishes the risk of error. Theseus's self-vindications, on the other hand, are sprawling and porous. Ironically, his favorite argument —that Aigeus died the sacrificial death of a true king—is the one that damages him the most. For, by explaining his father's death as a divinely motivated act, he elevates his lust for secular power to the spiritual level. At this point, there is little difference between him and Caligula, Tiberius's wicked successor in Rome. Theseus's punishment, like the whip and the bridle in Dante's *Inferno*, takes the form of re-enacting his sin: involuntarily, he comes to destroy the people closest to him.

Referring another Christian allegory to this drama, we see the Father performing Judas' role of betrayer when he ceases to be actuated by the spirit of love, or Holy Ghost. (The Christlike nature of Hippolytos, as we shall see, validates this mythical parallel.) Also implied in Theseus's punishment is his station as a priest-king: substituting self-love for love of God and for God's creation, he becomes an exiled spoiled priest, shorn of both the Holy Family and his own natural family. Other writers besides Mary Renault have seized upon Theseus's monstrous passion for power. Kazantzakis, in his play, *Thésée*,[22] describes this quality in Theseus as so overwhelming that Ariadne foresees his unconscious plan to show Aigeus the black sails. But Gide's Theseus does not even bother to justify his conduct: "I am sorry for the fateful slip by which I brought about his death—when I forgot, I mean, to run up white sails instead of black on the ship that carried me home from Crete. It has been agreed that I should do this if I were to return in triumph from my rash venture. One can't think of everything. But to tell the truth, and if I cross-question myself (a thing I never much care to do), I can't swear that it was really forgetfulness. Aigeus was in my way." [23]

The young king's first major challenge occurs directly after his father's funeral. As has been suggested, Mary Renault introduces at this point Prokrustes instead of burying him within Theseus's other conquests on the Isthmus journey. Her reason is dramatically and thematically sound: by delaying Prokrustes's single appearance in the myth until after the Cretan adventure, she both speeds the pace of the book and gives Theseus a chance to prove himself to the Athenian councillors. Because of Prokrustes's notorious practice of fitting his prisoners to his infamous bed, either by stretching them or by hacking off their limbs, he is the scourge of the Greek mainland. His late arrival to a policy meeting of the Athenian council is both an affront and a personal challenge to Theseus. Having slighted Theseus by neglecting Aigeus's funeral, he then opposes the young king's suggestion of sending Athenian troops to occupy Crete. Theseus quickly sees that, in order to gain the confidence of his countrymen, most of whom fear Prokrustes, he cannot ignore this insult. The episode forms an apt transition between the conflicting moods of the two novels. Not only does Mary Renault re-emphasize her commanding theme of life as challenge or action but, by placing Theseus in a position where he must fight Prokrustes before he can occupy Crete, she also forecasts the indirections and reversals that are to characterize so much of his reign.

Among other things, the first book of *The Bull from the Sea* is a mythical pageant, introducing several famous figures from Classical legend. The reviewer in the *Times Literary Supplement* took issue with Mary Renault's narrative treatment of these legendary figures, particularly Oedipus. The appearance of Oedipus, the reviewer complained, is too brief to warrant his presence.[24] In deference to this disclaimer, we must admit that Oedipus's single appearance does not excite as some of the other scenes in *The Bull from the Sea*. On the other hand, the reviewer misses the point by expecting movement and heightened conflict.

The interview between Oedipus and Theseus is consciously staged as a symbolic debate; and the action is carefully managed to convey poetic, rather than naturalistic, import. Growing out of this brief encounter are the following mythical themes: the killing of the father-king, the death of the king-in-exile, the loyal, devoted child (Antigone) who must later die for her father's excesses, the inscrutability of divine justice, and the conscious murder as a step to public power. As Theseus must do later in his life, Oedipus admits that his slaying of Laios, if not consciously planned, was consciously performed. Before he can expiate his crime, then, he must accept it as a deliberate act. T. S. Eliot states in *The Idea of a Christian Society,* "We need to recover the sense of religious fear, so that it may be overcome by religious hope." [25]

Ironically, the king (Minos, Oedipus, Theseus) has the force of character to elect his own daring acts; otherwise, he would be a follower instead of a leader. But his exceptional nature and stern refusal to languish in the commonplace also lead him to those deeds that violate man's law. The hero is the god's instrument to test and therefore ultimately to improve social justice. In the life of a true king, there can be no accidents, as Oedipus makes clear: " 'I was reared Polybios' son. But I never favored him. . . . Did I not know that every man or woman past forty must be my father or mother now, before the god? I knew. When the redbeard cursed me from his chariot's road and poked me with his spear, and the woman laughed beside him, did I not remember? Oh, yes. But my wrath was sweet to me' " (93). Burns also points out that the talk with Oedipus freshens Theseus's understanding of the idea of the king's royal death at the behest of the god.[26] Taking into account Theseus's unreadiness to grasp this cosmic imperative earlier in life, we must rule out the *Times Literary Supplement* reviewer's objection to Oedipus's appearance as mere showcasing. The scene, as brief as it is, compresses the main symbolic and mythical elements of the tragedy of kingship.

Other good scenes in the "Marathon" section of *The Bull from the Sea* include Theseus's meeting with Pirithoos and his trip to the land of the Kentaurs. Making use of etymology (words like *chiropodist* and *chiropractor* come to mind), the author renames Chiron, the Kentaur king, Old Handy; and, in line with the familiar legend, she portrays him as noble and intellectual in contrast to his brutish tribesmen. Here is Theseus's first impression of the redoubtable teacher of Jason, Asklepios, and Achilles: "I gazed long at his face. Whatever wild shape his guardian god had put on to beget him, some god was there. You could see it in his eyes. Dark and sad they were, and looked back a long way into the ancient days of the earth, before Zeus ruled in heaven" (76).

Although Chiron knew music and surgery, Mary Renault

stresses his healing powers. This motif, that of the physician-priest, foreshadows the emergence of Hippolytos and the changing nature of the king, a process Theseus delays with his short-sightedness. In contrast to the decadence of Knossos, Old Handy exudes a craggy, primitive dignity that makes him the standard of human excellence in the novel. Yet, like the other kings we meet, he too comes to grief. Although Mary Renault omits his self-sacrifice for Prometheus, Old Handy is unable to prevent the Kentaurs' drunken rout by the Lapiths. After this carnage, he retreats to the forest with a few fellow-survivors and is never directly heard from again.

The most important new force in Theseus's life, also introduced in the first book of *The Bull from the Sea*, is Pirithoos, the leader of the marauding Lapiths. Mary Renault retains the story of their meeting at Marathon as war-rivals: according to legend, Theseus challenged Pirithoos to single combat when Pirithoos tried to steal a herd of cattle from an Athenian farm. The fight between the two leaders never takes place, however, because each is so impressed with the other's valor and dignity. Mary Renault executes the scene brilliantly: although both heroes shrink from battle, neither loses face. The reader feels, as well, that this union produces a combined might that would have been halved by the destruction of either man. Pirithoos, a prince of great strength and daring, is a kind of double, or alter-ego, to Theseus. Theseus calls him "a daimon of my fate" (64); and with Pirithoos Theseus exercises his wanderlust. Together, the two men undertake fabulous trips to uncharted territories. Whenever Theseus is shackled by affairs of state, he refreshes himself by exploring a new land with Pirithoos: "For a long time the rover in me had been a slave and captive of the king; and now he was on holiday. My eye was as fresh as a boy's, and my heart was as light" (110).

The two men enjoy an ideal man-to-man friendship, as is brought out by their spontaneous teamwork during combat. This intuitive *rapport* looks back to the Cranes and looks ahead to the ideal sexual partnership of Theseus and Hippolyta, which completes, however briefly, Theseus's *moira*—both as a man and a king. In this regard, Pirithoos is a phase in Theseus's final adaptation. Theseus gladly gives up the friendship when he sees that Hippolyta answers all his human and kingly needs. Yet he falls back upon Pirithoos to fill the void in his life made by her death.

The tension in Theseus's life between the male and female principles, mentioned in the Author's Note (336), is personified in part by Pirithoos. Although his friend's appetite for raw experience complements Theseus's own male restiveness, Pirithoos misleads Theseus into ignoring both the claims of the Earth Mother and the feline virtues associated with Her spirit. Theseus undertakes many of his journeys with Pirithoos indiscreetly and at the cost of his public duties. It is no accident that the two men meet shortly before Theseus violates the Earth Mother's shrine, where Aithra, his mother, is shriving him of his numerous sins against Diana's worship.

We have seen elsewhere that the strongest moral imperative in the Renault canon refers to an individual's avoiding definitions. In *North Face* and *The Charioteer*, freedom means refusing to delimit oneself to a behavioristic pattern or category; Alexias is dwarfed in *The Last of the Wine* owing to his constant practice of interposing a father or father-surrogate between himself and moral responsibility. Dion rains calamity upon Syracuse in *The Mask of Apollo* by trying to resolve all problems of statecraft by reason alone. This moral theme attains new stature in *The Bull from the Sea:* both personally and politically, Theseus fails because he is too patently masculine. He had already, in *The King Must Die*, plotted Medea's death, overthrown the female worship at Eleusis, seduced and then deserted Ariadne, and laid waste the matriarchal structure of Knossos.

Although the inscrutability of the gods rules out easy answers, Theseus's failures as a king, a husband, and a father could have been averted had he nurtured the feminine graces of intuition, discretion, and sympathy. His one access to a balanced selfhood, Hippolyta, is taken from him. That Hippolyta herself has betrayed the Amazons by becoming Theseus's mistress (a typical Hegelian opposition of two goods, rather than one of a good and a bad) must also be noted. Diana's wrath explains Hippolyta's death as well as it does Theseus's inability to soften his masculine aggressiveness. This terror is intensified by Diana's waiting until the fates of Hippolyta and Theseus are enmeshed before destroying them in a single stroke.

To understand Theseus's resplendent failure with Hippolyta, we must return to the ceremony at the sacred grove where Aithra tries to prepare her son for the Earth Mother's forgiveness. The abortive ceremony suggests that Theseus not only fails to appease the goddess's wrath, but that he also aggravates it. The wild pig he uses as a holy sacrifice does not consent to its death; Theseus, bored during the anointing, indirectly kills an acolyte priestess when his amorous glance causes her to upset the screen in front of the sacred statue of the fertility goddess. After he commits the supreme sin of looking at the statue, a sight forbidden to all men, his despairing mother sends him away. Since Aithra never asks him to repeat the ceremony, we must conclude that, for the rest of his life, he is unpardoned.

Diana's curse is again invoked when he profanes the holy sanctuary of the Moon Maids in Scythia by watching the forbidden mystery and by stealing Hippolyta from the Maiden Crag. This episode is another example of the indirection and the power of the divine will. Hippolyta, the Amazon king, combines the peerless womanhood of Rider Haggard's Ayesha (*She*) and W. H. Hudson's Rima (*Green Mansions*). Theseus is so taken with her that he falls in love with her immediately. He then wins her in a fashion befitting his overwhelming passion and kingship. Their single combat, which they undertake in order to prevent the bloodshed of their followers, typifies the complexities of Theseus's reign. Whereas he simply killed Kerkyon, Phaia, and Asterion in *The King Must Die*, his battle with Hippolyta, staged as a fight-to-the-death, defies this easy solution. Already in love with her, Theseus must unarm her without either's incurring serious injury. As in *The Last of the Wine* and in *The King Must Die*, the fight incorporates Mary Renault's knowledge of weaponry, hand-to-hand combat, and the dynamics of human anatomy. And, when the fight is over, the author is just as adroit in honorably acquitting both warriors. Theseus wins his love, and Hippolyta keeps her difficult promise to return to Athens with him.

Their subsequent union, although never formally ratified by marriage, is the perfect match of two mighty chiefs. For the first time in his life, Theseus is content to be faithful to a woman. He and Hippolyta take up arms in the battlefield, discuss politics, and have a child together who is the ideal product of their ideal union. Their relationship, marked by a fresh, spontaneous mutuality, is fully satisfying: "it never needed speech between us, to share our thought" (178). Even Athens flourishes: owing to Hippolyta's in-

spiration, Theseus inaugurates the double reign of Artemis and
Apollo as the city's presiding deities. What is just as important,
Hippolyta cures him of his wanderlust and his chronic self-
assertiveness, thus freeing him for the duties of statecraft: "As for
my manhood, I reckoned it was proved by now and I could leave
such cares for others. . . . For her I was man enough" (153).
The imagery associated with Hippolyta celebrates her untamed
beauty and natural grace. Theseus compares her to a lion, a leop-
ard, a wolf, and a tiger—terms justified by her clashes with the
simpering ladies of the Athenian court.

Unfortunately, political expediency prevents her from ruling
Athens officially as Theseus's queen. By stages, he sacrifices her to
the demands of politics and, thereby, helplessly re-enacts his earlier ravages upon the female spirit. The first "death" he inflicts
upon her impinges on the military necessity of yoking Crete to
Athens. As his advisers explain, the only way Theseus can bring
Crete under Athenian law is to marry the Cretan princess,
Phaedra: "The fate I waited for had not stepped in to free me.
The girl was Minos' child; and Crete is too full of the old religion
to set aside the female line. If I gave her to another man high-
born enough not to disgrace her, he would have Crete in his hand;
if I gave her to a peasant . . . I should be disgraced myself, and
the Cretans would not bear my rule; if I kept her unwed, she
would be a lure for every ambitious king in Hellas and every lord
in Crete" (181).

Meanwhile, Athenian sovereignty is menaced by an impending
attack by the Scythians, who are led by Hippolyta's native tribe,
the angry Moon Maids. Mary Renault's imagery suggests a raven-
ous plague consuming all life in its southward path. The invasion
begins, it is thought, in present-day Ukraine; sweeps along with it
the tribes of Rumania, Bulgaria, and perhaps Yugoslavia; and
attains its greatest force as it crosses the ice-locked Hellespont into
mainland Greece. Just before the climactic battle against the
Scythian horde, Theseus senses his imminent death. He is wrong,
however; for he is not yet ready for the kingly death and union
with the god; Theseus cannot die until he is punished for his sins.
This cruel punishment unleashes itself upon his most cherished
possession—Hippolyta herself. By throwing herself in the way of
the arrow of Molpadia, her successor as the Amazon king, Hippolyta enacts her own regal *moira*. Just as she had given herself

body and soul to Athens's king, she sacrifices her life for the Athenian people.

As has been suggested, the supervening order asserts itself speedily in this powerful scene: in a single act, Hippolyta both affirms her vow to Theseus and atones for her betrayal of the Amazons. Her death is hedged by a double irony. As Theseus's scornful comment suggests, her love for him and her essential nature were finer than he is humanly able to imagine: "She had taken my death, lover for lover; she had been a woman at the last. She who was once a king should have known that only a king can offer for the people. The gods are just; but one cannot mock them" (234). Theseus's ignorance multiplies the ironies surrounding her death. Whereas her sacrifice is her most concrete expression of love, she would have done Theseus a better service by letting him die. He never rises to the height of her tragic renunciation; in fact, the Theseus of the last two movements of *The Bull from the Sea*, "Epidauros" and "Skyros," is so painfully disoriented that he is almost unrecognizable. The terrifying confusion and lostness he manifests after Hippolyta's death are augured by his closing comments to the second book. Although he professes to be describing himself, his mirthless revelation applies just as pointedly to the beautiful and noble Hippolyta: "She had saved her man alive to weep for her. But the King had been called; and the King had died" (234).

After Hippolyta's death, Theseus declines rapidly. Instead of reaching forward to embrace new values, he fitfully tries to recapture his romantic youth. He travels desperately to escape his painful memories, thereby besmirching his good name throughout the Aegean; he cannot sustain a relationship with a woman; shorn of his retinue and scorned by his servants, he must now run his own messages. The entire character of the man and his reign suffers a grisly change:

> That summer I sailed with Pirithoos . . . to sack the city of Thapsos. It was a night assault . . . . I could hear the watchman yelling. It was not "Theseus of Athens!" as it used to be, but "Theseus the Pirate! Theseus the Pirate!"
>
> I was angry, and the Thapsians paid for it. All the same, it set me thinking. All I had to show at each year's end, these days, was a load

of plunder, and a girl I would be weary of next year. Once it had been a hold of bandits cleared, the borders strengthened, laws broadened or fined down to a better justice . . . . It seemed, when I thought, that no one had been much the better for my life, this year, or last, or the year before. (252–53)

Theseus feels the sting of divine retribution in the "Epidauros" section of the novel. Like his father, he grows prematurely old and careworn under the enormous burden of the crown. And, while his old friends are all either dead or in distant lands, he must watch passively the collapse of his glorious deeds. Just before he dies, he recounts the various disasters that have broken the political unity he purchased with Hippolyta's death: "Crete broke away two years ago and more. . . . While I was sick, every man on the island knew that but I. Megara has found a prince of its ancient kindred; and they say that now when you cross the Isthmus, once more you need a guard of seventy spears" (324).

Every choice he makes after Hippolyta's death is infallibly wrong. These errors, which grow progressively self-deafeating in nature, are particularly damaging because they need not have happened. Theseus is given several fine opportunities to restore both himself *and* his derelict state. In the last two parts of *The Bull from the Sea*, Theseus, like Lear, is a painful anachronism who sows misery wherever he turns. By stubbornly clinging to his shattered vanity, he violates both the cosmological scheme and the freedom of his subjects. Theseus will simply not accept the end of his political effectiveness or the coming of an order grounded in principles different from his own. In *The King Must Die*, he voiced, in a moment of great clarity, the idea that true civilization begins with a creative merging of the male and female principles: "There is a measure in all things. . . . The Mother brings forth the corn. But it is the seed of the undying god that quickens her, not a mortal man doomed to perish. Wouldn't that be the greatest of all shows, to make them a wedding?" (141). Bearing in mind his own ravages upon the Daughters of Night, his failure to strike this important balance recoils upon him with galvanic force. Mary Renault develops this tragic theme through another just as compelling and timeless—the father-son conflict.

Theseus's envy of Hippolytos as a younger, taller, and handsomer man than himself, when the two men meet after a long separation, takes the form of a carping self-pity: "When I had been a child . . . trying to believe I was the son of a god, this was what I had prayed to grow into; but I had to make do with what I was given. Men have done worse with more" (241). Yet, while Hippolytos steadily acquires manly grace, Theseus's resentment moves from the physical to the spiritual order. Although Theseus fails to make the connection, Hippolytos embodies, both genetically and philosophically, the seeds of Athens's moral rebirth: "As we crossed the courtyard, I was thinking how often he spoke with reverence of Apollo now. Once it had been all the Lady. But he would have learned Paian's worship at Epidauros; they are brother and sister, after all" (271).

Hippolytos's feline sensibilities, which bear metaphysical import beyond Classical history, are brilliantly developed. Beginning with his childhood, Mary Renault describes his growth as part of a mythical-evolutionary drama. A climber of rocks and a votary of Artemis, the young Hippolytos blends in his hybrid personality the best of the male and female principles. While he repeats many of his father's daring childhood acts, he also emerges as a religious mystic: before he is ten, he builds his own private sanctuary to the Earth Mother and asks theological questions that confound Theseus. This absorption in and commitment to transcendent values gains symbolic expression through the larks which seem to accompany most of his appearances in the book.

A leitmotif just as persistent, however, and one which figures centrally in Hippolytos's burgeoning conflict with his father, is the horse. Mary Renault draws discreetly from the broad symbolic range horses have acquired over the centuries. A chariot driver and a healer of horses, Hippolytos receives his divine visitation while driving a horse-team: " 'I felt God going down into the horses, down through me' " (245). The strength, beauty, and nobility traditionally ascribed to horses are mirrored in his heroic appearance. Freud's symbolic representation of the horse as the castrating father applies directly to Theseus's rejection of Hippolytos's religious tenets. But the horse as a phallic symbol (one thinks of the stallions in Sherwood Anderson and Robinson Jeffers) is much more ironical. Although Hippolytos *is* a fount of prime energy, unlike his father he shuns both sexual and athletic prowess.

Theseus fears him for this very reason since he cannot understand him. Actuated by less immediate compulsions than his father, Hippolytos aspires to become a physician-priest, or medical missionary, in the service of Diana. (Most of the third Book of *The Bull from the Sea* takes place in Epidauros, the seat of the shrine of Asklepios, the Classical god of medical art.) The difference between Theseus as a priest-king and Hippolytos as an acolyte priest-surgeon suggests a mythical progression in the nature of the ruler. Ironically, Hippolytos stands closer to Old Handy than he does to his father: both physicians have a natural affinity to horses; they perform the same reflex action of dilating their nostrils at times of severe stress; and both heal sick children shortly after they are introduced.

This concept of the ruler as healer-priest was indirectly stated in *The King Must Die* when Minos, speaking of his youthful successor, said, " 'They sent a child to lead me' " (274). The destructiveness of Theseus's pride cannot be understood unless we note this faint echo from Christian mythology in *The Bull from the Sea*. Hippolytos's similarities with Christ, several of which have already been stated, suggest that Theseus's jeering disdain of his son may have delayed the birth of Jesus for fourteen centuries. Hippolytos is certainly a precursor. As a more fully developed being than his father, he embraces an ethic of power and justice so refined that it completely baffles Theseus: "He had been a riddle, I thought, since he was born" (244). "It ran to waste off him, this power over men he could have turned to mastery. . . . When the harvest ripened, he would give it away for nothing" (266). In addition to his charity, his virginity, and his antipathy for practical politics, the nature of Hippolytos's bond with Artemis adumbrates a true Christian ethic. That he has made no formal priestly vow reveals that he is bound by the spirit, not the letter, of canonical law.

Ironically, both the corroding Athenian state and its staggering king stand to profit by Hippolytos's example. Theseus's rejection of his son takes the immediate form of opposing the archetype of the father-search. Like Phaedra, Theseus chases Hippolytos all over the Aegean instead of letting his son pursue *him* and carve out an identity both within and beyond the natural father. By demolishing Hippolytos's *moira,* Theseus also violates something much more serious—the preordained harmony of the universe as an expression of human perfectibility. Suitably, this denial of the god's ability to exercise his timeless will through historical and evolutionary change backfires; for the less freedom he grants other people, the less free he becomes himself. Theseus's fitful acts of self-assertion end calamitously when he brings down Poseidon's curse upon Hippolytos. For accompanying Theseus's loss of faith in cosmic order is the total breakdown of his moral and physical world.

All kingly acts tally with each other: Aigeus's abortive poisoning of Theseus and Oedipus's assertion that nothing in a king's life is accidental show Theseus's slaying of his son as deliberate. This interpretation is also psychologically sound, considering Theseus's diminishing power, his combative nature, and his smouldering resentment against his son. Phaedra's bogus accusation of Hippolytos is both an exteriorization of his own wishes and a temptation he cannot resist. Instead of examining the evidence, Theseus welcomes her wild cries of rape as a chance to rid himself of his greatest rival. He does not acknowledge his error until after Hippolytos's death: "The sight of the woman rose before me. Bruised like a slave; a slave's terror too, and a slave's lies. If her tale had been true, she would have scratched his face, or bitten him. His torn tunic and dragged-out hair—he had been pulled at, not thrust away. Those weals upon her shoulders and her throat were the marks not of lust, but of his anger, the rage of the lion who sees the bars of the trap on every side" (301).

Theseus's exact visual recall of Phaedra's appearance during her accusation rules out his innocence; the havoc caused by his pride and self-deceit manifests itself immediately. He transgresses human bounds by invoking Poseidon for purely selfish reasons for the first time in his life, and the god punishes him by answering his invocation. Attempting to be more than man, he loses whatever scraps of manhood he has. His degrading marriage to Phaedra is only the starting point of his later decline. Theseus never suggests that he loves Phaedra; likewise, their marriage never advances beyond the political ruse that prompted it. Although his male vanity is piqued by the alleged rape, he cannot claim that his deepest loyalties have been blackened. Hippolytos dies a tragic death: bound by the spirit of his priestly vows, he cannot deny Phaedra's charge; but he dies happily, assured of his father's pardon and asking him to sacrifice a cock to Asklepios. Theseus, on the other hand, must endure life-in-death. The collapse he suffers after his son's dignified Sokratic death is even swifter and crueller than the one he underwent after the loss of Hippolyta. Immediately, he is stripped of his regal bearing. Even his compatriots are surprised to learn he is their king after he drives to the scene of Hippolytos's death: "They stared gaping, and knuckling their brows; they could not keep their eyes from running over me, a dirty unkempt man, haggard and stammering, whose face they had scarcely glanced at, one of themselves" (307).

Leaguing with Pirithoos—blindly retreating into his already overcharged male aggressiveness—is Theseus's stock defense against adversity and public responsibility. On one of their forays, he is seized with a paralytic stroke and then forced to languish for a number of years. His immobility, which is particularly painful to his active nature and his lust for heightened experience, marks his final retribution. Having offended both Apollo's injuctions against excess and the ancient worship of the Earth Mother, he must remain inert while his kingdoms decay. Theseus has gone full circle. When he recovers from his seizure, his name is held in such disgrace that he cannot return to Athens. He then resumes his exile and voyages to Skyros, an island suitably "shaped like a bull's brow" (326) and ruled by King Lykomedes.

Legend states that Theseus begged Lykomedes's protection after being driven from the throne of Athens by Menestheus; it has also been said that Lykomedes may have accepted a bribe from Menestheus to kill Theseus. Mary Renault refutes both this account and the conflicting claim that Theseus's death was accidental; her Theseus dies in Skyros, but more triumphantly. Although he dies after falling from a high rock, he dies the kingly death. Lykomedes's ancestry ("he was reared in the shrine of Naxos, and is the son of a priestess by the god" [327]) and his guest, the young warrior Achilles, indicate the forces comprising the major tension of Theseus's life. Theseus shrinks from meeting Achilles, the dauntless young hero of the new generation; and he does not attack the female worship personified by his host. In short, he is ready for the consenting death of a king.

His exhaustion and his expiation occur simultaneously. Now that he has outgrown the struggle of opposing wills, he is permitted to die. The night before his leap from the rock, he has a symbolic dream which compresses the major themes and energies of his stricken life. The accounts of the cosmic *realpolitik* are now balanced: the god sends a sign which explains to Theseus the meaning of his life, and Theseus reads the sign clearly. He remarks of his suicide the next morning, "It will seem like mischance, except to those who know" (331). The reader belongs to this knowing company.

In *A Portrait of the Artist as a Young Man,* Joyce distinguished sharply between tragic pity and tragic terror: while pity invites our sympathy for the human sufferer, terror reveals the secret cause of the suffering. Mary Renault's Theseus evokes real terror. Although he occasionally overlooks the secret cause regulating his actions, the reader is not permitted to make the same error. The concept of *moira,* the archetypes, and the elaborate supernatural machinery of the two novels reveal Theseus in the grips of a cosmic force that determines both his torments and his glorious achievements; and his privileges and punishments are phases of the same metaphysical necessity. His many crimes affirm the strength of the thread joining him to the secret cause: only after he fails to repent his crimes do the gods force repentance upon him. The terrifying remorselessness of his expiation, although theologically necessary, is not unjust. The gods do not thrust his painful translation upon him until his pride rules out voluntary contrition and redemption.

Mary Renault creates terror within the descriptive limits of narrative art. Although she describes the divine will as both all-encompassing and all-pervasive, she does not try to resolve questions like divine freedom. In that the gods give Theseus every chance to effect his own salvation, they seem free. On the other hand, the divine intervention that occurs after Hippolytos's death suggests that even the gods are limited by a supervening design. At times, Mary Renault seems to invite a natural explanation for the disasters that befall Theseus; but these events only heighten the divine paradox. Previous instances of the supernatural realm penetrating Greek politics and religion preclude terminal answers, and the theology of the two novels reaches as far as it can into the secular world. While Mary Renault discreetly avoids resolving universal problems, her sensitive, controlled artistry stirs our deepest perceptions. Her power to arrest and maintain our participation in a metaphysical enigma is a greater feat than any arbitrary answer.

Before judging the total performance of *The Bull From the Sea,*

I should like to discuss the tragic love-triangle of Phaedra, The-seus, and Hippolytos. Unlike earlier writers, Mary Renault vir-tually eliminates Phaedra's compassionate nurse—the Oenone of Racine's play. The same artistic impulse to adapt Phaedra's al-leged rape into her own mythical theme accounts for Mary Re-nault's other changes and omissions. Since Theseus is the control-ling point of view of the novel his indifference to Phaedra bars her from attaining both the beauty and the psychological complex-ity bestowed upon her by Euripedes, Seneca, and Racine. Al-though her suffering is real, we are made to see it merely as an outgrowth of her inherited sexual depravity. Mary Renault sacri-fices the warm humanity of Phaedra to the mythical-evolutionary struggle of Theseus and Hippolytos; we are not meant to sympa-thize with the forlorn Cretan princess.

Hippolytos, however, does follow Euripedes's model faithfully; but he is handled differently. For instance, he is not torn between the compulsions of Aphrodite and Artemis, whose speeches begin and end Euripedes's play. In that work, Aphrodite compels Phaedra to avenge herself against Hippolytos; but Theseus's divine ancestry and destructive pride eliminate the need for this super-natural machinery in *The Bull from the Sea*. Also omitted is Eu-ripedes's moral judgment that Hippolytos's death stemmed from his failure to shun excess. Mary Renault's Hippolytos, as has been mentioned, is no religious zealot. Accordingly, he is not the misogynist of Seneca's portrait, revolted by Phaedra's wild decla-ration of love; nor is he the lover of Aricia (or of any woman, for that matter), as Racine describes him. Mary Renault makes him a magnificent hybrid who reaches for the divine by dedicating him-self to human suffering—the meeting-point of man and God in the Christian experience.

Mary Renault's chief contribution to the Hippolytos myth con-cerns Akamas, the only one of Phaedra's children by Theseus ac-knowledged in the book. Frail, brittle, and sickly, Akamas stands in sharp contrast to Hippolytos and to the entire male genealogy of Theseus's kingly strain. He is the last living descendant of the corrupt Minoan aristocracy. Akamas's role in Classical history is so minor that Euripedes, Seneca, Racine, Bulfinch, Gide, and Graves all neglect to mention him. Mary Renault's device of choosing Akamas to explain Phaedra's treachery to his father is Theseus's greatest shame. Not only does Akamas have more courage and character than Theseus had credited; his ability to transcend his inherited decadence, a grave illness, and the risk of provoking his father's wrath also show how grievously Theseus has squandered his own advantages. That the heroic conqueror of Crete and Thebes must be enlightened by the least heroic character in the novel ironically completes the astonishing reversal of his public and private fortunes.

Although we have already rehearsed several of the great virtues of *The Bull from the Sea*—Mary Renault's creative use of myth, irony, psychology, point of view, and character deployment—we have not exhausted the novel's beauties. The descriptions of various artifacts and landscapes are just as lovingly wrought as the ones in *The King Must Die*, and the subtle parallels traced between Theseus and Shakespearean protagonists like Lear, Othello, Coriolanus, and the later Mark Antony imparts a believable timelessness to the nature of the hero. Nevertheless, it is hard to agree with Granville Hicks that *The Bull from the Sea* is as good a book as *The King Must Die*.[27] The reviewer in the *Times Literary Supplement* who called *The Bull from the Sea* "a string of interesting anecdotes rather than a shapely novel" strikes closer to home: the book suffers from a disjuncture of plot and narrative follow-through.

As the reviewer goes on to say, Mary Renault's portrait of heroic Hellas is markedly inferior to that of Knossos in *The King Must Die*.[28] Although Theseus is carefully intertwined with Greek life and even with Christian myth, too much of *The Bull from the Sea* is asserted into existence rather than dramatized. This subordination of description to explanation is fatal to the novel's artistry. Many of the crucial events are either omitted or summarized; the paragraphs are usually much shorter than the ones in *The King Must Die;* the time shifts are much bolder. Theseus reports a great deal of the important action from the perspective of a bystander, like the incidents at the Kentaurs' camp and the holy rites at Troizen and Scythia. Mary Renault also forfeits many fine narrative opportunities by merely alluding to several of the great moments of Theseus's reign—his battle against Prokrustes; his second expedition to Crete; his conquest of Thebes; his rivalry with his successor, Menestheus; and the political intrigue at Athens before Hippolyta's death. Because the novel lacks the controlling unity that the Cretan episode gave *The King Must Die*, its structure is uneven and jerky with no single action sustained long enough to invite our imaginative participation.

An example of the book's tired, scrappy structure is the friendship of Theseus and Pirithoos. It has already been said that Pirithoos is central to Theseus's downfall and that Theseus calls him "a daimon of my fate" (64). Since he personifies the combative male acquisitiveness in Theseus's unbalanced nature, he is thematically essential. We cannot argue with Mary Renault's dramatic intention, for ancient myth has been so fascinating to recent writers precisely because it compels so many interpretations and treatments. If she sees Theseus's tragedy as a failure to strike a healthy tension between his male and female instincts, she is perfectly free to do so. But a novelist must always convey moral statement through mood, motive, and character interplay in order to make it dramatically valid. As a character whose appearances in the novel are both infrequent and brief, Pirithoos does not generate this lifelike authority. After the men meet on the Marathon plain, Mary Renault progressively dissolves their friendship into bald summary. In the process, Pirithoos becomes a minor character whose thematic function runs counter to his reality as a person.

The following passage reflects her tendency to diminish character, event, and theme by uninteresting narrative technique: "I have sailed the seas since then, and sacked many cities. Unless there was war, I went roving with Pirithoos every year. To see new things, and live from day to day, is better than wine or poppy, and fitter for a man. I have passed through Scylla and Charybdis by the smoking snows; and off the Siren Rocks, where the wreckers send their girls to sing you over, I have caught a siren and lived to tell. Women I have had in plenty, though none for long" (237).

The entire moral and metaphysical weight of *The Bull from the Sea* rests on Theseus's radical decline after his return from Crete. Had Theseus's pride not addled his reason, Mary Renault would have had no mythical plot. Her chief task, therefore, was to make his meteoric career artistically convincing and of a piece. A comparison with Arnold Bennett's *The Old Wives' Tale* shows the extent of her failure. Bennett developed the personalities of the two Baines sisters alongside a mode of provincial British life by introducing, in his words, "an infinite number of infinitesimal changes" [29] over a period of forty-five years. In *The Bull from the Sea*, the changes Theseus undergoes are not infinitesimal or gradual. Mary Renault takes great liberties with her time sequence and replaces Bennett's technique of close observation with irrational actions. And whereas we feel, in spite of their numerous shifts in fortune, that the Baines sisters have remained basically the same from the ages of sixteen to sixty, the same cannot be said of Theseus. His grating inconsistency makes us ask whether the battler who overthrew Eleusis and Crete could have sunk to the self-defeating idiocy of his later years; for there is not enough sound connective tissue between the two books to convince us that the two Theseuses are the same man.

But Mary Renault's Theseus is not only self-contradictory; he is also dwarfed. Plutarch praised the charity Theseus extended to the distressed and the deprived. More than eighteen centuries later, Graves praised him for being the first Athenian king to mint money and for founding a unified Greek commonwealth.[30] Mary Renault mutilates Theseus by omitting this compassion and political vision. Most of his actions are reactions; and, rather than instigating action, he becomes the kind of man things happen to. The general weakness of *The Bull from the Sea* can be traced to faulty artistic selectiveness. Mary Renault continued to write about Theseus after he had ceased to interest her. He can no longer surprise her in *The Bull from the Sea* by assuming a life of his own and by taking charge of the narrative. The momentum established by *The King Must Die* did not suffice to command her best artistic efforts.

III *Conclusion*

Except for *North Face*, a tour de force that cracked under the weight of its motive impulse, *The Bull from the Sea* is probably Mary Renault's weakest book since *The Middle Mist*. On the other hand, successes like *The Last of the Wine* and *The Mask of Apollo* indicate that the Classical mood is now her natural milieu. Critically, she cannot be ranked alongside the more popular type of historical novelist as a writer of sheer adventure tales based on history. Although her classical novels bristle with excitement and adventure, the action is carefully monitored by technique. The first-person narrative in the four classical novels creates a critical perspective, deepened by time, from which to view the action, and it does so without any corresponding loss in dramatic impact. Stylistically, too, Mary Renault's classical fiction overtakes the conventional romantic legend or adventure story. The sonorous cadences of the two Theseus novels match the heroic exploits described in the books. But *The Mask of Apollo,* Mary Renault's latest book, succeeds best in aligning style and subject matter. While less flowing and colorful than the language of *The King Must Die* and *The Bull from the Sea,* the novel's harsh, angular style stands closer to the events it reports. This genius for clinching language to theme allows Mary Renault to use historical fiction as a comment on her own times. If her reputation rests on the five novels published since 1956, justice will be served; for they both enlarge and dignify the tradition of historical fiction. Worth noting in the context of this achievement is the fact that few artists, indeed, can boast of having revolutionized the mode in which they did their best work.

Mary Renault is both a seasoned and accomplished storyteller. She may still write the epic masterpiece augured by her most recent work. But it is idle to speculate about the future: unless she shifts her narrative focus as sharply as she did after *North Face,* any books she writes will be couched in the heroic vein. Judging from her last five novels, once again, posterity will praise her for her brilliantly documented Classical settings and her ability to infuse modern themes into ancient history. How long it will take literary scholars to awaken to her art is another matter. The prevailing critical animus against homosexual fiction and historical fiction has already delayed the recognition she deserves; but I sincerely hope that my book will change this unfair trend.

Notes and References

Although there is no uniform edition of Mary Renault's novels, the dates, titles, and pagination referred to in the text correspond to the first American printings.

Chapter One

1. My information about the social and intellectual climate of the 1930's comes largely from the following works: Robert Graves and Alan Hodge, *The Long Week-End: A Social History of Great Britain 1918–1939* (London, 1940); Christopher Isherwood, *Lions and Shadows* (London, 1938); John Lehmann, *The Whispering Gallery* (London, 1955); C. Day Lewis, *The Buried Day* (London, 1960); Malcolm Muggeridge, *The Sun Never Sets* (New York, 1940); George Orwell, *The Road to Wigan Pier* (London, 1937); Stephen Spender, *World Within World* (London, 1951); Julian Symons, *The Thirties* (London, 1960).

2. For an account of right-wing politics in England in the 1930's, see Colin Cross, *The Fascists in Britain* (London, 1961).

3. Day Lewis, p. 212.

4. Isherwood, pp. 65–66.

5. Justin Replogle, "The Gang Myth in Auden's Early Poetry," *Journal of English and Germanic Philology*, LXI, 3 (July, 1962), 489.

Chapter Two

1. Bill Casey, "Nurse Novels," *Southwest Review*, XLIX, 4 (Autumn, 1964), 335, 338.

2. This distinction was first developed by Edwin Muir, "Novels of Action and Character," *The Structure of the Novel* (London, 1928), pp. 7–40.

Chapter Three

1. Among Miss Renault's many acts of kindness to me was the permission to quote her remarks on Julian's paternity. Her letter, addressed from Cape, South Africa, is dated Boxing Day [1965]:

Yes, Julian's old mum *is* telling him he is the actor's child. That is really supposed to be the key to her behaviour throughout the book. As long as he is willing to be a country gentleman he is *her* son and she will accept him; the moment he commits himself to his father's calling, she not only rejects him but projects on him all her ancient stored resentment at the insult to her pride. When she talks about the pregnant servant-girl who had to be helped out of her 'difficulties' she means that *he* was *her* 'difficulty.' He sees this, and she means him to see. His putative father is supposed to have married her knowing she might be pregnant by the other man, but, like many people at that period, never actually discussing it in so many words, and, of course, not highly delighted when Julian turned out the image of his real father. As you have probably noticed, these resemblances are often very strong in new-born babies, more so than later on.

2. Gilbert Ryle, "Introduction," in A. J. Ayer, W. C. Kneale, G. A. Paul, *et al.*, *The Revolution in Philosophy* (London, 1963), p. 11.

3. [Plato,] *Phaedrus*, in *Four Dialogues of Plato Including the "Apology of Socrates,"* trans. by John Stuart Mill, introd. by Ruth Borchardt (London, 1946), pp. 84–85.

Chapter Four

1. Landon C. Burns, Jr., "Men Are Only Men: The Novels of Mary Renault," *Critique*, VI, 3 (Winter, 1963–64), 108.

2. M. I. Finley, *The Ancient Greeks: An Introduction to Their Life and Thought* (New York, 1964), p. 41; see also H. D. F. Kitto, *The Greeks* (Baltimore, 1964), pp. 64–79.

3. Kitto, p. 252.

4. Stringfellow Barr, *The Will of Zeus: A History of Greece from the Origins of Hellenic Culture to the Death of Alexander* (New York, 1965), p. 169.

5. Kitto, p. 151.

6. *Ibid.*, pp. 158–59.

7. Burns, pp. 106–7.

8. Edith Hamilton, *The Greek Way to Western Civilization* (New York, 1962), p. 134.

9. Barr, pp. 167–68.

10. Christopher Isherwood, *The Last of Mr. Norris*, in *The Berlin Stories* (Norfolk, Conn., 1963), p. 86.

11. Barr, p. 224.

Chapter Five

1. Northrop Frye, *Anatomy of Criticism* (Princeton, 1957), pp. 33–52.

2. Kitto, p. 54.

3. Robert Graves, *The Greek Myths* (Baltimore, 1955), I, 59.

4. Burns, p. 121.

5. Mircea Eliade, *Cosmos and History: The Myth of the Eternal Return,* trans. by Willard R. Trask (New York, 1959), p. 42.

6. Graves, I, 338–39; André Gide, *Two Legends: Oedipus and Theseus,* trans. by John Russell (New York, 1950), pp. 73–74.

7. Plutarch, "Theseus," *The Lives of the Noble Grecians and Romans,* trans. by John Dryden and revised by Arthur Hugh Clough (New York, n. d.), pp. 6–7.

8. Graves, I, 329.

9. Burns, pp. 112–13.

10. Gide, p. 72.

11. Plutarch, p. 5; [Thomas Bulfinch,] *Bulfinch's Mythology* (New York, n. d.), p. 124; Graves, I, 325.

12. Burns, pp. 111–12.

13. Graves, I, 10.

14. Although the Cranes included both males and females in their membership, the origin of the team has never been ascertained. In *The King Must Die,* Theseus decides to call the team the Cranes when he sees a crane flying above the Cretan tribute ship. Plutarch states that the Crane was a dance, "consisting in certain measured turnings and returnings, imitative of the windings and twistings of the labyrinth" (13); according to Plutarch, Theseus and the Cranes performed this dance on their return from Crete to Athens. Graves defines the Crane as a dance "which consists of labyrinthine evolutions" (I, 342) and which Theseus brought from Knossos to Athens. See also Agnes Carr Vaughan, *The House of the Double Axe: The Palace at Knossos* (New York, 1959), pp. 158–59.

15. Leonard Cottrell, *The Bull of Minos,* introd. by Professor Alan Wace (New York, 1962), pp. 115–16. For more exhaustive studies of the Minoan culture, see Sir Arthur John Evans, *The Palace of Minos,* 7 vols. (London, 1921–36); Charles Henry Hawes and Harriet Boyes Hawes, *Crete, The Forerunner of Greece* (London and New York, 1922); J. D. S. Pendlebury, *The Archaeology of Crete: An Introduction* (London, 1939); and Joan Evans, *Time and Chance* (London, 1943).

16. Cottrell, p. 192.

17. Vaughan, p. 226.

18. Sir James George Frazer, *The Golden Bough: A Study in Magic and Religion,* one volume, abridged ed. (New York, 1963), pp. 452–53.

19. Kevin Herbert, "The Theseus Theme: Some Recent Versions," *Classical Journal,* LV, 4 (January, 1960), 176.

20. Burns, pp. 114–15.

21. *Ibid.*, p. 119.

22. Nikos Kazantzakis, *Thésée,* in *Tragedies grecques: Melissa, Thésée* (Monaco, 1953).

23. Gide, p. 63.

24. "King of Athens," *Times Literary Supplement,* March 16, 1962, p. 181.

25. T. S. Eliot, *The Idea of a Christian Society* (New York, 1940), p. 63.

26. Burns, p. 117.

27. Granville Hicks, "Theseus Speaking, Man to Man," *Saturday Review,* February 17, 1962, pp. 21–22.

28. "King of Athens," p. 181.

29. Arnold Bennett, *The Old Wives' Tale* (New York, n. d.), p. vi.

30. Plutarch, pp. 23–24; Graves, I, 349–50.

Selected Bibliography

PRIMARY SOURCES

1. Novels

Promise of Love. New York: William Morrow, 1939.
Kind Are Her Answers. New York: William Morrow, 1940.
The Middle Mist. New York: William Morrow, 1945.
Return to Night. New York: William Morrow, 1947.
North Face. New York: William Morrow, 1948.
The Last of the Wine. New York: Pantheon, 1956.
The King Must Die. New York: Pantheon, 1958.
The Charioteer. New York: Pantheon, 1959.
The Bull from the Sea. New York: Pantheon, 1962.
The Mask of Apollo. New York: Pantheon, 1966.
Fire from Heaven. New York: Pantheon, 1969.

2. Children's History

The Lion in the Gateway: The Heroic Battles of the Greeks and Persians at Marathon, Salamis and Thermopylae. Ed. by Walter Lord. Pictures by C. Walter Hodges. New York: Harper and Row, 1964.

3. Article.

"Amazons," *Greek Heritage,* I, 2 (Spring, 1964), 18–23.

4. Review

"A Man Who Survived Tradition," *The New York Times Book Review,* August 15, 1965, pp. 1, 20 [Nikos Kazantzakis, *Report to Greco*].

5. Radio plays

Typescripts of three unpublished radio plays, "The Day of Good Hope," "The God of the Crossroads," and "Song of Troy" are located in the Humanities Reference Room, Love Memorial Library, University of Nebraska, Lincoln, Nebraska 68508. "The Bounty Mutiny," a radio script in eight parts of thirty minutes each is in the possession of Curtis Brown, Ltd., 13 King Street, Covent Garden, London W. C. 2.

SECONDARY SOURCES

BURNS, LANDON C., JR., "Men Are Only Men: The Novels of Mary Renault," *Critique,* VI, 3 (Winter, 1963–64), 102–21. Studies character, theme, and the use of classical myth in *The Last of the Wine, The King Must Die,* and *The Bull from the Sea.*

CASEY, BILL. "Nurse Novels," *Southwest Review,* XLIX, 4 (Autumn, 1964), 332–41. Formulates a mock esthetic for nurse fiction since World War II.

HERBERT, KEVIN. "The Theseus Theme: Some Recent Versions," *Classical Journal,* LV, 4 (January, 1960), 175–85. Compares Mary Renault's *The King Must Die* unfavorably with André Gide's *Theseus* and Nikos Kazantzakis's *Thésée.*

"RENAULT, MARY," *Current Biography Yearbook* (New York, 1959), pp. 379–81. Briefly summarizes the life and literary career of Mary Renault.

Index